BI 3559912

D1765736

WEEK LOAN

Remember to return on time **or** renew at
https://icity.bcu.ac.uk/ or
http://www0.bcu.ac.uk/library/public/
or **24 Hour Renewals: Tel 0121 331 5278**
Items in demand may not be renewable

Elizabeth Bowen:
New critical perspectives

Elizabeth Bowen:
New critical perspectives

Edited by
Susan Osborn

First published in 2009 by
Cork University Press
Youngline Industrial Estate
Pouladuff Road, Togher
Cork, Ireland

British Library Cataloguing in Publication Data

    Elizabeth Bowen : new critical perspectives
        1. Bowen, Elizabeth, 1899–1973 – Criticism and
        interpretation
        I. Osborn, Susan
        823.9'12
        ISBN-13: 9781859184356

The authors have asserted their moral rights in this work.

Typeset by Tower Books, Ballincollig, Co. Cork
Printed by Athenaeum Press, UK
www.corkuniversitypress.com

To my mother

Acknowledgements

This book owes much to early spirited discussions about Bowen's work with Robert Caserio and Barry Qualls. Their refusal to accept the commonplace was a gift for which I remain indebted. I would also like to thank my daughter, Alana Osborn-Lief, for her perceptive and challenging comments about Bowen's fiction.

It has been my good fortune to work with Catherine Coughlan, Sophie Watson and Tom Dunne at Cork University Press, all of whom expressed special interest in Bowen and her work. I am especially grateful to Catherine Coughlan for her enthusiasm and support.

This book is particularly indebted to Julian Moynahan, with whom I have enjoyed many stimulating conversations about Elizabeth Bowen and Ireland, about Bowen's work and reputation, and about her time spent in Princeton while she was teaching at Princeton University. His passionate and intelligent insight into the more complicated facets of her work and his understanding of her reception here, in North America, and in Ireland and Britain galvanized, in many ways that he would disavow, the production of this collection.

Susan Osborn
Princeton, New Jersey
September 2008

Contents

Contributors

Brook Miller is Assistant Professor of English at the University of Minnesota, Morris. He specializes in twentieth-century British literature, with emphasis upon turn-of-the-century fiction and modernism. He has published on a variety of topics, including the work of Elizabeth Bowen, Joseph Conrad, Henry James and George Bernard Shaw. He is currently completing a manuscript on turn-of-the-century Anglo-American cultural politics. *Luke Elward, Phil Kollar* and *Tessa Hempel* are students at the University of Minnesota, Morris, and were members of a course on twentieth-century British women's fiction.

Sinéad Mooney is the author of *Samuel Beckett* (Northcote House, 2006) and the editor of *Edna O'Brien: New Critical Perspectives* (Carysfort, 2006), and has written numerous essays on Beckett and on Irish women's writing. She is currently working on a monograph on Beckett, translation, and self-translation, and holds a Research Fellowship from the Irish Research Council for the Humanities and Social Sciences for 2008/9. She is a lecturer in the Department of English, National University of Ireland, Galway, where she teaches modernism, women's writing and Irish literature.

Susan Osborn is a critic, novelist and poet who lectures in the Department of English at Rutgers University, New Brunswick, New Jersey. Her last novel, *Surviving the Wreck*, was published by Henry Holt and Company and Econ Verlag. She has published articles on topics including early British modern literature and literary theory, feminist theory, the Irish Gothic tradition, and pedagogical theory and practice; her essays and book reviews have appeared in over thirty publications including *Modern Fiction Studies*, *Literature & History*, *Rhetoric Review*, *The Irish Literary Supplement*, *The New York Times*, and elsewhere. She also guest edited the Summer 2007 issue of *Modern Fiction Studies*, the first issue of a scholarly journal exclusively devoted to the work of Elizabeth Bowen. In addition to grants from the Princeton Research Forum, the Virginia Center for the Creative Arts, Byrdcliffe and Dorset Colony House, she is the recipient of awards from the New Jersey State Council on the Arts and Rutgers University. She is currently working on a study of Bowen's relationship to Bloomsbury and her engagement with the aesthetic and philosophical developments of the time, and completing a collection of stories.

June Sturrock is an Emeritus Professor of English at Simon Fraser University, Vancouver, where she continues to teach occasionally in the Graduate Liberal Studies Programme. Her publications include about sixty articles and book chapters, *Heaven and Home: Charlotte Yonge's Domestic Fiction and the Victorian Debate about Women* and an edition of Jane Austen's *Mansfield Park*. Forthcoming are a book on nineteenth-century domestic fiction and several more articles.

Eluned Summers-Bremner is Senior Lecturer in English at the University of Auckland, New Zealand. She has published *Insomnia: A Cultural History* (Reaktion Books, 2008) and is currently writing *A History of Wandering* (Reaktion Books), and *Ian McEwan: Sex, Death and History* (Cambria Press) and is working on studies of trauma, the affective work of love and reading and a project on war trauma in mid-century British fiction.

Shafquat Towheed is Lecturer in English at the Open University, where he is also Project Supervisor for the Reading Experience Database, 1450–1945 ('RED'), an AHRC-funded project (http://www.open.ac.uk/Arts/RED). He is the editor of *The Correspondence of Edith Wharton and Macmillan, 1901–1930* (Palgrave Macmillan, 2007), *New Readings in the Literature of British India, c.1780–1947* (Ibidem Verlag, 2007), the forthcoming Broadview Edition of Arthur Conan Doyle's *The Sign of Four*, and, with Mary Hammond, is co-editor of *Publishing in the First World War: Essays in Book History* (Palgrave Macmillan, 2007). He is the current chair of the SHARP DeLong Book History Prize committee, and is also writing a book on Vernon Lee.

Shannon Wells-Lassagne is Associate Professor at the University of South Britanny in Lorient, France. She specializes in twentieth-century

British and Irish literature and on film adaptation studies. She is the author of articles on Elizabeth Bowen, Graham Greene, Ford Madox Ford, and forthcoming books on Elizabeth Bowen and co-editor of a collection on film adaptation.

Introduction

SUSAN OSBORN

Although Elizabeth Bowen was first praised as a writer of sensibility and classed with E.M. Forster and Henry James as a psychological realist, upon reviewing the criticism of her earliest readers, one quickly perceives a sense of interpretive strain: at the same time that these readers herald her work as an instrument in the solidification and advancement of a specific artistic practice, they simultaneously, and often with considerable discomfort, underscore Bowen's lack of success in mediating many of the imperatives of the conventions of the realistic fiction to which her work was by them consigned. We need look no further to see evidence of this strain than Jocelyn Brooke's *Elizabeth Bowen* (1952), the first long study of her fiction published during her lifetime. Brooke recognizes Bowen as one of the three or four most important novelists writing in Britain at the time, and he notes approvingly, as had other critics, that her 'way of seeing' was, like Forster's and James's, marked by imperatives generally assigned to context and class. But he is also troubled by Bowen's divergence from realist practice, and especially by the abundance of excessive and extraneous stylistic tics apparent in her work that interrupt the reader's unproblematic absorption in and validation of the text. Certainly her narratives are, as he approvingly writes, concerned with the 'social behaviour of highly civilized men and women' especially as those highly civilized men and women are threatened by 'the pretentious, Philistine middle-class' (10); some of her narratives '(almost) [sic] [seem] drawing-room comed[ies]' (16). But at the same time, he is distressed by the apparently unassociated, confusing and exaggerated effects that he finds in her work, including her 'occasional use of the supernatural' (19), her 'tendency to "thicken" her

1

stylistic effects' (18), the 'distorted fragmentary effect' apparent in some of her work (25), and her 'highly wrought' (12), 'idiosyncratic' (18) and 'convoluted style' (26), which he ultimately likens to a 'neurotic impediment, a kind of stammer; [that] occasionally . . . lead[s] to actual obscurity' (26), all problematic estrangements that disturb the familiarizing work expected of this class of fictions; irregularities, in other words, that are at odds with some of the imperatives of the discursive practices of the conventional realism to which hers was most often compared.

The praise and blame in Brooke's account work jointly to identify certain aspects of Bowen's fiction that make her work uncommonly difficult to conceive, describe, and evaluate and that make the terms of appreciation and analysis unusually difficult to apprehend and apply. That Bowen's work has been considered worth reading since the publication of her first collection of short stories, *Encounters* (1923), has never been doubted. However, while her earliest interpreters have concurred with Brooke's praise, like Brooke, they have also invariably been less enthusiastic about her tendency to complicate her management of the things that she should be managing. Especially dismaying, as noted by Brooke, are her 'distortions', 'convolutions' and the abundance of 'distracting detail', her 'decorative elaboration' as William Heath (1961), another early commentator, described these apparent mismanagements, her 'pointless verbal excess' (44) as he complains with exasperation about Bowen's early novel, *The Last September* (1929).

Broken down, what Brooke is troubled by, and what has been echoed by almost all of Bowen's past critics, is that, while some elements in Bowen's fiction assure an unproblematic representation of the reader's social experience in the world, others interrupt the naturalizing work expected of this class of fictions, in particular, by Bowen's corruption of the boundary between the essential and the contingent and/or the 'pointless', the familiar and the strange. In other words, the realist novel's prestige and the reader's confidence in the literary mimesis inscribed in realism is linked to certain initiatives and prospects that supposedly had been achieved during the nineteenth century. When well managed, literary realism as practised by Forster and James, for example, overcomes a sense of artificiality and intimations of excess and uncontainability by the ways the representation selects and arranges essential or representative patterns of experience that reveal a sense of the world in its innermost intelligibility; in other words, by the way the representation confirms the distinction between the probable and the possible, the imperative and the extraneous and arbitrary. The resulting verisimilitude is largely sustained by means of collective agreements and can be conceived of as a kind of contract: the reader gives credence to the mimetic claims of the text in return for confirmation by the writer of the reader's expectations. But there is something in Bowen's fiction that unsettles what Eco has termed the reader's 'prior stipulation of pertinence' (1976, 225), something that seems fashioned for purposes other than those solely of consensus that threatens the set of agreements between reader and writer as to what forms faithful representation, an unregulated quality that had supposedly been settled by the likes of Forster and James and which points to a presumably cast off and more indeterminate heterogeneity of the real that is both difficult to approach and to analyse and that challenges the reader's efforts to control the interpretive field. And yet it is precisely the extra charge produced by this corruption, a charge that is felt as both enigmatic and occasionally burdensome, that lends to her work its most penetrating influence, constitutes its most baffling and salient effects, and grants to her stories and novels a protean strength and allure not easily neutralized by conventional exegesis or by their proper classification.

Within the last two decades, more complex modes of reading involving issues of gender, class, ethnicity and nationhood and their multiple intersections have combined to create a more complicated understanding of some of the less familiar and more provocative valences in Bowen's work that together reveal some of the less transparent, potentially subversive currents apparent in Bowen's fiction. Distributing Bowen's fictional narratives across an ideological spectrum bounded by Irish nationalism (pursuant to the Bowen family's material status and class) at one end and a more progressive if coded feminism/lesbianism at the other, historical interpretations range from those that regard Bowen's writing as a conservative and largely disciplinary apparatus to more nuanced approaches that steer a middle course between ideological extremes. Such readings carry considerable weight and force and have done much to galvanize interest in Bowen's work. Among these are readings that look more broadly at the conservative topoi of Bowen's fiction and the more disquieting implications that can be drawn from her writings. These include Phyllis Lassner's *Elizabeth Bowen* (1990), in which Lassner regards Bowen's class with its investment in patriarchal ideology as a legitimate bar to anything beyond a moderate or conservative feminism. As she writes, Bowen's discursive practices are connected to women's 'struggle[s] with autonomy, dependence, and self-expression', struggles that 'reflect . . . [Bowen's] position as outsider both culturally and as a woman of her time' (153, 145). Likewise, in his ambitious *The Novel in England 1900–1950: History and Theory* (1999), Robert Caserio suggests that Bowen's female characters are indelibly marked by imperatives attributable to class and patriarchy. For example, in his analysis of *The Last September*, he connects the female characters' gender status to their 'beleaguered vulnerability as colonialists', and, using Fredric Jameson's notion of the political unconscious, suggests their 'subversive alliance' with the rebellious members of the Irish Republican Army (251). These explanations, often with a good deal of technical competence, open new avenues of inquiry that allow, for example, an examination of the prospect of qualitative change for women, retrospectively; in other words, through the lens of recorded history. But where such criticism falls short is precisely in its assumption that Bowen's practice was bounded by and sometimes identical to the purposes of social regulation identified by the historical context within which the reader's argument is framed. There is no doubt that when reading Bowen's narratives, we must be mindful of the imperatives of gender, class, ethnicity and national conflict that we can, with some degree of confidence, speculate make Bowen's work in some ways responsive to topical imperatives and local claims of propriety which, during the first half of the twentieth century, promoted women's culture, for example, as a small and restricted circle circumscribed by imperatives dictated overtly and insidiously by class and patriarchy. Likewise, it would be just as irresponsible and disingenuous to ignore probable influences on Bowen's work of the rise of and various manifestations of oppositional sentiment that erupted in Ireland following the 1916 Easter Rising and the 1919 meeting of Dáil Éireann, generally understood to be embodied in and symbolized by Sinn Féin and the paramilitary operations of the Irish Republican Army and directed at both the British colonizers and the by-and-large Protestant gentry, of which Bowen was a member, owners of Ireland's 'Big Houses'. Nor can we overlook probable influences on Bowen of both the Second World War and the Blitz. However, by interpreting Bowen's *oeuvre* as social or political texts from which they cannot be disjoined, such historical readings make Bowen's work answerable to given contexts instead of appreciating them as contexts in themselves in which history works to dilate and complicate competing pressures and inchoate forces already present in the work. In other words, rooted as these readings are in the known facts from which Bowen's work is in some ways inextricably linked, such readings are limited to modes of interpretation and to conclusions that square with the particular historical and/or social contexts upon which they are based. Consequently, Bowen's achievement is then read as a representation that works in only one register and to one single purpose. As such, these readings consistently stress the conservative, largely regulatory work of her fiction, over and against any other prospects they may hold, especially those nascent and intimated within the troubling excess, those instabilities of form, language and composition that lend to her work its uncommon elusiveness and that makes it uncommonly resistant to conventional historical, generic and ethnic incorporation. Not surprisingly, as with Bowen's earliest readers, the infrequent times that Bowen's late twentieth-century readers do note the narrative and formal estrangements that discomfited and sometimes offended and obstructed Brooke and some of Bowen's other early interpreters from forming the kind of apodictic and totalizing interpretations presented by these readers, they are most often dismissed or derided, as they had been in the past, as unaccountable gaffes, obscuring distractions unworthy of sustained critical attention.[1]

Within the last decade, Bowen's readers have sought to recuperate her fiction by focusing their analyses precisely on those aspects of her work that produce the sense of interpretive strain early identified by Brooke and others, those problematic exchanges caused by the ungainly irregularities, the improprieties and 'thickened' stylistic effects that produce her works' uncustomary recalcitrance and that continue to challenge readers' interpretive abilities. Of special interest to these readers are many of the conspicuous and unruly excesses identified by Brooke, albeit in different terms, including Bowen's weird and inconsistent mimeticism, the dramatizations of impasse and non- or dissolved presence, and the elliptical dialogue and lacunae in plotting that both invoke and discredit a sense of meaning, the way the concatenation of extravagant and conventionally employed forms, in provocative and sometimes impudent ways, confuses distinctions. For example, in her recent study, *Elizabeth Bowen: The Shadow Across the Page* (2003), Maud Ellmann explores some of the less regulated aspects of Bowen's narratives, including the author's disruptive and disconcerting 'addictions', as she refers to the representational incongruities, the 'frictional disjunctions' (4) and florid 'clashes between literary forms' (3) apparent in Bowen's work. In his recent historically based study, *Elizabeth Bowen: The Enforced Return* (2004), Neil Corcoran attends to the 'arresting strangeness' in her work and situates his interpretation in his notion of Bowen's awkward and transgressive 'bilocality', by which he refers to her living 'between' Ireland and

England (13). Corcoran is especially interested in the ways in which the 'peculiar [and] disconcerting ethics' in her work, revealed by the ways the works' heretofore unexplored 'gaps, ellipses, absences, hauntings, silences, and aporias' produce 'arrestingly strange, but intelligible' narratives, unexpectedly inflected with affirmation (13). In what is undoubtedly the most audacious recent reading of Bowen's work, *Elizabeth Bowen and the Dissolution of the Novel* (1995), Andrew Bennett and Nicholas Royle, citing many of the especially strange and resistant aspects of her mimeticism, argue against all previous readings of her work and suggest instead that Bowen's fictional narratives

> are open to fundamental rereadings . . . which at once transform the status and importance of Bowen's work and effect a deconstruction of everything that is seemingly most conventional and reassuring about the very notion of the novel. (xvi)

Citing in particular Bowen's under–examined and undervalued novel *Eva Trout or Changing Scenes* (1968), they suggest that Bowen's work undermines the epistemological foundations of the novel, necessitating 'a new critical vocabulary' (142), one that eludes all externally imposed vocabularies.

However, while the radical narrative and formal transgressions erratically displayed and written into Bowen's narratives are often felt to be urgent demands to be recognized as irreducibly other, Bowen's works' resistances and the unfamiliar and often irregular problems that the non-identical elements of her work present seem less indicative of an irreducible otherness or a conceptual or lexical failure than they do of the persistent uncertainty that readers share about how to approach and represent the competing pressures apparent in Bowen's art. Because the identical and the non-identical in Bowen's work insist, as early noted, at times hyperbolically, on their mutual entanglement, her work challenges us to make sense of the unruly and often egregious interdigitation in her work of the regular and the irregular, the familiar and the strange. Above all else, Bowen's narratives are marked by the central linking of well-governed and less well-governed elements whose interpretation is dependent both on laws peculiar to themselves and laws commonly recognized, and whose representation consequently sometimes but not always exceeds the orbit of the conventional conceptual categories used to interpret them. Indeed, one wonders if the derision still apparent in some Bowen criticism might be explained in part by what is perceived by some to be the intolerable pressure of contradictory compulsions that form the signature of Bowen's style, a pressure that places her work, as Paul Muldoon suggests, along with Joyce's and Beckett's, at 'some notional cutting edge' (25). The most exciting aspect of this unusual quality of her work derives from the various ways that the categorical excesses offer new horizons of possibility that require ways of reading and modes of interpretation in which the works' resistance is felt to be both empowering and impoverishing. In other words, because the relation between the non-identical and the identical in Bowen's work cannot be reduced or stabilized into an opposition between antithetical forces, her narratives resist commonly employed metaphors of complimentarity and coordination; simply put, it is difficult to smother her work with our preconceptions because so much of what the work does and how it does it resists them. Consequently, among other things, Bowen's work offers unfamiliar ways by which we might reconceptualize the relationship between realism and modernism, the ambiguities of identity, and the obscuring effects of many familiar critical assumptions, including those pertaining to canonicity, notions of genre, and the representation of gender, sexuality, class, nationhood and ethnicity in literature.

Recognizing that it is the uneasy and often unexpected interlinking in Bowen's narratives of the familiar and the strange that casts the strongest claim to comprehending the represented reality into critical relief, the essays collected here elaborate recent discussions of Bowen's work by attending to the unexpected, often contradictory pressures and relations in Bowen's work. While the essays are varied and do not provide a complete spectrum of contemporary responses, they are primarily concerned with two salient characteristics of Bowen's work: her at times intimidating artistic, linguistic and substantive difficultness, and her more recently recognized aesthetic, moral and cognitive complexity and distinctiveness. Specifically, these essays examine and analyse in considerable detail some of the stranger pressures and unfamiliar tensions heretofore dismissed or ignored, tensions that make her work uncommonly difficult to conceptualize, describe, and evaluate, and that make the terms of appreciation and analysis difficult to apprehend and apply; to present fuller and more nuanced accounts than were previously available of a number of these tensions; and, partly on the basis of these two endeavours, to begin to develop ways of thinking about and developing terms for understanding the novelty, force, difficulty, and significance of Bowen's work, and to develop the implications of these ideas for our thinking about a wide range of contemporary concerns.

The ingenuity and complexity of many of these arguments testifies to both the complexity and originality of Bowen's art. In the first essay,

'Unstable compounds: Bowen's Beckettian affinities', Sinéad Mooney
begins the work of setting aside the edifice of social realism that has
obstructed critical efforts to represent Bowen's narrative strangeness
through an exploration of the striking similarities apparent in the two
writers' work. In particular, Mooney attends to the asymptotic
approaches to zero that generate both writers' novels, and pays special
attention to the ways that the writers' stylistic investment in the
'nuances of negativity' – she sees in Beckett's 'depleted moribunds' parallels to Bowen's many suspended protagonists – discountenance
classic realist narrative form. Particularly useful is Mooney's exploration of the suggestive correspondences apparent in two of the writers'
'unreadable' novels, Beckett's *Watt* (1953) and Bowen's *Eva Trout or
Changing Scenes* (1968). While Bowen's 'defective' or non-identical protagonist has generally been read as a kind of monster (her
representation has been criticized for being too bold, too brutal, too
chalky, too inconsistent), Mooney unmoors Eva from certain vehicles
of ideology, notably the conventional realist plot, that have interfered
with readers' appreciation of this problematic character and this
strange and difficult novel. Instead, Mooney reads Eva as a 'proto-postmodernist younger sister of . . . Watt', both of whom suffer a 'loss of
filiation' from conventional linguistic structures. While the odd concatenations in both of these novels alternately provoke and resist a
search for encompassing connections and apodictic readings, Mooney
attends instead to the various stylistic disruptions and panicked linguistic atmosphere apparent in both and discusses ways that these
irregularities dislocate fragile structures of identity and jeopardize
readers' confidence in hermetic structures of meaning.

   In the second essay, '"How to measure this unaccountable darkness between the trees": the strange relation of style and meaning in
The Last September', Susan Osborn examines one of Bowen's early
novels, one most often read as a realistic novel concerned with the
conflagration caused by Britain's division of Ireland in 1920.
However, Osborn examines some of the ways that Bowen's troublesome and problematic stylistic irregularities undermine the ideological
work represented as being achieved in such readings, and suggests
instead that the novel's most affecting dramas and the distinctive
strain involved in interpreting this novel's protean allure result in
large measure from the provocative and disordered ways that the prose
violates rules of mimetic representation and realistic discourse while
establishing a relationship with them. Where there are departures
from the commonplace, the expected sites of agreed-upon meanings,
there occur interpretive challenges, but, as Osborn contends, much of

the interest of *The Last September*, and of Bowen's fictional narratives generally, lies in the ways that Bowen acknowledges these problems not in terms of reductive psychological categories, but by the way her representation estranges commonly conceived and represented relations among the 'real' and the 'fictional', the phenomenal and the noumenal, and by the ways she sometimes but not always disjoins the imbricated real thus produced from the social context of practical knowledge. By so doing, Bowen produces a novel that is driven as much by the epistemological suspensions that are formed among reader and text as it is by the action represented as occurring in the narrative's manifest plot.

In the third essay, 'Dead letters and living things: historical ethics in *The House in Paris* and *The Death of the Heart*', Eluned Summers-Bremner examines some of the ways that the contradictions in Bowenian omniscience and the opacity and fluidity of 'the real' that they corporately foster disturb the traditional hegemonic compact between the reader and the text. While the classic realist text ensures the position of the reading subject in a relation of dominant specularity, Summers-Bremner traces some of the privileged spatial and temporal dislocations that in *The House in Paris* (1935) and *The Death of the Heart* (1938) encourage a kind of reading practice which is in ways at odds with the realist imperative to clarify or dominate. At the same time, using a Lacanian concept of trauma, Summers-Bremner explores ways that the sufferings of the two children in the two novels, Portia and Leopold, are interconnected with the convoluted structures of Bowen's syntax and grammar and analyses ways that these odd joinings conduce to create her narratives' peculiar relation to history, a relation in which the readers' and characters' sense of retrospection and possibility are largely interdependent.

As earlier noted, the realist privilege is tied to a suppression of the extraordinary and the improbable; its practice inoculates itself to irruptions of the other and to an attenuation of the probable by admission of tempered variety and managed accident. And yet, upon reading Bowen's work, we often experience a dreadfully exciting and disconcerting feeling, not unlike that felt upon reading supernatural fiction, that the wall, let's call it, which governs or regulates the visiting privileges between various domains is not always working in a customary or consistently reliable fashion. As a result, when reading, we sometimes feel that we have 'stepped unnoticingly over a threshold into some . . . world drawn up alongside [and] at times dangerously accessible to the unwary' (Bowen, *Collected Stories*, New York, 1981, 151). It is this queer, 'provisional' quality, as John Bayley once observed, 'not quite like sleep, not quite like the future' (166), this strange admixture of the 'opposing' realms of the awe-full and the awful in Bowen's stories that the next two essays address.

In 'Mumbo-jumbo: the haunted world of *The Little Girls*', June Sturrock examines the critical unease provoked by Bowen's penultimate novel, *The Little Girls* (1964). This strange novel has received little sympathy from critics who tend to find its characters fey and its situations unrealistic. As with many of Bowen's narratives, there is no terribly compelling story line in *The Little Girls*, little sense of cumulative progression. Yet Sturrock suggests that the near universal critical discomfort provoked by this novel is due precisely to the novel's success in communicating its lack of faith in the representational systems used by the narrator, the author and the characters. Sturrock is especially interested in Bowen's use of an uncertain representational language that, as in *A World of Love* (1955), continually alludes to and verges on the supernatural, without ever abandoning the rationally explicable. The narrative incongruities here, seen especially in the concatenations of the strange and the ordinary that are frequently represented in a language of haunting and enchantment, simultaneously present horizons of possibility that are as closely akin to the Romantics' commitment to a discourse of the imagination and to the 'romantic' claim of modernity to awaken the mind's attention from the lethargy of custom as they are to realistic discourse's commitment to the quotidian and consensual. As such, the novel's conflicted representation allows for certain possibilities in the text and in the modes of reading instilled, in excess of the aims and teleologies typically assigned to both Romantic and modern narratives.

In its desire to grasp Bowen's narratives 'whole', if you will, and generally in terms of the works' 'thematics' or psychology of depth, criticism of Bowen's work has tended to be impatient with the apparently decorative detail, the 'claptrap' seen in her work that often draws our attention away from the inside and holds it on to the surface of her narratives. Consequently, readers have left unexplored some of the most characteristic and daring aspects of her fiction. In '"She-ward bound": Elizabeth Bowen as a sensationalist writer', Shannon Wells-Lassagne examines the proliferation of competing, non-privileged representational discourses used in Bowen's work and, as others collected here have emphasized, examines ways in which Bowen's narratives are made of partial or indeterminate orders that resist common modes of interpretative adjudication and understanding. Wells-Lassagne is especially interested in Bowen's use of techniques from popular or 'lowbrow' genres, including the detective story, the Gothic novel, the sensation novel and the Victorian quest romance, and she focuses in particular on the use of visceral language and characteristic turns of plot that combine to create an uneasy tension that exists among the strange, intransitive two-dimensionality often seen in Bowen's characters and her more conventional fictions of physical, personal presence. Finally, she discusses ways that the interdigitation of these techniques foregrounds issues of ontology in the reader and the text, while at the same time subduing or subverting explanatory structures that might, in a realist or modernist text, control, explain, or direct affectivity.

Recently, fictional narratives written during the 1940s in Ireland and England are interpreted through the lens of recorded history and are commonly understood to be produced by that history. For example, the stories collected in Bowen's *The Demon Lover* (1945) are most often read as narratives of exposure, stories in which the members of the discrete world of the upper middle class are, by virtue of the consequences of the Blitz, no longer able to seclude themselves. But in 'Territory, space, modernity: Elizabeth Bowen's *The Demon Lover and Other Stories* and wartime London', Shafquat Towheed charts ways in which the fluid and overlapping fictional terrains represented in these stories, be they physical spaces (parks, streets, bedrooms) or emotional (fear, desire, claustrophobia, anomie, alienation), unsettle the coherent coordinates and benchmarks that have plotted our conventional sense of scale regarding psychic and physical space since the Enlightenment. Of special interest to Towheed is the importance of positive–negative space, the 'glassless windows', to quote Bowen's story 'In the Square', that frame 'hollow inside dark' and the *gnomons*, to borrow a term first applied to Bowen's work by Ellmann, the physical and emotional remainders that have indicative potential even after the removal of the causative agent, and in the ways the changing, contingent, elastic nature of physical and psychic space represented in these stories offers avenues for thinking about new interpretive cartographies.

In the final essay, 'Narrative, meaning, and agency in *The Heat of the Day*', Brook Miller et al. examine *The Heat of the Day* (1948), the novel widely known as Bowen's 'Second World War' novel. Typically the interpretive challenges the novel presents are cited as naturally occurring, even predictable reactions to a catastrophe conceived as a historical event. But in this essay, the writers question the idea that the war creates the conditions that foster the epistemic and ontological crises experienced by the characters. In particular, the authors are interested in exploring ways the representation, as conventionally interpreted, cannot account for the uncustomary migratory relationship that is represented as existing among humans and objects. This fluid or hallucinatory exchange of aspects or partial aspects of essences represented in all of Bowen's fiction, Bowen's 'expressionistic' or non-naturalistic, contradictory and distorted mapping of inner experience or character 'psychology', and the inconstant and compounded struggle for reliable object status represented have often provoked snide derision from Bowen's earlier interpreters. But in this essay, the commentators examine the representation of character more as a mediation, a dilemma in response to a perceived sense of contingency, than as an identity in relation to inter-subjective and ideological pressures. Focusing primarily on Roderick, whom they suggest is the most 'porous' of the many leaky characters in *The Heat of the Day*, the writers track ways that the characters resist being narrated and examine the ways whereby they escape absorption by conventional historical interpretations and thereby elude any sense of final definition despite pressures often interpreted as irresistible or finalizing by prior readers.

As is apparent, the essays published in this collection are not intended to represent a continuity of the writer's endeavour, nor do they suggest the growth of an operative consciousness. While the essays do attempt to articulate a diverse range of vital if under-examined tensions in Bowen's narratives, they do not culminate in a single account of Bowen's extraordinary achievement either. Rather, by providing more carefully nuanced accounts of relationships in Bowen's work, relationships that have typically not been given a substantive role in interpretation, it is hoped that these essays underscore a plea inherent in Bowen's work for fine and flexible discrimination and provisional appreciation as they simultaneously broaden and complicate our understanding of the many unsettling energies of her art.

1
Unstable compounds:
Bowen's Beckettian affinities

SINÉAD MOONEY

The work of Samuel Beckett frequently has been gestured towards by critics making efforts to do justice to Elizabeth Bowen's striking narrative heterogeneity. Maud Ellmann, for instance, aligns Bowen's interest in nothingness with Beckett's 'long declension into nullity'.[1] Neil Corcoran links *A World of Love* to *Waiting for Godot*, as 'a remarkable representation of the desuetude, melancholy, exasperation and resignation attendant on "waiting"'.[2] W.J. McCormack suggests that *The Heat of the Day* might belong to an Irish Protestant literary lineage: 'Yet comfortable belonging is a feature this distinctly Protestant "tradition" (merely hypothesised here) might on principle disavow, all the more so if Samuel Beckett's *Watt* or *Molloy* were to be considered for admission'.[3] Many such efforts, however, end by being recuperated into configurations of Bowen's interest in social realism. There has not, therefore, been an extended attempt to explore Bowen's Beckettian 'affinities', which are not, on reflection, so unexpected, but which are, this essay will argue, enormously productive in setting aside the edifice of realism in Bowen, the better to focus on her narrative oddities, frictions, and gaps, and her elusiveness in the standard accounts of 'classic' realism and modernism.

This essay aims to read certain recurrent tropes in Bowen's fiction through the lens of its affinity with Beckett's writing. While attempting to avoid what Beckett in the opening of his 1929 appreciation of Joyce's *Work in Progress* dubbed 'the danger [of] the neatness of identifications', it will discuss dramatizations of impasse, paralysis and lack of presence, deliberate narrative unpicking, actions repeatedly arrested or aborted, and will suggest a way of approaching Bowen's petrified *ingénues* through Beckett's depleted moribunds, with particular reference to

Murphy and Bowen's *The Hotel*.[4] Finally, it will read *The Heat of the Day* and *Eva Trout* alongside Beckett's *Watt*.

Despite the frequency of brief Beckett references throughout Bowen criticism, the 'affinity' at first seems an unlikely, even strained one: Bowen's urbane social comedy, her mannered, post-Jamesian style, her nostalgic conservatism, her dangerous *ingénues* and Big Houses are an apparently odd match for Beckett's savage retrenchments of form in the novel and drama, his philosophical farce, his denatured tramps, waifs and strays, his bin-bound geriatrics, his investment in ignorance and impotence. While she has frequently been recruited to one of the more genteel varieties of conventional realism, and is described by her biographer Victoria Glendinning as 'what happened after Bloomsbury . . . the link that connects Virginia Woolf with Iris Murdoch and Muriel Spark', Beckett has insistently been aligned with existentialism, absurdism, a heroically renunciatory modernism, and postmodernism.[5] (In fact, the twin charges levelled at Bowen by dislikers of her characteristic style – intractable opacity and a wilful disordering of English syntax – are virtual signatures of the kind of writing we know as 'Beckettian', but they attract in Beckett scholarship none of the opprobrium with which they are associated in studies of Bowen, where they have tended to be seen as symptoms of 'feminine preoccupation with technique'.[6])

Bennett and Royle's 1995 *Elizabeth Bowen and the Dissolution of the Novel*, in its denunciation of the conventionalizing blurb to Bowen's novels, suggests 'alternative blurbs', deliberately designed to shock, which include 'Bowen's novels are like Jane Austen on drugs' and 'Together with Beckett's, Bowen's are the greatest comic novels written in English this century'.[7] The joke appears to be one of juxtaposition of unlike terms: 'Austen on drugs' is clearly meant to be understood as structurally equivalent to the unlikely yoking of Beckett and Bowen – except for the fact that this yoking prefigures Bennett and Royle's argument that Bowen's fictions 'embody nothing more and nothing less than the dissolution of the twentieth-century novel'. The *apparent* joke-opposition reveals, if not a similarity, then a deep-seated affinity.

If we set aside, then, the virtual caricatures of the gloomy Parisian naysayer and the post-Bloomsbury novelist of manners, can the affinity between Beckett and Bowen be sustained beyond critical asides? In what ways can Bowen's work be read as 'Beckettian'? Perhaps first and foremost, Bowen is, like Beckett, a specialist in inertia, a sculptor of the void, a word which figures largely in both their writing. Harold Bloom notes that, in Bowen's short stories, 'what never happens is more nuanced and vital than anything that does take place'.[8] Both operate a perverse endorsement of negative states and demonstrate a strong sense of underlying identification with stillness, paralysis, and states of abeyance. Beckett's early English fiction is weakly dominated by solipsistic protagonists who seek paradigmatic states of mental and physiological immobility. As this essay will demonstrate, *Murphy*'s thanatological urge towards the catatonia of the lunatic asylum and its withdrawn inmates sits curiously easily with the *Dubliners*-like petrification of *The Hotel*, where the somnambulistic heroine Sydney is attracted to the lethargic Mrs Kerr, in a narrative where stasis is everywhere preferred over forward movement. Maud Ellmann rightly compares the 'deconstructive logic' of the end of *The Hotel*, by which all relations and connections established during the course of the novel are unravelled again, to the chess game in Beckett's *Murphy*, in which the madman Endon attempts to return the pieces to their original positions on the board in a virtual ballet of disengagement.[9] This, however, is no isolated instance. In fact, Beckett's continual self-unweaving or intentional undoing of a text's origins – influentially dubbed the 'intent of undoing' by S.E. Gontarski[10] – has its counterpart throughout Bowen, whose novels are full of holes, elliptical dialogue, lacunae in the plotting and moments of aporia, as a pervasive nothingness appears to bring itself to bear on the textual fabric, or as though the author were repenting of her originary disclosure.

More than this, however, the work of Beckett and Bowen, both repetitive writers, with a limited repertoire of what Bowen in 'Out of a Book' terms 'addictions, pre-dispositions',[11] appears to share an all-assimilating instinct towards annihilation or a return to the womb, reminiscent of the Freudian death wish. Freud's well-known argument in *Beyond the Pleasure Principle* is that the compulsion to repeat reveals 'an urge inherent in organic life to restore an earlier state of things'. Repetition acts in the service of this urge by resisting and, as it were, giving as little ground as possible to the contrary urges 'which push forward towards progress and the production of new forms'.[12] This drive towards womb or tomb is everywhere thematically evident in Beckett, whose questing geriatric, Molloy, drags himself on crutches in search of his mother's room in order to undo the original sin of having been born, while *Waiting for Godot*'s Pozzo asserts '[t]hey give birth astride of a grave'.[13] More intimately, however, this thanatological urge is evident in the oddities of Beckett's syntax, where obligation and impotence work together, as Beckett first sets out in the *Three Dialogues with Georges Duthuit*; there is in his aesthetic not only a struggle towards expression, but also an equally powerful one

against expression. That there is 'nothing to express' and yet the 'obligation to express' is the central aporia of Beckett's work, which figures
itself in his work's endless reiterated guilt at sullying the empty page,
and the oddities of his aporetic syntax as the writing appears to wish
to 'void' itself.[14] These, of course, are the hallmarks of the Beckettian
stylistic signature.

However, Bowen's work, while remaining more involved with its
realist business, is almost equally invested in staging a drama of life-
lessness: her obsessive interest in manners and the elaborate artifice of
her fictive societies signals an anxiety that her characters risk being con-
sumed by the vacancy that surrounds them and from which, at times,
they detach themselves with reluctance. Harrison, the spy who haunts
Stella in *The Heat of the Day*, apparently goes 'into abeyance, just as he
was, with everything he had on him, between appearances. "Appearance" in the sense used for a ghost or actor, had indeed been each of
these times the word'.[15] Despite an apparent investment in melodrama,
nothing ever quite gets started, or, if started, properly under way; *The
Heat of the Day*, despite its sensational thematics of war, espionage and
betrayal, is notable for its almost total lack of event, evoked in a diction
frequently almost unreadable in its oddity. Furthermore, the various
forms of erotic fruition posited in Bowen are generally sidelined in
favour of death-in-life relationships such as the 'deathly yet living stillness, together' of Eva Trout and her comatose schoolmate, which
constitutes, in this novel as well as many other Bowen texts, the
'requital of all longing'.[16] Her equally characteristic contorted syntax,
on the other hand, with its tortuous double negatives and inversions,
its velleities of nuanced deadliness, appears to do subtle battle with a
devouring nothingness which resists expression: the struggle to resist
and contend linguistically with an underlying void makes its way into
the grain of Bowen's language, as it does Beckett's.

More crucially, while obviously avant-garde or postmodernist texts
flaunt their own strangeness, in novels such as Bowen's, where aspects
of the mimetic persist, most critics have seemed inclined to view the
text in mimetic terms, or to move from the basis of a mimetic reading
to other forms of reading. While some developments have recently
taken place which move Bowen criticism further from this basis,
baffled and hostile responses to Bowen's last novel, the strikingly
strange *Eva Trout*, suggest even in critics well disposed towards Bowen
a certain unease at the breaking of the established realist contract
between author and reader. Beckett's writing has, arguably, suffered
from the opposite problem, in that his critics have often tended to
ignore the manner in which, if it does deviate from narrative norms, it

also retains marked traces of those norms. Despite the iconoclastic, radically dislocated nature of Beckett's writing, the works, particularly the drama, frequently emerge from and rest upon a relatively traditional substructure, which is never entirely evacuated from the final work; *The Unnamable*'s refusal to grant any form of epistemological certainty to the first-person pronoun could not work as well without the traces of the autobiography it conjures up and refuses, while *Waiting for Godot* achieves important elements of its dramatic effect through juxtaposition with the 'well-made' play.

To juxtapose Bowen with Beckett, therefore, is productive in the first instance in aligning her writing with that of a considerably less orthodox author; it points up, I would argue, that her novels belong to what Frank Kermode has influentially called the 'problematical middle ground between the "classic realist text" and the *scriptible*'.[17] Bowen is an exemplary instance of a writer who exists in a hinterland between different kinds of writing, uncomfortably assimilated to forms of orthodox mimesis. In the midst of her stylish comic realism, there is an alien, outlandish, even monstrous element at work, the 'lunatic giant' of the famous passage from *The Death of the Heart*, whose 'knockings and batterings' keep Bowen's house of fiction from mere urbanity.[18] R.F. Foster points out that there is, even in the drawing-room elegance of the first part of Bowen's career, another voice, 'a vein of uncompromising brutality, and an alien humour', which exists in a state of tension with that elegance.[19] Observant Bowen criticism needs to recognize that any adequate response to Bowen involves a reading that is alert to her work's disunities and incoherences, and recognizes the importance of such instabilities within her narratives, which not only resist norms but deploy them in order to resist them. Bowen's readers, more so than Beckett's readers, are continually aware of the temptation to convert her fictions back into a more familiar form, to attempt to reconcile the ways in which they are visibly at odds with themselves as narratives, to smooth the roughnesses of narrative surfaces. However, it is precisely the lack of epistemological certainty that is the point. I will return later to this in my discussion of Beckett's *Watt* and Bowen's *Eva Trout*.

This is not, of course, to argue that Bowen's output as a whole in any obvious way resembles Beckett's writing, or to set aside her work's investment in representation or verisimilitude; Bowen's Beckettian affinities are certainly, on the whole, more easily divined in her wartime and post-war work. However, even in the earlier novels, in which Bowen is at her most obviously socially attuned, one can see certain points of resemblance, especially to the early Beckett, who has not himself at this point entirely relinquished conventional narrative modes, particularly in terms of the preoccupation with inertia already mentioned, and an ambivalent commitment to realism. Beckett's *Murphy* (1938) is the key text here. Retaining considerably more elements of representational writing than any of his other work, *Murphy* is narrated in the third person and nods towards certain conventions of the comic novel and *Bildungsroman*, even while it exposes them; much of the novel's vitality comes from this interplay of competing impulses, towards and away from conventional novelistic representation. The eponymous Murphy is a solipsistic anti-hero, a 'chronic emeritus' who follows 'no profession or trade' (M, 14, 16), and who instead devotes most of his energies to pursuing a life of complete solitude and inertia, first by studying a method of stopping the heart, then by binding himself to his rocking-chair, and later being drawn to the suburban mental hospital whose padded cells he regards as 'indoor bowers of bliss' (M, 103). In his idleness, he resembles Bowen men such as Victor Ammering in *The Hotel* and *Friends and Relations'* Rodney Meggatt, whose 'bent had not declared itself' (FR, 19), as well as the Bowen *ingénue*, eternally on the edge of a life that often seems an only ambivalently attractive prospect. Alongside his project to seclude himself entirely from the outside world and its irritations of physical desire, as personified by the wistful prostitute Celia and her carnal 'music', runs a broadly comic subplot involving a Dublin quartet all seeking the elusive Murphy for diverse reasons surrounding the fulfilment of romantic love. The farcical *ronde* of unrequited love which links Neary to 'Miss Dwyer, who loved a Flight-Lieutenant Ellmann, who loved a Miss Farren of Ringaskiddy, who loved a Father Fitt of Ballinclashet, who in all sincerity was bound to acknowledge a certain vocation for a Mrs West of Passage, who loved Neary' (M, 7) in fact resembles the distinctly algebraic love-rectangle of *Friends and Relations*.

Of course, Beckett's *Murphy* is an elaborately allusive philosophical farce, which makes far more evident gestures of dissent towards causality and verisimilitude, interpolating relatively conventional passages of narrative with chess diagrams and lists. However, under its more obviously realist carapace, Bowen's *The Hotel* also evokes mutual confrontations between silent and speaking, immured and transient, solitaries and crowds, catatonia and alertness, as well as between verisimilitude and curious 'abeyances' or lapses into the various forms of catatonia discussed by Bennett and Royle. The novel is summed up by the appalling, bookish child Cordelia Barry, who rebukes a clergyman who claims to have come on holiday 'for the people': 'How funny! I only like people in books who only exist when they matter. I think it is being in danger or terribly in love or discovering treasure or revenging yourself that is thrilling, and for that you have to have people. But people in hotels, hardly *alive* . . . !' (TH, 137). *The Hotel*, despite having been recruited by many to the Forsterian school of social comedy it superficially resembles, is considerably more interested in pursuing this anatomy of the 'hardly alive', those 'people' who are attenuated to the extent that they query the possibility of character, in impasse and immobility, than it is in the romantic ending it decisively rejects in favour of a disjunctive dispersal of all the characters it had assembled. Bowen's people, like Beckett's, are considerably less likely to discover treasure, fall in love or revenge themselves than they are to be on the verge of abeyance.

The Hotel, for instance, bears certain resemblances to *Murphy* in placing its half-anaesthetized or 'paralysed' protagonist Sydney Warren between Mrs Kerr, the entrancingly immobile older woman she idolizes, and the transient irritations of romantic desire represented by her brief engagement to the clergyman James Milton. The nameless Mediterranean hotel in which the novel is set plays something of the same part as *Murphy*'s Magdalen Mental Mercyseat. Associated with death and an ambivalently desired withdrawal throughout, it is compared with the adjacent cemetery, in terms of a *Godot*-like atmosphere of eternal waiting 'for some new arrival that never arrived' (TH, 8). Both novels share an ambiance of stale negativity: *Murphy* begins with the eviscerated cliché 'the sun shone, having no alternative, on the nothing new' (M, 5), while *The Hotel* opens with a vacant lounge: 'not a movement among the shadows . . . Not a shadow crossed . . . Not a sound came . . . ' (TH, 7). Mr Endon (his name is Greek for 'within'), the catatonic schizoid whose alienation fascinates Murphy, has his equivalent in the monstrously disengaged Mrs Kerr, who languidly presides over the generalized inertia of the hotel, and to whom Sydney is strongly attracted. Mrs Kerr is only one of the recurring, death-dealing older women in which Bowen specializes, and which include the more obviously vampiric Madame Fisher in *The House in Paris*, and who also anticipates the recurrence of the literal *femme fatale* in late Beckett plays such as *Rockaby* and *Footfalls*. As Murphy, looking into Endon's unseeing eyes, ultimately finds himself horrifyingly unseen, 'stigmatised in those eyes that did not see him' (M, 140), Mrs Kerr finally neglects Sydney in favour of reunion with her son, merely expecting her at intervals 'to take form somehow out of a limbo to which forgetfulness had consigned her' (TH, 9). As noted earlier, Maud Ellmann's comparison of the concluding impasse of the novel, after an obstructed motor expedition leads to a lengthy standstill during which Sydney breaks off her engagement and the novel's few tentative connections are entirely unravelled, to the 'deconstructive logic' of the disengaged chess game between Murphy and Endon is an apt one. Inertia and disengagement defeat the demands of realism.

If what Hermione Lee dubs Bowen's 'Burkean conservatism', the lingering snobbery of her monomania for the 'humanistic, classic and disciplined' her essay 'The Big House' associates with her Ascendancy forebears, is difficult to relish, it is nevertheless sharply undercut in her fiction (as distinct from her essays), much as her investment in staging the void pulls against her mannered-realist style.[20] Bowen's Big Houses are finally less Jamesian or Forsterian than they are Beckettian, in their reliance on a tradition which is revealed as only a somewhat dignified 'habit' or repetition, for Beckett 'the guarantee of a dull inviolability . . . the ballast that chains a dog to his vomit'.[21] If Bowen seems often in thrall to the perceived 'dignity' and 'beauty' of Ascendancy history, her work – particularly her 'historical' novel of paralysis and impasse, *The Last September* – none the less shows a trenchant awareness of the relationship of this 'history' to mere collective habit, an automatized repetition which allows an ordering of existence without the necessity of taking action. *The Last September* resembles Beckett, particularly his *Endgame*, in its asymptotic approaches to zero, all the time approaching it but never quite reaching it: 'something is taking its course', and is moving relentlessly towards some endlessly receding end. The characters in *The Last September* are half-conscious that they are in an endgame, caught in a running-down or diminishing cycle, moving towards certain extinction, yet, like the recurrent allusions in Beckett's *Godot* to the coming of Godot, some kind of tension is created; all is 'nearly finished', as *Endgame*'s Hamm phrases it (*CDW*, 93). Beckett's characters have recourse to mechanical repetition, re-enacting situations without perceiving any significance in the repeated actions, like Pavlov's dogs; the painkiller, the ongoing story, the ritual back-and-forth dialogue of *Endgame*, to choose only one example, resemble the deadly world of *The Last September*. In this world, the army, according to Sir Richard, 'has got into the habit of fighting'; the Danielstown dinner table is deadly 'certain of its regular compulsion'; visitors are 'superimposed on the vital pattern' of the house, 'till a departure tore great shreds from the season's texture'.[22] There is an obvious political dimension in this novel to the dignifying of habit into tradition in the face of imminent dissolution, but Bowen's minute attention to the significance of decorum in 'going on' continues as a trace throughout her career.

Such habit, and its elevation into 'custom' or 'tradition', may be the only form of ordering possible in a universe in which agency is a consoling fiction. As Sean O'Faolain has noted, the prose of *The Last September* is notable for its diminishment of human agency; with its hypnotic reliance on passive verbs (while, oddly, objects recruit to themselves a form of volition usually associated with the human, as Bowen shares Beckett's fascination with the inanimate), it approaches a Beckettian 'syntax of weakness'.[23] Habit, as Beckett's Vladimir remarks, is 'a great deadener' (*CDW*, 84), a formulation which is both predicament and solution, in that it insulates against experience with its own brand of tedium: Danielstown, 'spread like a rug to dull some keenness, break some contact between self and sense perilous to the routine of living', protects its inhabitants against 'some crude intrusion of the actual' (*LS*, 67, 44). *The Last September* anticipates *Watt*'s baffled and baffling account of ritual, in which the entirely senseless ceremonies of Mr Knott's quasi-Big House – the elaborate rituals by which he dresses and dines, by which he changes his sleeping position every night to make a complete annual circulation on his round bed, and by which his surplus food is disposed of – appear to have an arbitrary though regulating power of their own, in the novel's satire on inherited and assumed forms of social custom which present themselves as laws, and which, in *Watt*, include language. Ritual even structures forms of inaction and unexpressed feeling, leaving 'no opportunity for what [Hugo] must not say to be rather painfully not said' (*LS*, 138). It is not just that, as Lois, who likes 'to be in a pattern', opines, 'just to *be* is so intransitive, so lonely' (*LS*, 98), but that just to *be* is impossible without the succour of habit, the 'stately furniture and long mild meals' which are 'earth to Lois's roots' (*LS*, 171). In a novel saturated with negatives – in which Marda's engagements 'have all come to nothing', Hugo opines that the Anglo-Irish position in the war is 'no side', and Lois, despite her addiction to 'pattern', longs 'to be enclosed in nonentity, in some ideal no-place' (*LS*, 85, 82, 89) – habit wards off vacancy, even while Lois and Danielstown, the paralysed *ingénue* and the death-dealing house, 'penetrat[e] each other mutually in the discovery of a lack' (*LS*, 166).

Both Bowen and Beckett's significant 'lack' of credentials as sufficiently Irish writers has been problematic for many of their critics. In this, both bodies of work are entangled with the biographies of their authors. Bowen's equivocal position as an Ascendancy daughter who spent most of her life living in, and writing about, England finds a parallel in Beckett's urban Protestant distance from 'Irish Ireland', his lifelong exile in Paris, his rejection of identifiably Irish settings for his

works, and his espousal of the French language as the original medium
for much of his most enduring writing.[24] Beckett's writing comes to
occupy a strange, literally outlandish *Zwischenwelt* lying between languages and national identities, as Bowen, while remaining within
English, continually probes the position of cultural disorientation, the
dilemma – with its resonance both in terms of her problematic Anglo-
Irish heritage and of the post-Second World War refugee – of the
'displaced person'. While the critical 'repatriation' of Beckett, whose
Irishness was in dispute at the time of his being awarded the Nobel
Prize in 1969, has been continuing apace since the 1990s and has
perhaps had its culmination in the Dublin celebrations of his cente-
nary in 2006, Bowen's reclamation as Irish has been a more tentative
and problematic affair. She is on the one hand regarded as an essentially Irish exemplar of the 'heart-cloven and split-minded state' her
friend and sometime lover Sean O'Faolain associates with her,[25] or, on
the other, according to the crude formulation of the Aubane Historical Society's *North Cork Anthology* (in which Bowen's name appears on
the contents page with a line of cancellation drawn through it),
deleted from being considered as an Irish writer because of her
ancestry, long-time English residence, and wartime work for the Ministry of Information.[26] In some sense Bowen's position as wartime
political 'collaborator' and 'double agent' crystallizes her work's deep
uncertainty about identity and nationality and 'home', and obsession
with belonging and betrayal, and – alongside Beckett's linguistic
'betrayal' of his mother tongue for French – reveals ambivalent
responses to both writers as perceived threats to received notions of
identity, selfhood and philosophical coherence.

Bowen herself mentions Beckett as one of her Anglo-Irish 'us' in
Pictures and Conversations as part of her disquisition on the characteristics of Anglo-Irish literature: 'As beings, we are at once brilliant and
limited; our unbeatables, up to now, have been those who best prof-
ited by that: Goldsmith, Sheridan, Wilde, Shaw, Beckett.'[27] R.F. Foster,
writing about *Seven Winters*, argues that its characteristic diction 'holds
a Beckettian uncertainty, reflected in language that sometimes reads
like proto-Beckett. "So having been born where I had been born in a
month in which that house did not exist, I felt that I had intruded
upon some no-place".'[28] Both Bowen's own and Foster's recruitment
of Beckett here are interesting: Bowen's highlights the exilic nature of
Anglo-Irish writing, its performance of its Irishness for a foreign audi-
ence in a way which has parallels with the self-conscious performance
of Irishness in her novels, while Foster's draws attention to Bowen's
investment in negativity and uncertainty, as well as gesturing towards

Bowen's lack of 'fit' with contemporary Dublin, and as a form of (entirely apt) shorthand for the 'uncertainty' both of the locations of Bowen's childhood and Bowen's location as an Irish writer.

While Bowen never made Beckett's crucial break with his mother tongue and semi-permanent allegiance to another language of composition, her disquisition in *A Time in Rome* (1959) on the curious 'ease' of disorientation – 'Anywhere, at any time, with anyone . . . one may be seized by the suspicion of being alien—ease is therefore to be found in a place which nominally is foreign: this shifts the weight' – suggests a deep comprehension of its necessity for the modern writer.[29] Beckett writes famously of Jack B. Yeats that '[t]he artist who stakes his being comes from nowhere', while Bowen's 'Notes on Writing a Novel' (1945) appears to contradict this, in one of her characteristic double negatives: 'Nothing can happen nowhere' (*MT*, 39).[30] Her insistent self-identification with her Anglo-Irish 'race', and concomitant lack of interest in the constitutive act of Irish modernist severance from the nets of family, nation and religion, *à la* Joyce and Beckett, has been, I would argue, one of the contributory factors to Bowen's elusiveness within the standard accounts of modernist literature.

If her pronouncements on her absolute sense of her own Irishness seem to protest too much, they are subtly contradicted by the ways in which her fiction explores a more genteel version of the wandering of Beckett's tramps, visiting as an existential predicament. 'Visits terminate, visitors have to go', says the displaced orphan Eva Trout of her position as paying guest at Larkins (*ET*, 11). The Italian cemetery (in which it 'costs a great deal to be buried permanently') and hotel are aligned in *The Hotel* as spaces of enforced transient community.[31] Hugo and Francie in *The Last September*, their shared life advancing 'uncertainly, without the compulsion of tragedy . . . delayed, deflected' (*LS*, 15), strikingly foreshadow the Beckettian pseudo-couple, mutually and nastily dependent, locked together in a paralysis which paradoxically involves continually shifting about. Asked by a teacher whether she still finds her new school 'strange', the teenage protagonist of Bowen's final novel *Eva Trout* responds, in one of Bowen's characteristically skewed locutions, 'Anywhere would seem strange to me that did not' (*ET*, 58). Bowen's characters, like Beckett's, are always in transit, paradoxically, between conditions of stasis. The closest either author approaches to any form of permanence is their obsessive redeployment of, or 'enforced return' to, images of Irish landscapes and childhood, which, however, in both is made strange or edged towards a nowhere. Neil Corcoran rightly points out that Bowen's evocation of the Shannon estuary in County

Clare at the end of A *World of Love* – 'a mad void utter rocky declivity
to the West' – suggests less a specific Irish setting than 'a kind of Beckettian nowhere'.[32] This kind of return is less invested in verisimilitude
than in the uncanny.

Yet, if Beckett and Bowen's work makes frequent literal and
metaphorical detours to Ireland, amidst the prominently fore-
grounded aporias which characterize both *oeuvres*, their shared vision
of the second half of the twentieth century as dislocated, dispossessed
and denatured was confirmed on a vast scale by the Second World
War; arguably, both were 'made' as writers by the war. It is not coinci-
dental that larger numbers of critics make more confident and
totalizing comparisons to Beckett in relation to Bowen's wartime
writing. Barbara Bellew Watson notes for instance that 'in its
unflinching treatment of the dire losses of certainty of our century . . .
Elizabeth Bowen's war novel shows a vision closer to those of Kafka,
Pirandello, Camus, and Beckett than to that of Jane Austen'.[33] W.J.
McCormack in turn views the Second World War as a turning-point
in Irish self-consciousness, 'not only a consciousness of being Irish, or
as Ireland as a distinct entity, but also a consciousness of the Self as
problematic', which he sees in the work of other Irish writers like
Flann O'Brien, Dennis Johnston, Louis McNeice and Francis Stuart,
as well as Beckett and Bowen.[34] This 'crisis of selfhood' is evident in
The Heat of the Day's exploration of the spy, notions of loyalty and allegiance, and the narrative movement between the Irish Big House
Mount Morris and London in the Blitz, where the depredations of
war and the ambivalences of Bowen's Anglo-Irish background under-
write one another and fuel her increasing interest in the supernatural.
In a considerably more oblique and idiosyncratic manner, Beckett's
Watt is also a study of the dislocation of itinerant subject from hermetic environment.

While in most respects utterly dissimilar, Beckett's *Watt* (1953) and
Bowen's *The Heat of the Day* (1949) have a shared root in the Second
World War. *The Heat of the Day* is obviously 'about' war, with its Blitz
setting and espionage plot, while *Watt*, though similarly written
during the conflict – as Beckett said, 'to get away from war and occupation'[35] – concerns a gentle eccentric's time as a servant in the
mysterious house of a Mr Knott, and makes no reference whatsoever
to war, concerning itself primarily with philosophical farce. However,
the two novels have in common an attempt to engage with the horrors
of war in terms of specifically *linguistic* alienation and dislocation, and
the manner in which the problematic relationship between war and
language has considerable repercussions for the individual subject.

Constituted through language, the subject is placed in a critical situation through that language's inability to contain or express the experience of war. *Watt* constitutes a classic, if idiosyncratic, example of how, in causing disruption to the established order, war challenges the strategies through which the subject makes sense of the world, and prevents the confident articulation of a position within that world. It is a novel obsessed with the intimate workings and failures of language: as Beckett's last novel to be written in English for many years, the text, with its pervasive Gallicisms, is testament to a linguistic identity under severe pressure.

More crucially, against the barbarism of the Europe of the 1940s, Watt's mobilization of ridiculously 'rational' strategies in order to make sense of Knott's domain is entirely emblematic of a world gone mad. As Watt attempts to find words for his experience, which seems to resist language, the normal, obscured workings of language are exposed by the rupture of war, and the ever-present gap between signifier and signified is uncomfortably revealed. Objects consent to be named, if at all, with reluctance, like the pot of which Watt can say only 'It resembled a pot, it was almost a pot, but it was not a pot of which one could say Pot, pot and be comforted' (W, 78). This uncertainty creates an instability that dislocates the fragile structures of identity:

> As for himself, though he could no longer call it a man, as he had used to do, with the intuition that he was not perhaps talking nonsense, yet he could not imagine what else to call it, if not a man . . . But for all the relief this afforded him, he might just as well have thought of himself as a box or an urn. (W, 80)

Linguistically speaking, the signifiers remain the same but the signifieds have changed: linguistic strategies for survival have failed. Watt's fate, as he evolves his private cryptic language, is the fate of the refugee who, in letting go of the framework of normality, is brought face to face with the unbearable 'reality' of war.

The Heat of the Day, while paying far more lip-service than *Watt* to the externals of war, via the novel's central trio of Stella, Robert and Harrison, is an essentially static novel, not one primarily interested in external event. W.J. McCormack has pointed out its essentially linguistic focus, which, he argues, replaces the 'vacuum caused by the absconding of action, or the abjuring of it by the author'.[36] It is at its most trenchant as a critique of the effects of war if it is released from a strictly realist template, and if, like the dementedly explicit syntax of *Watt*, its syntactical dislocation is viewed as symptomatic of a more general upheaval. It is perhaps the Bowen work in which her relentless stylistic investment in the nuances of negativity is most paradoxically, and poignantly, successful, in conveying the unthinkable bereavements of war: 'Not knowing who the dead were, you could not know which might be the staircase somebody for the first time was not mounting that morning' (HD, 154). Language, because of the ominous press of this nothingness, is threateningly unstable throughout, from the ambiguity of Cousin Francis's will to the novel's very Beckettian concern with the repetition or near-repetition of names, whereby Kelway and Harrison, hunter and hunted, share a Christian name and Stella's son Roderick Rodney and Louie Lewis's name are repetitive variants – to the extent that, amidst a panicked linguistic atmosphere, in a novel about deception, this near-convergence jeopardizes the reader's confidence in individual identity. Like Watt's pot, which offers no 'comfort', names offer no protection against the wartime erosion or erasure of individual selfhood, or individual or collective structures of meaning.

Beneath its surface control, The Heat of the Day presents a set of deeply encoded anxieties about the disruptions of war. The sophisticated, urbane Stella Rodney appears an unlikely Watt-equivalent, but Louie Lewis sees Stella as a 'soul astray' (HD, 249) – a phrase also used of the child Anna in The Death of the Heart – while Colonel Pole recognizes Stella's 'refugee glance' at Cousin Francis's funeral (HD, 68). Furthermore, it is she as refugee who receives the novel's unsettling ultimate linguistic lesson from her spy lover Robert Kelway: 'What is repulsing you is the idea of betrayal, I suppose, isn't it? In you the hangover from the word? Don't you understand that all language is dead currency?' (HD, 270). The narrative thus emphasizes the impossibility of defining or controlling such powerful and essentially meaningless terms as 'love', 'loyalty' and 'betrayal'. When one man's treason is another man's loyalty, and when language is revealed to be a fundamentally inadequate medium, the possibility of ontological security and certainty is comprehensively destroyed. As a result, not only is the status of language as a common measure of experience severely compromised, in both Watt and The Heat of the Day, but language itself splits into a number of distinct, even opposed, positions of enunciation.

An imagery of war, evoking in particular fragmentation and ruination, renders some of Bowen's statements on war and writing increasingly similar, and increasingly Beckettian. Beckett's 1946 'The Capital of the Ruins', intended for broadcast on Irish national radio, about his experiences as a volunteer at the Irish Red Cross hospital in

Saint-Lô, Normandy, 'bombed out of existence in one night', is one of his first statements of the post-war sense of physical and moral desolation of which his work, particularly his drama, would be received as a major expression.[37] The 'violent destruction of solid things, the explosion of the illusion that prestige, power and permanence attach to bulk and weight' that Bowen writes of in her introduction to *The Demon Lover*, gesture towards both her account of the difficulty of writing at a time of dislocation – 'These years rebuff the imagination as much by being fragmentary as by being violent'[38] – and her increasingly fragmented post-war narrative techniques, with their insistence on nothingness and desuetude. Both Beckett and Bowen's work, in different ways, testifies to their fascination with objects. If for Bowen this is bound up with her continued allegiance to the detailed, thing-filled settings of realism, while the scant bicycles, sucking-stones and greatcoats that loom large in the Beckettian universe do so precisely because of his far weaker commitment to realist textual fabric, their representation of objects has in common what Maud Ellmann, discussing Bowen, calls an 'elegiac' treatment of appurtenances. These 'stand, like Freudian fetishes as monuments to lack and loss'[39] – here Bowen is remarkably similar to the plangent treatment of objects in *Endgame*, where, in a world running down, there is 'no more pap', 'no more bicycle wheels' and, eventually, 'no more nature' (*CDW*, 96–7). The destruction of objects mirrors the dismantling of form; the 'minor trickle of dissolution' which succeeds the explosion in the London house of 'The Happy Autumn Fields' continues to be heard in formal terms throughout Bowen's post-war work, even when detached from war themes or settings, as her writing becomes increasingly irreducible to notions of psychological realism, narrative unity and coherence.[40]

While Bowen's approach to character and narrative convention pulls further away from realism than her pre-war novels, it obviously stops short of Beckett's near-total evacuation of these props. Beckett dismisses the realism of Balzac as a 'chloroformed world' of 'clockwork cabbages' and praises instead, in his review of Sean O'Casey's *Windfalls*, O'Casey's discernment of 'the principle of disintegration in the most complacent solidities', a 'dramatic dehiscence' he regards as the most significant achievement of his fellow dramatist.[41] Bowen remains, meanwhile, evidently attracted to order and symmetry, yet her talent is for a scrupulous delineation of dislocation and derangement. Her wartime short stories she describes in terms of blast damage, in a manner not dissimilar to Beckett's violent imagery of 'dehiscence'; they are 'disjected snapshots', 'flying particles'.[42] There is

an evident match between Bowen and her period when she can write
that '[o]ur century, as it takes its frantic course, seems barely habitable
by humans: we have to learn how to survive as we learn how to
write'.[43] Beckett, in one of his rare manifestos, said he hoped to find a
form to 'accommodate the chaos'.[44] In a 1950 radio interview Bowen
said that she aimed

> to give the effect of fortuity, of a smashed-up pattern with its frag-
> ments impacting on one another, drifting and cracking [. . .
> because of] the horror beneath the surface, the maintenance of the
> surface of a subject fascinates me. In fact, the more the surface
> seems to heave or threaten to crack, the more its actual pattern fas-
> cinates me.

In the same interview, she goes on to say that she had wanted the
action of *The Heat of the Day* to resemble 'the convulsive shaking of a
kaleidoscope, a kaleidoscope also of which the inside reflector was
cracked'.[45] Beckett's emphasis is on trying to found a form in which
the chaos will not be tidied or falsified, Bowen's is on the tension
between the 'lunatic giant' knocking away within, in its underworld of
uncertainty and fragmentation, and a barely maintained veneer of
order; the tension is clear as far back as the closing passage of *The Last
September*, in which, as Danielstown burns, every object in the landscape has each 'its place in the design of order and panic' (*LS*, 205).
However, there are texts in both the Bowen and Beckett canons in
which panic appears to overcome design, and it is to a discussion of
two notable examples of this, *Eva Trout* and *Watt*, that the remainder
of this essay is dedicated.

Eva Trout (1968) is, arguably, Bowen's most 'Beckettian' novel. For
Neil Corcoran it is, along with *A World of Love*, the work where she
finally 'loses touch with classic realism and its customary methods'
and, significantly, after the stylistic excesses of the preceding *A World
of Love*, constitutes the result of a 'process of intense writerly scruple
[like] the disciplines of abstinence which characterise the later prose of
Samuel Beckett'.[46] Given the lack of obvious 'abstinence' in *Eva
Trout*'s style, this scruple appears to make itself felt in Bowen's
refraining from aspects of the hallucinatory realism she has previously
employed. However, it is in relation not to late Beckett, but to his
earlier *Watt* (1953) – the strikingly odd 'ugly duckling' of a novel he
wrote during the Second World War – and his final novel, written in
(Gallic-inflected) English before his turn to French, that I want to
view Bowen's final work.[47] *Watt* and *Eva Trout* are both, in a sense,

novels about culture shock, about an individual hopelessly estranged from group identity, cultural economy and the language which might allow a subject's self-positing. Both novels operate via a form of narrative and epistemological shock tactics and gain a large part of their peculiar effects by their parodic and somewhat embattled relationships with previous works by their authors. *Watt* moves beyond the demented verisimilitude of *Murphy* into a full-blown parody of narrative realism driven by a tirelessly explicit style heavily reliant on enumerations of possibilities, while *Eva Trout* has most often been greeted, as Patricia Craig does, as Bowen 'parodying herself', allowing her 'mannered manner to run away with her'.[48] The generative force of both novels appears to be less their odd, episodic plot and their incoherent, inconsistent characters than their differently overweening styles, and the disruption or ruination of a classic form.

Both *Watt* and *Eva Trout* have as protagonist a linguistically baffled, questing grotesque, somewhat reminiscent of Bowen's Vassar short story notes on 'the Innocent'. Here Bowen defines the 'Innocent' as child, 'arrested', 'defective' or 'simpleton', her definition of 'simplicity' in this case being that which 'handicaps a character in his or her ordinary traffic with the world'.[49] She goes on to note that the short story, 'with its non-explanatory nature', is the best form in which to deal with this 'Simple Soul', the novel requiring a *'rational* character'. However, *Watt* and *Eva Trout* centre notably 'non-explanatory' novels on their central innocents; both constitute forms of enquiry into language and subjectivity and are, arguably, held together primarily by disjointed burlesque and abortive or pastiche *Bildungsroman* which cut across their already half-hearted concessions to narrative continuity, and where style operates as a force which papers uneasily over the cracks of internal disorder. Watt is one of Beckett's terminal procession of bemused elderly waifs, a questing rationalist who may not actually be a man at all, but a 'carpet for example, or a roll of tarpaulin', and of whose '[n]ationality, family, birthplace, confession, occupation, means of existence, distinctive signs', the novel claims to be in 'utter ignorance' (*W*, 14, 19). The scarcely human, eponymous heroine of *Eva Trout* is a 'monstrous heiress', a 'giantess', and possible hermaphrodite (*ET*, 62, 5, 48), who wears a 'massive coat' and is attached to her anthropomorphized bicycle in a suggestively Beckettian manner. Both can only make quasi-autistic approximations at appropriate human responses: Watt leaves those at whom he smiles 'in doubt as to what expression exactly was intended' (*W*, 23); Eva, unable to weep since childhood, is baffled by 'a bewildering, blurring filling up' (*ET*, 300).

However, what both novels hold most in common is that they confront their arrested or defective protagonists with an initiation into a resistant, exclusive or inadequate language. Eva Trout, who cannot find a home in language, is in fact a proto-postmodernist younger sister to Beckett's Watt, suffering his 'loss of filiation' from linguistic structures.[50] Watt, written when its author was both an expatriate and an internal exile in unoccupied France, manifests an anxious preoccupation with language's desertion of the self. Words literally fail Watt, as his world becomes ineffable: superficially straightforward events, such as the visit of the Galls to 'choon the piano', modulate into events that 'resisted Watt's attempts to saddle them with meaning' (W, 67, 75). Events and objects become recalcitrant, intractable, incapable of either being mollified into meaning with words, or of themselves yielding 'semantic succour' (W, 79). Bowen's orphaned heiress, left without a mother tongue by her neglectfully international upbringing, is another of Bowen's dangerous innocents – like Watt, who, the Addenda to the novel tells us, has 'never been properly born' (W, 248), Eva is an adult infant (in-fans), as Maud Ellmann points out, in that she can barely speak. Her dispersed upbringing has left her expressing herself 'like a displaced person', in an 'outlandish, cement-like conversational style' (ET, 10). The heiress appears to have no linguistic heritage: 'unable to speak—talk, be understood, converse', her diction is 'wooden . . . deadly . . . misbegotten', as she herself is (ET, 62, 64). In fact, Eva's strangely autistic or 'deadly' language bears a striking resemblance to the lexicon of Beckett plays such as Waiting for Godot and Endgame: in lieu of a polite enquiry into the health of her guardian, at one point she asks, Beckettianly, 'Are you deteriorating?' (ET, 104).

While Watt, baffled and astray in the world of Knott's house, finds himself 'longing for a voice . . . to speak of the little world of Mr Knott's establishment, with the old words, the old credentials' (W, 81), Eva does not suffer from this form of linguistic nostalgia; she has never had such 'credentials' and has always been an être manqué. She confesses to Iseult, the teacher who tries to induct her into language, of having once had hopes '[t]o be, to become—I had never been . . . I was beginning to be' before being sent 'back again – to be nothing': 'I remain gone. Where am I? I do not know—I was cast out from where I believed I was' (ET, 203). Without language there can be no interiority, as Eva observes when she repairs to the National Portrait Gallery to be galvanized into the realization that '[t]here was no "real life"; no life was more real than this' (ET, 216). Despite the novel's multiple settings in London, Paris, Chicago and Kent, Eva Trout shares with Beckett's *habitués* of urns, limbos and dustbins a condition of 'goneness' which is inextricably linked to an inability to speak the self in language, to a linguistically panic-stricken displacement. Memory is another, related, way of possessing and accumulating the past into a form of subjectivity, and Proust is an important forebear for both Beckett and Bowen. However, by *Eva Trout* even this weak form of agency has become impossible; the amnesiac Eva remembers, as she speaks, 'disjectedly': 'To reassemble the picture was impossible; too many of the pieces were lost, lacking' (*ET*, 42). The amnesiac subject, all sure grasp of the past dissolving, has the dubious freedom to rearrange *ad nauseam* the elements of a posited selfhood into some new form, the self becoming an endless series of such refashionings, or nobody at all, the fear that is behind Eva's endless spinning of lies, fictions and fantasies. Eventually, her 'mistrust of or objection to verbal intercourse', and the discovery that her adopted son is deaf-mute, leads to a temporary, wordless existence of 'sublimated monotony', like that of a Beckettian pseudocouple (*ET*, 207, 208).

If *Eva Trout* falls short of *Watt*'s maniacal intransigence – crowned, famously, by the presence of a set of 'Addenda' containing 'illuminating material' omitted due to 'fatigue and disgust' (*W*, 247) – Bowen's novel chooses not to 'reassemble the picture' and remains, as Bennett and Royle characterize it, 'awkward, disjunctive, convulsive'.[51] It incorporates themes familiar from previous Bowen works – the dangerous innocent abroad – but, with techniques newly disjunctive, consciously sets its sketchy, patchy self up against the greater richness of the past, particularly in comparison with Dickens, on whom the failed novelist Iseult Arble muses in the Broadstairs section of the novel. If the always halting narrative movement of *Watt* frequently grinds to a halt under the baroque weight of its own syntax and its related tendency to unfold itself into increasingly elaborate edifices of possibility before collapsing again, *Eva Trout* frequently seems almost equally baffled before its own incoherent procedures, its uncomfortable admixture of genres. Like *Watt*, its register is often one of bafflement. It is compounded of lacunae: we never know precisely what occurs between Eric Arble and Eva, or how the 'missing' four hours are spent by Jeremy and Iseult Arble; we never discover the true story of Eva's 'unspecified bridegroom' (*ET*, 39), nor how she acquires Jeremy. Iseult, writing to her correspondent, Constantine, can express gladness that their 'non-relationship was as ever, unimpaired, static, stable . . . All had been nothing' (*ET*, 228), while Eva's alternating periods of frantic movement and stasis paradoxically suggest, as she vouchsafes herself, 'I continue going away' (*ET*, 249). In a novel which concerns an innocent being birthed into language, Iseult, the substitute mother who fails to induct Eva into language, also fails to write a novel which she describes as 'born dead' (ET, 253), and which thus bears a striking resemblance to Eva Trout (as well as to the succession of Beckett creatures 'not properly born'), which refuses ever quite to cohere into a novel, though at times looking as though it may.

Finally, the novel approaches a Beckettian ethics of failure. The strikingly cinematic finale – the 'child star' in his 'ballet enactment of a crime passionel' in front of 'audience-minded' bystanders 'not obstructing, they hoped, the rigged-up cameras' (ET, 298) – moves the denouement out of the realm of a language found wanting, a lurch away from words into a picture or cinematic still, a final, late modernist admission that, as one of its minor characters says 'Words do not connect' (ET, 218). Eva Trout, like Watt, stops but has no end, not having progressed far beyond Eric Arble's initial verdict on the savagely innocent protagonist: 'Nothing . . . makes sense . . . She makes sense as much as else' (ET, 19). If, ultimately, there is a comic relation to be sketched between Beckett and Bowen, it is that there is something inherently funny about meaninglessness or absurdity, for which one might ascribe the Freudian explanation of the pleasure of no longer having to invest our energies in the labour of making sense.

Writing about The Heat of the Day, Neil Corcoran notes the knowing allusiveness of Harold Pinter's screenplay made from the novel for a TV film by Christopher Morahan, which features the following concluding stage direction:

> They sit in silence.
> After a time the All Clear sounds.
> They do not move.

'They do not move' is also, of course, the final stage direction in both acts of Waiting for Godot, after Estragon each time proposes departure, indicating that Pinter's screenplay implicitly recognizes a Beckett–Bowen affinity in this pervasive sense of scarcely postponed departure, immobility and refusal of closure.[52] This essay has attempted to sketch some of the more prominent ways in which these two very dissimilar oeuvres might be aligned in terms of a shared commitment to nullity, disconnection, and a strongly Proustian recognition that, as Bowen remarks in her 1952 preface to The Last September, it is 'those very periods of existence which are lived through . . . carelessly, unwillingly or in boredom that most often fructify into art' (Mulberry Tree, 124). Both writers share a limited range of themes – isolation, disorientation, loss, ending, decline, impasse, the uncanny proximity of the other. If Bowen's work does not exhibit the savage truncation of the human form, the generic bleeding or the radical denaturing of language which characterizes Beckett's later work, it none the less mounts a strikingly modernist attack on the metaphysics of presence. Gaps continually yawn between self and world, different parts of the self, different parts of a life. A characteristically Beckettian state of non-presence recurs continually throughout Bowen: Janet in *Friends and Relations* experiences in Alex Thirdman 'a glimpse of vacancy', and he reciprocally sees her as 'never among them, a positive no-presence' (*FR*, 31, 33); Iseult in *Eva Trout*, face to face with Constantine, finds that 'nothing authenticated him as a human being . . . To be with him was to be *in vacuo* also' (*ET*, 41). If Beckett's delineation of the void is primarily comprehensible in the nakedly philosophical terms from which his work never entirely departs, in the continual, apocalyptic lapping of nullity around her characters' involvement in desire, Bowen's often richly farcical writing abolishes any real ontological security. Continually practising stylistic and structural experiment, deliberately injuring her disjointed, self-reflexive narratives in order to inoculate them against empty elegance, Bowen is a writer deeply attuned to the aims of high modernism, even if she never entirely loses touch with classic realism and its more customary methods.

2

'How to measure this unaccountable darkness between the trees':

the strange relation of style and meaning in *The Last September*[1]

SUSAN OSBORN

Despite Elizabeth Bowen's emergence as a seminal figure in several key areas of contemporary study, much of her fiction is still considered difficult and resistant to interpretation. In large measure, this is because Bowen's past commentators have paid almost exclusive attention to historical and thematic aspects of her fiction, perhaps above all to her ascribed interest in women's experience as that experience was shaped by early and mid-twentieth-century Irish and English historical crises. Yet critical attention to such concerns has always brushed aside an immitigable fact of Bowen's writing: her notoriously strange style, which produces in almost every sentence – either explicitly or subliminally – some disorientation of sense, some deviation from standard meaning. The focus of this essay, then, is precisely on Bowen's troublesome stylistic practices and their influence on and relation to meaning formation. Although the ideas here presented have degrees of applicability to all of her novels and stories, this essay will be primarily restricted to a discussion of Bowen's as yet under-examined and under-appreciated *The Last September* (1929).

In the past, *The Last September* was most often read as a realistic novel concerned with the conflagration caused by Britain's division of Ireland in 1920. While some interpreters read the novel as a denunciation of the British colonialists, others read it as a condemnation of the resistance fighters, and still others, including, most recently, Maud Ellmann, read the novel as a critique of the Protestant Irish, who are generally represented as anachronisms, destroyed by defects attributed to morality or class (*Shadow*, 52–67). For example, in Hermione Lee's seminal study, she writes that the novel has to do with Ireland's time of the Troubles and the tragedy(ies) inherent in and to internecine warfare and colonialism (*Estimation*, 42–3), while Heather Bryant Jordan asserts that 'the main subject of the novel is . . . the war of independence, or revolution'; the book's theme concerns the 'demise of the Protestant ascendancy' (*Elizabeth Bowen*, 54, 49).[2] In a complimentary reading, Neil Corcoran (2004) interprets the novel as a Big House 'comedy of manners', albeit one marked by unexpected ellipses and lacunae, one which forms part of Bowen's effort to interpret the experience of being 'bilocated', by which he refers to the experience of living 'between' Ireland and England during the Troubles (39, 13). Other interpreters, including Phyllis Lassner (1989), have found feminist themes in the novel and have read it as a reflection of Bowen's concern with women's 'struggle with autonomy, dependence and self-expression' (153). In one of the most complex feminist readings of *The Last September*, Robert L. Caserio connects the female characters' gender status to their 'beleaguered vulnerability as colonialists'. Using Fredric Jameson's notion of the political unconscious, Caserio (1999) suggests their 'subversive alliance' with the rebels (251). In a similar reading, renée c. hoogland (1994), suggests that the novel's female protagonist discloses the 'intertwined operations' of the opposing realms of 'phallogocentric gender and nationalist discourses personified by [her fiancé] as oppressive and exclusionary practices' (69).[3]

Yet, as interesting as these interpretations are, the enigmas surrounding *The Last September*, the novel's shot-through queerness, give few grounds for any optimistic good faith or trust in any such comprehensive and competent handlings. Certainly these interpreters ably contract the area of unknown that exists in and around the novel, but there is an unfamiliar and unruly quality to this novel, something that oscillates between the formed and the perceived that cannot be well represented or neutralized through the logical coherence of a theory. The novel is fraught with a sense of suspense and danger – one cannot escape the sense of proximity to dangerous, unknown forces – and an exquisite tension is set up between the rational modern world and a sense of long-forgotten forces acting within it. As a result, when we read, we respond intensely, even in ways viscerally, to the press of something not always made manifest in the language of the story. Yet whatever it is remains unknown and inchoate. The sense of illogical, disruptive, archaic forces skulking through and around the story is perhaps the story's most prominent characteristic and yet it is not always apparent. This extra charge grants to the novel its most baffling and salient effect and undoes our efforts at conceptual clarity in ways different from and beyond the familiar polysemy of language. By so saying, I don't mean to suggest that past thematic or historical

interpretations of The Last September are 'wrong'; in fact, there is much
that is right and challenging about them. Rather, that the ideological
or suasive work represented as being achieved in these readings is
undermined by the provocative and often defamiliarizing narrative and
formal irregularities in the novel, irregularities that undermine the certainty upon which these readings rely for their force, and that bar us
from forming conclusive statements about how the story might have
been legislated prior to its writing, as well as from making statements
about its ultimate justification or meaning. That we cannot, with anything akin to certainty, attribute the vague sense of awe and dread that
we experience upon reading The Last September to either the manifest
political conflict or the personal conflict embedded within the more
public context is perhaps what disturbs us most powerfully upon
reading the novel.[4]

That said, it is not surprising that critics have trouble articulating
just what it is that makes The Last September so strange. A review of the
manifest plot of The Last September reveals little that might account for
the strange sense of proximity to ill-defined and unfamiliar forces that
we experience when reading the novel.[5] The novel is strangely unbur-
dened of content, the putative subject – the engagement of a member
of an Irish landowning family, Lois Farquar, to Gerald Lesworth, a
British subaltern – is quotidian, and the characters, intellectually considered, are not very striking.[6] Events thicken and accrete, and we have
a sense, upon completing the novel, that something momentous and
unmediated has taken place, but there are no clearly discernible climaxes.[7] Certainly, the war is most often cited as the motivating theme
in The Last September and, on occasion, the characters do attribute
noises emanating from the woods to skirmishes between the republi-
cans and the subalterns, but this in no way proves that Sinn Féin or its
paramilitary wing, the Irish Republican Army, is the cause of the characters' unease. In fact, outside of two scenes – the mill scene in which
the man in the mill is assumed by most readers to be a member of the
IRA, and one scene in which a house guest's watch is taken and
returned by an unseen character who is not identified in the story as a
member of Sinn Féin but who is presumed by most readers to be associated with Sinn Féin – the supposedly malevolent rebels are never
seen and the war takes place completely 'off stage' and is never reified
in the narrative. Indeed, the war seems more a mechanical motif
perhaps used to lend credibility or plausibility to a larger, darker
texture of events. Even though the homeowners and their guests
ascribe the family's fears to aspects of the politically motivated conflict, one cannot help feeling that there exists, beyond the manifest

world represented, a world or system whose workings are only partially revealed, a system, if you will, potentially malignant, certainly sinister, and implacable under whose persecutions the family is suffering. Upon finishing the story, we are chilled by a sense of something far more ominous than the fire raging at the Big House on the hill. How then, as Lois asks, can we account for the 'living silence', the 'darkness between the trees'?[8]

In the past, perhaps from a sense of critical largesse, the few uncertain readers who addressed Bowen's prose style saw in it most often an imperfect approximation of Woolf's.[9] Certainly, a case could be made for their similarity. Like Woolf's, much of Bowen's prose has a 'transparent', numinous quality that suggests the existence of deeper zones below the highly articulated surface. As with Woolf's, a great deal of the beauty of Bowen's 'good' prose springs from undulation. In other words, the sense and sound of multiple periods rise together and both fall away in a mutual, rhythmical cadence. The periodic rhythms control and direct the force of the sentences – a stage of thought finishes with a stage of rhythm, a thought member with a rhythmic member.

Look, for example, at the much-acclaimed first paragraph of Bowen's widely admired *The Death of the Heart* (1938 [New York, 1955]):

> That morning's ice, no more than a brittle film, had cracked and was now floating in segments. These tapped together or, parting, left channels of dark water, down which swans in slow indignation swam. The island stood in frozen woody brown dusk: it was now between three and four in the afternoon. A sort of breath from the clay, from the city outside the park, condensing, made the air unclear; through this, the trees round the lake soared frigidly up. Bronze cold of January bound the sky and the landscape; the sky was shut to the sun—but the swans, the wings of ice, the pallid withdrawn Regency terraces had an unnatural burnish, as though cold were light. There was something momentous about the height of winter. Steps rang on the bridges, and along the black walks. This weather had set in; it would freeze harder tonight. (3)

What wants special attention here is the almost poetic continuity of this passage, the uninterrupted skein of the reader's heightened attention and of the verbal beauty which excites it, the effect of the periodic prose, in other words, on the vivacity and susceptibility of the reader's attention. As is typical of much of Bowen's well-mannered prose, the passage is composed of impressionistic descriptions and presents a series of sentences of tempered variety free (except for 'cracked') of any harsh rhythmic or phonemic intrusions. The language dwells sensually on the scene described and is beautiful in its unobtrusiveness, in the way it, for the most part, leaves its calculation and skill unobserved. The description is heavily burdened by assonance and alliteration, the erotic 'mouth music' that ties Bowen's work to that of poets like Heaney. The repetition of the initial and medial consonants, especially the 's's and 'l's, creates easy and sensible swells through which the reader slides. The periodic rhythm controls and directs the force of the sentence; its predictability is clued to the hope of the shapeliness of things. The punctuation and sound patterns create an architectural momentum of imaginary weights and transported presences: the peculiar grace and expressive meaning is composed of recognizable rhythmic details and even visual grace. As is typical of much of Bowen's prose, the infrequent moment when the language does call attention to itself, it does so only by its continuous slight heightening and deft coordination; it is unmarked, in other words, by any strongly marked features – eccentricities, inelegancies, and inaccuracies of expression – which might contort or grotesque the surface. By reducing the number of sounds, selecting them from a limited range, and restricting the rhythms of the periods, both Woolf and Bowen – at least in places – numb our analytic attention and allow us to move inattentively over the surface of many of their sentences, as the punctuation of sound patterns creates implications of meanings which appear and disappear as the sounds and rhythms change and we adjust to the changes. The activity of both creates and leaves behind not a material object, but an imaginary one. 'Somewhere between the realms of ornamental sound and representative statement, the words pause and balance, dissolve and resolve' (Blackmur, 1986, 75). Like ice into water, words deliquesce into meaning.[10]

And yet, as is well apparent in *The Last September*, unlike Woolf's, there is also much about Bowen's prose that invites our derision. With wilful disregard for the reader, she often inserts ugly sounding words into otherwise mellifluous sentences when more euphonious ones would do just as well if not better; her syntax is often anfractuous and strained; her images are frequently bizarre, unexpectedly macabre, in places, even nonsensical; and her punctuation is so often ungoverned that one wonders, at times, if the errors were intended or the result of negligent proofreading. Sentences and phrases such as 'In their heart like a dropped pin the grey glazed roof reflecting the sky lightly glinted'; 'His singleness bore, confusing, upon her panic of thoughts her physical apprehension of him was confused by the slipping, cold leaves'; '. . . the sound moved shakily, stoopingly, like someone running and crouching behind a hedge'; 'Chinks of sunlight darted up her like mice and hesitated away like butterflies'; 'Split light, like hands, was dragged past the mill-race, clawed like hands at the brink and went down in destruction'; and 'They approached the doorway that yearned up the path like an eye-socket' appal and confound us (*The Last September*, 78, 213, 33, 45, 155, 105). How are we to account for these *bizarreries*, this kind of useless and confusing 'decorative elaboration', 'this pointless verbal excess' as an abashed William Heath once asked (1961, 43)? It is certainly tempting to read these apparently underworked or overworked sentences, as have earlier readers, as inadvertent errors, embarrassing evidence of authorial carelessness that somehow escaped the governing eye of the editor or proofreader. How else can we account for the often apparently arbitrary use of punctuation; the odd, seemingly rash and indiscriminate word choices; the convoluted and at times insensible syntax – the whole ungainly thing? Certainly, the want of 'finish' exhibited in these brief excerpts, the ways these strangely wrought sentences seem conceived and executed with a blatant disregard for the accepted norms of intellectual decorum, grammatical and syntactical coherence and technical competence, those formal properties intended to assure an easy concord between reader and text, seems indefensible. Could these injudicious word choices, the unfamiliar syntax, the unexpected punctuation be the result of inexperience, as Bowen's biographer, Victoria Glendinning, has suggested (*Biography*, 1978, 76)? Or are they, as Sean O'Faolain declared, merely the indecorous products of Bowen's unaccountable penchant for the shocking and sensational: '[Bowen's] sensibility', he noted, 'can be catty, even brassy, too smart, like an overclever décor for ballet . . . on occasion vulgar' (1957, 167–8)? Or perhaps they are simply the unbecoming and ill-advised efforts of a writer whose ambition is, as Virginia Woolf averred, in excess of her talent: 'In some passages you are in danger of being too clever' (Pippett, 1955, 182).[11] The want of artistic discipline exhibited here, the uninhibited way in which these irregularities are displayed and the troubling excessiveness apparent in these transgressions have bothered many of Bowen's more recent readers as well, including the admiring Hermione Lee, who worries that Bowen's stylistic infelicities become 'uncomfortable, especially in [their] syntactical mannerisms':

> Ever since the preciousness of *Friends and Relations*, Elizabeth Bowen has been in control of her idiosyncratic manner, which she has disciplined. In *The Heat of the Day*, for the first time, it begins to look like affectation; and although this was her most successful novel, it

> was after its publication that critical objections to 'the unusually evasive surface', 'the proliferation of detail that is fascinating in itself but ultimately distracting' began to be commonplace. Both *The Demon Lover* stories and *The Heat of the Day* overuse double negatives, inversions, the breaking-up of natural sentence order, passive constructions . . . such effects are all too easy to parody . . . and they look irritating . . . (*Estimation*, 165)[12]

While Lee ultimately tries to recuperate Bowen's style in *The Heat of the Day* by analogizing it to the strain she sees apparent in the novel's plot, she, like Maud Ellmann, who fears that Bowen's descriptions can be 'somewhat overstated' and who suggests disapprovingly, that Bowen's 'glorified addictions' and 'overheated' syntax inexplicably 'atrophy into strangulating mannerisms', obstructing affectations (*Shadow*, 2003, 189) and Neil Corcoran, who suggests that Bowen has written some of the most 'fearful' prose in modern history, shares a widespread concern that, as Corcoran writes, the 'writer herself may not remain in control of the [stylistic] riot' (Corcoran, 3).[13] Were it not for these lapses in taste or judgement, these untoward exaggerations, reads the subtext of these interpretations, many of her novels and stories might be declared master works, or at least be considered exceptional examples of their genre. Were it not considered the result of ineptness or a want of personal resolution, her style might be declared as strikingly complex and original as Joyce's or Beckett's, perhaps even more so. As it is though, the distaste and derision elicited by Bowen's stylistic practices suggest that, as arresting as her style is, it has not been considered coherent enough, meaningful enough, or intended enough to warrant thorough examination and analysis.

A careful examination of these readers' remarks suggests that there are two conspicuously occurring features of Bowen's prose style that most trouble her readers and interfere with their appreciation of her prose. The first and perhaps the most challenging is a general one concerning the diverse and often unfamiliar ways that the irregular aspects of her prose style interrupt the easy concord between the reader and the writer. In other words, generally, the reader gives credence to the mimetic claims of the text in return for confirmation by the writer of the reader's expectations. But what Lee is saying, and what has been echoed by almost all of Bowen's past critics, is that while some elements of Bowen's prose style confirm and validate the unproblematic circuit of response between reader and text, others are deemed extravagant or excessive because they estrange the familiarizing work expected of this class of fictions. That is, if we assume a sociological understanding of the process of reading and accept the

Barthian notion that the 'subject' of mimesis is an inter-subjective entity issuing from a shared set of cultural codes, a collaboration dependent on interactive systems of mutual knowledge inscribed in representational discourse, then, even with certain latitudes allowed, the lack of cooperation on the part of Bowen's prose, and specifically, the way Bowen unsystematically applies artificial, elaborate and unfamiliar tropes and images which frequently but not always confer onto the representation unusual, unexpected and sometimes apparently arbitrary emphases and values that sometimes but not always resist being assimilated into the work of representation produces in the reader an unfamiliar and often frustrating contest between absorption and distraction. In other words, by producing in places a sense of opacity rather than the expected intelligibility, the unusual imbrication and interdigitation of conventional and less conventionally referential and syntactical properties in Bowen's work disturb the traditional hegemonic compact between the reader and the text by interrupting what Frank Kermode refers to (adopting a concept of Leonard Meyer's used in relation to our responses to music) as the generically determined 'probability system' (Kermode, 1975, 119) within which the practice of literary mimesis is inscribed. Instead, as Ellmann notes, Bowen's 'addictions' and unacceptable 'mannerisms' disrupt and estrange the cultural codes through which these readers expect the text to be realized in the act of reading. Historically, the indignation and derision expressed by Bowen's readers are most often related to this insolent recalcitrance; in other words, to the peremptory ways that many of her tropes often but not always affront the logic encoded in these probability systems by resisting or refusing to be absorbed into the *subjectum* of the intellect. The difficulties that these unusual and inconsistently employed irregularities create present perhaps the greatest challenge to those readers such as Lee and Ellmann who most believe in her abilities, as the inequality of execution apparent in Bowen's prose, the unsystematically employed irregularities, sometimes but not always resist hermeneutical penetration, thus making it difficult to reconcile her prose with generally held demands for narrative effectiveness.

Yet here lies the chief virtue and central challenge of Bowen's prose. As has been well remarked, in Woolf's writing, her well-mannered and well-executed periodicity is clued to the hope of the shapeliness of things. As Robert Caserio has noted, Woolf's narratives 'solidif[y] [the] disjunction[s]' among various narrative elements (Caserio, 1999, 272); 'the contrast of opposition[s in Woolf's work]', writes Kathleen McCluskey, 'enables an equilibrium between opposing

forces in [her] text[s] as in the world' (McCluskey, 1986, 124). But in
Bowen's fiction, we see no such global attempt to superimpose a
harmony or to consistently or evenly distribute the weight of meaning
and emphasis across individual sentences or narratives, but nor do we
see any consistent disruption of the formal coherence of the novel or
its individual elements (such as diction, grammar and syntax). Rather,
the complex effects of Bowen's prose, the potent yet relative and
uncustomary legibility of The Last September, the novel's enigmatic and
burdensome charge and the distinctive strain involved in interpreting
that charge result in large measure from the unsystematic ways that the
prose transgresses expected processes of signification and from the
ways it confuses when it does not undermine many of the conventions
of mimetic representation, especially the expected reciprocity at the
level of the symbolic. In other words, because Bowen's prose unsystematically violates rules of mimetic representation and realistic
discourse while establishing a relationship with them, the prose both
permits logical conceptualization and challenges it. As a result of these
estrangements, many of the commonly employed interpretive binaries
that we generally rely on to help us read and interpret works of literature such as the customarily conceived relation between form and
content, sign and signifier, are deprived of much of their force and
value, without being rendered completely meaningless. This is not to
suggest that there is anything 'wrong' with The Last September, although
there is – this novel and all of her fictional narratives are characterized
by all sorts of rhetorical improprieties – but that it is Bowen's inconsistent and unsystematic employment of representational and formal
irregularities that threatens the stability of conventionally conceived
historical interpretations and that also lends to The Last September its
strangely transformed air, its sense of being about something other
than itself, at times beyond the control of intelligence. In order to
appreciate and better understand the protean strength and allure of
Bowen's fictional narratives, then, we must look not just at her regular
or 'good' prose or at her irregular or 'bad' prose, but at the ways the
unusual linking of the expected and the unfamiliar both invokes and
discredits a sense of meaning, at the way the concatenation of extravagant and more traditional forms, in provocative and sometimes
impudent ways, effaces areas of expected significance and confuses distinctions, thereby vitiating our attempts to control her narratives or
even to think about them in conventional ways.

Take this short passage, for example, which describes The Last September's homeowners, the Naylors, and their guests gathering for
dinner:

In the dining-room, the little party sat down under the crowd of portraits. Under the constant interchange from the high-up faces staring across—now fading each to a wedge of fawn-colour and each looking out from a square of darkness tunneled into a wall—Sir Richard and Lady Naylor, their nephew, niece and old friends had a thin, over-bright look, seemed in the air of the room unconvincingly painted, startled, transitory. Spaced out accurately around the enormous table—whereon in what was left of the light, damask birds and roses had an unearthly shimmer—each so enisled and distant that a remark at random, falling short of a neighbour, seemed a cry of appeal—the six, in spite of an emphasis in speech and gesture they unconsciously heightened, dwindled personally. While above, the immutable figures, shedding into the rush of dusk smiles, frowns, every vestige of personality, kept only attitude—an outmoded modishness, a quirk of a flare, hands slipped under a ruffle or spread over the cleft of a bosom—canceled time, negatived personality and made of the lower cheerfulness, dining and talking, the faintest exterior friction.
In Lawrence's plate of clear soup six peas floated. (24–5)

Unlike the earlier excerpt reproduced from *The Death of the Heart*, on first reading this odd, inexpedient passage plunges us into a vortex of linguistic confusion. The paragraph has an unfamiliar density to it, not a depth, but a kind of weird gumminess that resists penetration. Indeed, what strikes one first about this description is its strangely imperious and peremptory facture, the ostentatious way that the paragraph seems to call attention to its bizarre and disorienting execution. Certainly, the description is nuanced and individual parts of the passage are given precise and rigorous form, but just who or what is being described and by which parts of this description? While conventional syntax is intended to help us explicate the world and our ideas about it – it provides a kind of guarantee that, through its proper application, a real and fulfilling comprehension of the intelligible may be had – the disorder and formlessness of these passages at first confronts the mind with absurdity. Certainly a progression of phenomena is represented, but with its disrupted periods, syntactical inversions, amphibolies, odd words and words used oddly ('enisled'?, 'dwindled personally'?), the shape of both that which is represented and the mode of its representation is difficult to apprehend clearly. Indeed, while reading this verbal filigree, one has the sense that the suturing of the various parts of this description was not necessarily impelled by any desire to conform to conventional or logical notions of succession or clarity. Instead, separate elements of phenomena are connected but are often placed in an obscure and even, in places, an apparently random relation to one another. Of special note are the proliferation of commas and dashes; normally refinements of meaning, here they isolate groups of words that often appear arbitrarily, incompletely, or imperfectly expressed. In other words, while the plethora of dashes and commas, adverbs, and other syntactical tools are all clearly circumscribed and differentiated in themselves, in this passage, they do not clearly delimit persons, things, or portions of actions or events in respect to one another. As with the separate elements represented, the relationships between and among elements in this description (i.e. their temporal, local, causal, consecutive, antithetical and conditional limitations) are also often but not always confused and obscured by the punctuation and syntax. As a result, the apparently random formation that we find many of the words in, the uncustomary and irregular use of subordination and hypotaxis, challenges but does not completely prohibit our desire to highlight key or consistent concepts or to form one-to-one correspondences that might reliably help us gauge and reinforce our interpretations. In other words, oddly, for all its spectacularness, this description is, by and large, only unevenly or might we say uncertainly legible. And while one might imagine that the return to the mannerly and the regular at the beginning of the subsequent paragraph would moderate the abruptness of the disjunction between the more certainly understood and the less certainly understood parts of this description, that isn't the case. Rather, by focusing our attention on the hyperbolic concatenation of the two, it exacerbates our sense of the disjunction. In other words, the interdigitation of various modes of representation in the same passage refuses to allow the 'good' or the customary and the 'bad' or the uncustomary to simply contrast with one another; one could not reduce or stabilize their relation as a simple opposition between the 'good' and the 'bad'. Rather, the representation insists on their mutual entanglement.

In large measure, the unexpected virtues of this passage and passages like it derive from the ways that they do not broadcast their intentions, from the ways that the descriptions or parts of the descriptions sometimes but not always seem to have no immediately available sense. In other words, descriptions such as the dining-room one are nuanced, but we couldn't say they unfold. As a result, what ought to be obvious is not. Here are three more. In the first, a group from the house sets off on a walk:

> Out, at last, through the window, dazzled, threading and separating between the flower-beds, the party dispersed with their cigarettes. Large to themselves, to each other graduating from a

little below life-size, to an eye from the mountain antlike—but smaller and less directed—or like beads, tipped out . . . The sense of a watcher, reserve of energy and intention, abashed Laurence, who turned from the mountain. But the unavoidable and containing stare impinged to the point of a transformation upon the social figures with orderly, knitted shadows, the well-groomed grass and the beds in their formal pattern. (147)

The second describes a moment during a walk that Lois takes with her fiancé:

She stood perplexed at the edge of the path; he kissed her with frightened violence. The laurels creaked, as in her arms, she bent back into them. His singleness bore, confusing, upon her panic of thoughts her physical apprehension of him was confused by the slipping, cold leaves. (213)

And the last describes a guest upon her arrival in the drawing room after she dresses for dinner:

Vague presence, barely a silhouette, the west light sifting into her fluffy hair and lace wrappings so that she half-melted, she gave so little answer to one's inquiry that one did not know how to approach. (21)

As with the dining-room description, these descriptions are explicit – they don't fail to deliver – but what they deliver is often incongruous and difficult to tease out. In other words, if the scene of mimesis unfolds within networks of interpenetrating and interpretive schema within which the reader and writer participate in a series of collaborative exchanges, then, even allowing for a degree of 'poetic licence' on the part of the author, the estranged and unfamiliar syntactical and grammatical arrangements used here undermine the stability of the participatory endeavour upon which the success of the mimetic enterprise depends, and challenge our ability to find apt terms to conceptualize, describe, evaluate and analyse her prose.

There is another way of thinking about these passages that warrants mentioning. You could say, as many have, that these passages are dreadful and, with their multiple distortions, that they have a dreadful quality about them. We have a sense, in other words, given the vast wealth of beautiful periodic prose from which they arise, that they have 'come out of nowhere' and that they intrude in an uncomfortable way into the norm of the rest of the prose. It is almost as if the language of the novel had been invaded by something that was not supposed to come out into the open, something other that should not have appeared. And while many of the sentences ultimately submit to rational paraphrase (for example, of the second short passage reproduced, we could say that Lois's feelings about her fiancé are confused and somehow made more acute by aspects of the physical environment), they remain strikingly unfamiliar, and their placement within the rest of the prose of the paragraph and story, which is, by and large, familiar and mannerly, gives the entire narrative an uncanny quality whereby the familiar and unfamiliar are interdigitated, the probable and the possible placed in proximity, and the dreadful aspect of the story, the other, lies not only 'out there', in the plot or a character or somewhere beyond the text, but exists out there and 'in here', in the prose, in the sentences that supposedly serve the function of representing the dreadful outside of itself. In other words, in *The Last September* and all of Bowen's fictional narratives, the quotidian is no less genuine for containing the strange. Bowen's smudging of boundaries which typically keep separate the seemingly distinct and contradictory realms of the beautiful, periodic prose and the rude, poorly executed and sometimes even seemingly meaningless prose threatens to disrupt not only the ordinary tension between the known and the unknown, inside and outside, the familiar and the strange, and estrange that tension so that it seems unfamiliar, strange, unknown, and unknowable in the story, but also threatens the fixed laws of nature encoded in mimetic literature, laws intended to safeguard us against the unplumbed and unapprehended, and the putative transcendent stability of the prose is both evoked and disturbed by the syntactical indeterminacy, the dynamic interaction of the forms of the prose.

The second conspicuous reservation expressed by Bowen's past readers specifically concerns the 'distracting' 'proliferation of detail' that Lee noted, referring to the apparently undisciplined ways that Bowen's prose sometimes draws the reader's attention away from the 'inside' of the sentences, the place where the meaning is supposed to lie, and holds it instead on the surface, the word level or the 'top' of the prose, that level of the representation that is supposed to be passed through to get to the meaning 'behind'. This is an interesting reservation, as it concerns the inconsistent ways in which Bowen's language sometimes appears to seek to deny itself as language, to the often unfamiliar and distracting ways that Bowen's language sometimes defamiliarizes the conventional role of the signifier in the performance of the act of reference, thus diminishing the importance of the 'meaning' by instead conferring much of the glamour and fascination with which meaning is usually endowed onto the words themselves, the patterns of signs that are conventionally supposed to represent the more interesting (and privileged) meaning 'behind'. In other words, in narrative realism, words generally trace a reality without suggesting an architectural presence. When successful, the signs diffidently efface themselves before their referents in order to create what Barthes has described as the work's reality effect ('L'effet de réel', 1968, 84-9). We say the writer has succeeded, then, when the reader enjoys the sense of being faced not with words but with things; in other words, with reality itself. But in *The Last September*, the putative immateriality of the signs is called into question. Words which are meant to 'dissolve' and disappear into meaning sometimes seem burdened by a strange, unexpectedly bossy, Braille-like tangibility, an unfamiliar sense of 'material obtrusiveness' as Ellmann has noted (x). Indeed, one often has the sense of having felt Bowen's words before reading them and this unnatural sense of prominence sometimes makes us experience even the smallest compositional details not as flat, but almost as sculptured forms that emerge towards the reader. This strange materiality is more often associated with plastic arts than written, arts in which we more often find a salient concern with the relation between flatness and depth. Because one frequently feels a preponderance of a word over its meaning, many of the words in Bowen's prose appear curiously more substantial than the passage as a whole and direct us to their definitions, the denotation in front of the meaning. For example, here is the opening of *The Last September*:

> About six o'clock the sound of a motor, collected out of wide country and narrowed under the trees of the avenue, brought the household out in excitement on to the steps. Up among the beeches, a thin iron gate twanged . . . (3)

The first sentence would form a plausible beginning to any realistic novel. As with the passage reproduced from *The Death of the Heart*, Bowen's scrupulous and economical rhetorical and syntactical choices emphasize proportion and stability and demonstrate the writer's aesthetic competence and taste. The fidelity to detail, their precision and fastidiousness, provides a sense of the expected congruity between the representation and that represented and establishes a sense of the solidity, the materiality of external reality. In particular, Bowen's extensive use of the assonance which spans these phrases, especially the repetition of the seductive and suggestive 'o' and 'ou' sounds, along with their complex echoes, enhances our apprehension of the orbit of meaning, while at the same time investing the words' literal meanings with heightened emotional significances that the words would not bear if read in isolation.

However, the most disturbing aspect of this short passage comes from the word 'twanged', from the way in which it seems to surface as a mark on the page, almost as some separate part of the prose. In other words, by comparison with the words around it which quickly dissolve into meaning, 'twanged' assumes a strangely insistent quasi-materiality, a graphic indissolvability that distinguishes it from the more 'transparent' others. As a result, our attention is arrested by the word long after it ought to have been absorbed into the loam of signi-fication. In part this happens because the word's obtrusiveness disrupts the sentence's anticipated arc of suspension and momentarily stops our forward momentum through the narrative. But also, its unexpected appearance here grants 'twanged' too much emphasis as a word, a discrete combination of sounds separate from all the rest. As a result, the word diverts attention away from the 'reality' that the word transcribes and onto the verbal surface (the 'top') of the prose, thus disturbing the typically unimpaired movement from sign to sig-nified. In other words, here and throughout *The Last September*, the unexpected substantiality of much of Bowen's diction creates a highly stylized representation in which individual words sometimes seem to obtrude in an almost material way into the familiar immateriality of the language. Often these are chunks of words with an almost gras-pable solidity and cut to them such as 'twanged', or heavy-sounding verbs such as 'clotted' or 'flanked' or 'clapped' or nouns or adverbs such as 'alacrity' and 'implacably', words that contain a superfluity of aural contradictions in themselves and rapidly alternate soft and spiky tin-can consonants and sibilant vowels in a quick rhythmic mix that contrasts with the rounder fit of most of the other words in our mouths. Rather than providing the reader with a sense of wave-like unendingness that soothes and continues to promise continuing expansions and graceful transformations, these words suddenly and with a strange impertinence contract the periodicity of their sentences and emphasize the infiltration of the strange and unexpected into the ordinary daily world. Momentarily, inside the complex musical, rhythmic, grammatical and syntactical labyrinth of these sentences, these surprising intrusions become unmanageable and pantomime physical shock that may or may not have any relation to the plot. Yet one cannot help but feel that the shock value is less intended as an aid to representation as it is used as a striking force directed at us, the readers. Further, 'twanged's' unexpected emergence here (guitars twang, while iron gates more often clang) grants to the word an emotional surcharge which is difficult to avoid while at the same time it liberates a rude aural value to the word that it would not necessarily bear were it used in a more customary way. But the way it is here deployed suggests excess while its rudeness simultaneously mocks the conventional eloquence established by the first signature sentence.

Because Bowen's diction sometimes but not always thwarts our desire to entertain illusions about entering fictive depth (the place where in mimetic narratives we expect to find meaning hiding or at least the beginning of a promise of meaning revealed by the tracks, the words), it thus creates a perpetual interchange between words as words and words as signifiers, apparitions which can be passed through to meaning. As a result, when we read, we vacillate between the gravitational pull of the representation into the vortex of meaning and an almost impertinent decorative quality to some of the words, as the prose inconsistently 'vanishes' into meaning or sense and comes forward in an almost physical way. Consequently, the representation is confused and deprived of a number of its conventional functions, as almost all parts of the composition – every formal element – are subjected to two different forces: 'decorative' two-dimensionality and 'realistic' three-dimensionality. Released, then, from conventional ways of functioning, a strange affinity between words and things is created in Bowen's fiction whereby the words' quasi-palpability sometimes occludes or at least hinders our search for deeper or hidden meaning. This unusual and unconventional rhetorical manipulation lends to Bowen's prose a strange and continuous multi-dimensionality that forces the reader to slip from one plane of experience of the language to another, her being caught in a kind of strange and strenuous *perpetuum mobile*.

Put somewhat differently, Bowen's fictional narratives are written in a queer, opaque style that realizes itself not solely as a style to be looked *through* but as a style to be looked *at* as well;[14] what is unsettling about her narratives is as much a function of their surfaces as it is of the various depths they conceal. In large measure, it is this strange, inconsistent, fluctuating motility, these unexpected and at times contradictory movements that take place within the same story, that give Bowen's fictional narratives their sense of inchoate pressure and force. And while 'twanged' does not completely prohibit recuperation into the representational schema, it does dramatize the innate recalcitrance, not as openly admitted by more conventional realistic discourse, that materiality presents to the shaping imagination while, in various ways, it simultaneously emphasizes the arbitrariness of closure.

While Bowen's fiction has most often been likened to that of a diverse range of turn-of-the-century and mid-twentieth-century writers typically associated with social and psychological realism such as E.M. Forster, Henry James and Graham Greene, the strange and inconsistent imbrication and erratic concatenations of surface and depth in Bowen's fictional narratives bring into the open one of the salient dilemmas that defines the problematic field of modern literature. Just as Manet's peony still lifes could be said to define the problematic field of modern painting – the flowers appear to shed brush strokes not petals, and this undisguised facture anchors the painting to its surface and thwarts illusions viewers have about entering fictive depth – because the substantiality of many of Bowen's words throws the substantiality of things into question, just as the substantiality of things throws the substantiality of words into question, her prose could be said to define the problematic field of modern literature.

In the space remaining, I would like to discuss one more aspect of Bowen's prose style that contributes to the hermeneutical uncertainty that characterizes *The Last September* and that makes the terms of appreciation and analysis uncommonly difficult to apprehend and apply. Despite modernist and postmodernist critiques of mimeticism and the prevailing suspicion of its ontological and ideological entrapment, generally contemporary criticism has yet to abandon ideas about mimeticism's referential imperatives, ideas originally outlined by Aristotle and admirably consolidated by Ian Watt in his remarkable study, *The Rise of the Novel*.[15] A reference is distinguished from other linguistic categories in a work of literary mimesis in that its purpose is to identify a particular individual member of a class of entities. While the topic of reference remains controversial, it is generally held that the conditions of a reference include a set of grammatical and contextual constraints on the capacity of an expression to perform this function. The idea of reference involves an existential presupposition: one can only refer to something that is held to exist in the world. By thus exploiting the referring properties of language, the mimetic text ensures that process of recognition whereby the reader connects the world produced by the text with the world of which she herself has direct or indirect knowledge. Reference, then, belongs to mimesis as part of a general process of reminding, a recognizing of the object as the same again; a work of literary mimesis maintains its intelligibility when the referential language used re-presents in ways that keep the criteria of identity intact. To the extent that such an agreement is unsupported by the representation or becomes impossible, the realistic effect is compromised. As Leslie Hill has argued, the success of the mimetic enterprise is then assured by virtue of reader and writer engaging in a 'contract of mutual recognition', a contract which accords with those general networks of agreements from which a society demarcates its boundaries between sense and nonsense, the typical and the anomalous, the normal and the abnormal (Hill, 1990, 336). In other words, by suppressing and excluding anything arbitrary or fanciful and instead favouring descriptive verisimilitude, the mimetic enterprise reinforces rather than contradicts what is generally accepted as truthful and relevant without distortion or overt or conspicuous stylization. Stated somewhat differently, the mimetic enterprise gains its force from the way its use of referential language encourages certitude about the bond between the object of knowledge and the discourse about it, by the many ways it reinforces rather than contradicts our sense of congruity between the signified and the sign. As a consequence, mimesis tempts the intellect into believing that what is copied is the extent of the real.

But while the similarity and appropriateness of the sign to the signified are the criteria for mimetic effectiveness, in *The Last September* similitude is often rejected in favour of jarring and unsettling inaccuracies and improprieties. Consequently, many of the intellectual disturbances effected by Bowen's prose are due to the unexpected ways in which the representation sometimes confuses, estranges or renders inadequate the set of socially constructed typifications in respect of which the world is supposed to function in certain more or less regular and predictable ways, thus forcing us to reconsider them or abandon them in favour of more transgressive comparisons of dissimilitude. Look, for example, at the passage that describes the terrain through which Lois and a guest drive on their way back to Danielstown from a neighbour's:

> . . . Lois . . . drove home briskly. To the south, below them, the demesne trees of Danielstown made a dark formal square like a rug on the green country. In their hearts like a dropped pin the grey glazed roof reflecting the sky lightly glinted. Looking down, it seemed to Lois they lived in a forest; space of lawns blotted out in the pressure and dusk of trees. She wondered they were not smothered; then wondered still more that they were not afraid. Far from here, too, their isolation became apparent. The house seemed to be pressing down low in apprehension, hiding its face, as though it had her vision of where it was. It seemed to huddle its trees close in fright and amazement at the wise light lovely unloving country, the unwilling bosom whereon it was set. From the slope's foot, where

Danielstown trees began, the land stretched out in a plain flat as water, basin of the Madder and Darra and their fine wandering tributaries, till the far hills, faint and brittle, straining against the inrush of vaster distance, cut the droop of the sky like a glass blade. Fields gave back light to the sky—the hedges netting them over thinly and penetrably—as though the sheen of grass were but a shadow on water, a breath of colour clouding the face of light. Rivers, profound in brightness, flowed over beds of grass. The cabins lifting their pointed white ends, the pink and yellow farms were but half opaque; cast doubtfully on their fields the shadow of living. Square cattle moved in fields like saints, with a mindless certainty. Single trees, on a rath, at the turn of the road, drew up light at their roots. Only the massed trees—like a rug to dull some keenness, break some contact between self and senses perilous to the routine of living—only the trees of the demesne were dark and exhaled darkness. Down among them, dusk would stream up the paths ahead, lie stagnant on lawns, would mount in the dank of garden, heightening the walls, dulling the borders as by a rain of ashes. Dusk would lie where one looked as though it were in one's eyes, as though the fountain of darkness were in one's own perception. Seen from above, the house in its pit of trees seemed a very reservoir of obscurity; from the doors one must come out stained with it. And the kitchen smoke, lying over the vague trees doubtfully, seemed the very fumes of living. (78–9)

And here is another that again describes the country through which Lois and a guest drive:

... [S]he drove home briskly. On the bright sky opposite, Mr. Montmorency's pale face hung like an apparition's. She took the curves of Mount Isabel Drive with a rattle: the trap rocked on its axle, the traces creaked. Beyond the gates light lay flat and yellow along the hedges where brambles showered, hard red blackberries knocked on the spokes and swung back, shining. She took the short way, over a shoulder of mountain; the light pink road crushed under the wheels like sugar. Coming up out from the lanes, they bathed an hour or so in the glare of space. Height had the quality of depth: as they mounted they seemed to be striking deeper into the large mild crystal of an inverted sea. Out of the distance everywhere, pointless and unrelated, space came like water between them, slipping and widening. They receded from one another into the vacancy. On the yellow furze-dust light was hard and physical; over the parching heather shadow faded and folded tone on tone, and was drawn to the sky on delicate brittle peaks.

The road bent over a ridge, the trap ran down on the pony's rump, he and she shifted back up their seats. (73)

Of all of Bowen's difficult passages, it is no surprise that these intimidating, hard-to-approach 'nature' descriptions, these peculiar light and landscape accounts that constitute some of the most complex and intense moments of her fictional narratives, have been virtually banned from the territory of critical scrutiny, for it is here where we most often find the security of the assumptions which underpin the mimetic project most dramatically called into question, where we see the problem of the relations among representation, origin and referent most dramatically encountered in Bowen's work. While reading these descriptions, the entire matter of our making sense is experienced as strange and is defamiliarized. Certainly these descriptions appear grounded in realism – the represented world is minutely described and the descriptions seem true enough, up to a point. But what are we to make of a landscape where space comes like water, where trees exhale darkness, where lawns are blotted out by the pressure of trees? Where are these places where height has the quality of depth, where houses press down in apprehension and hills strain against the inrush of distance? Just what parts of Ireland do they describe? At any point in the system of mimesis, we should be able, in principle, to infer the unfolding of causal sequences that allow us to recognize the represented objects as the same again, and that consequently lends to the work its sense of teleological coherence. As earlier noted, the authentic mimetic work refers to and arranges essential or typical patterns of experience and, in so doing, grasps laws underlying reality and history, putatively revealing the world in its innermost principles of intelligibility. When successful, the formalized representation of this capacity includes the deductive inferences of logic and the inductive inferences of science; to the extent that the work of literary mimesis is shaped by these modes of reasoning, it rests on exceptionally durable intellectual foundations. But because these frequently encountered light and landscape descriptions do not consistently obey the laws of logic, identity, or causality, nor do they consistently follow the grammar of intention, finding a map, if you will, for reading these descriptions is extremely difficult. These landscape descriptions hardly resemble the domesticated lower altitudes found in realistic fiction, but nor do they represent the foreign yet natural terrain of exiled excess.[16] Unlike the recognizable landscapes in realistic fiction, these landscape descriptions appear to invite us to decode them, to make meaning of them, and yet that being described often eludes recognition. Objects are clearly defined yet, for all their specificity, these descriptions are curiously unkenable, not invisible but in ways hard to 'see'. In other words, because they sometimes but not always escape the cartography of consensus upon which our comprehension depends (which are the contingent parts? which are the essential?), they only irregularly avail themselves of our cognizance, and then often only relatively. One almost has the impression reading the strange way the narrator describes the world (square cows?, pink and yellow farms?, faint hills that cut the droop of the sky like a blade?) that we are not reading a description of natural geography, but rather are reading an imaginative interpretation of an expressionistic landscape painting or even of an evocative dream. Certainly this is not reality, or is it?

We often find these ambiguous descriptions in *The Last September* and in all of Bowen's fictional narratives, descriptions that move fluidly between the conscious mind with its symbolic resources and the unconscious with its subliminal significations or the semiotic where words may be nonsense and images meaningful. Because these descriptions make it difficult to uphold the distinction between the probable and the possible, in ways they work to expand and de-centre meaning itself for, if we accept, as the descriptions insist that we do, the existence of a foreign or ambiguous or hard-to-discern reality existing alongside or among the recognizable reality represented, our acceptance has the paradoxical effect of undermining the authority with which one asserts the principle that guides our assertion of the queerness or improbability of parts of the description in the first place.

Here is another passage, which describes a derelict mill:

> The mill startled them all, staring light-eyed, ghoulishly, round a bend in the valley . . . The river darkened and thundered towards the millrace, light came full on the high façade of decay. Incredible in its loneliness, roofless, floorless, beams criss-crossing the dank interior daylight, the whole place tottered, fit to crash at a breath. Hinges rustily bled where a door had been wrenched away; up six storeys panes still tattered the daylight. Mounting the tree-crowded, steep slope some roofless cottages nestled under the flank of the mill with sinister pathos . . . The sun cast in through the windows some wild gold squares distorted by the beams; grasses along the windowsills trembled in light . . . Split light, like hands, was dragged past to the mill-race, clawed like hands at the brink and went down in destruction. (151, 152, 153, 155)

And here is one more, which describes Lois walking outside in the evening:

> A shrubbery path was solid with darkness, she pressed down it. Laurels breathed coldly and close: on her bare arms the tops of the

leaves were timid and dank, like tongues of dead animals . . . High up a bird shrieked and stumbled down through the darkness, tearing the leaves . . . Fear curled back in defeat from the carpet-border . . . Now, on the path: grey patches worse than the dark: they slipped up her dress knee-high. (36)

There is a monstrous incompatibility to many of Bowen's images – laurels breathe, leaves are like tongues, light claws like hands – and a shocking taint of primitivism, of pressures exerted by energies more typically repressed, that provokes unease and anxiety and suggests a freedom of association that borders on anarchy. As with those earlier explored, much of the power of our experience of reading these images derives from their spectacular obscurity, from the fact that the mental image or meaning created by the words cannot always be judged similar, analogous, or even identical to what we know about the world from sense data directly ('Fear curled back in defeat from the carpet-border'?), or from the words (ditto). To a great extent, these descriptions' originality consists neither in their referential purity nor in the fantastic quality of their content but rather in the often florid contingency and interdigitation of the recognizable, the nearly recognizable, and the unrecognizable. Because these descriptions combine obscure, evocative language with more conventionally referential language of description without, despite their occasional syntactical regularity, a consistently convincing force employed to mediate between the words and the sentences and the words and the meaning, these descriptions are often unknowable or rather only relatively knowable, as they depend for their force on an occlusion not created by any theorized 'failure of the signifying order', but by the irregular concatenation in the prose of the natural and supernatural, the familiar and the strange, the known and the unknown, the recognizable and the unrecognizable. In other words, where the mimetic project relies on the certitude engendered between the object of the representation and the discourse about it, much of the power of Bowen's bizarre images lies precisely in the way that many of them refer to no one thing, neither a known and recognizable material phenomenon nor an historical reality. In fact, the critical interest and indeed, in ways, the comprehensibility of these passages resides in the ways that they are fashioned for something other than a reality effect, in the ways that they are fashioned for something other than the purposes of consensus.

Yet the intellectual disturbances effected by these images are due not only to the inappropriateness of the sign for what is signified, but also to the ways that Bowen's weird images often undermine the

mind's confidence in similitude and mimesis as criteria of language
and cognition. A common aspect of many of Bowen's aesthetic defor-
mations is that they take mimesis as their target; rather than presenting
the mundane as the real, by creating instead unions that are grotesque,
anomalous and excrescent, the deformed images destabilize the ontological status of 'copy' by at times eliminating or compromising the
known world and its differentiations. The semantic conceptual anom-
alies produced not only menace our expectations about comparison
and signification, but call attention to and undermine our confidence
in customary processes of signification. In other words, by denying or
at least questioning the putative stability of the form of the relation
between language and the object world, Bowen defamiliarizes a fundamental theoretical support of mimesis. While the rhetorical excess in
these descriptions arouses in us an expectation that the base reality represented will be, through understanding, transmuted into a 'higher'
form of truth or understanding 'outside' or beyond itself, by sometimes but not always locating a dimension of meaninglessness within
the very vehicle of meaning, Bowen disconcerts and sometimes subverts the reader's expectation that the visual description can be
translated into a pattern of knowledge, a cognitive structure or information (on the basis of the assumption that the visual description is
assumed to promote or project the creation of a verbal text which is
materialized in various kinds of commentary and which can be translated back into the prior verbal text, the description in the story).

That said, some of Bowen's most effective images are those that are
least weighed down by the dross of similitude. Look, for example, at
this passage that describes Lois and a house guest walking along a path:

> They approached the doorway that yearned up the path like an
> eye-socket. A breath of peat-smoke, of cold trodden earth, of the
> ghostly dark of white walls came out from the cottage. Danny took
> form in the darkness, searching with his one eye. He stood with
> his white beard, helpless and eager. 'Well!' exclaimed Hugo. Then
> Danny broke out this was young Mr. Hugo, wasn't he a lovely gen-
> tleman, as fine and as upstanding as ever. And here was his wife he
> brought with him, the beautiful lady. And trembling and
> searching, he took Marda's hand. He declared that she brought
> back the sight of youth to his eyes. (105)

The most startling image in this passage is of course the first. '[T]he
doorway yearned up the path like an eye socket'? It's hard to imagine
what we might do to 'correct' that image, to make it yield or be assimilated into the work of representation. If there is congruence here, it

is so estranged from the unities of identity that we have learned to take for granted and that are assumed in realist formulation that it is unfathomable to us. Like many of Bowen's images, the transgressive nature of this image, the way it combines parts from two discrete categories, in this case the inanimate (the door) and the animate (the human), suggests an outrageous mixing of categories of being established by science and logic and alludes to a frightening and disconcerting interpenetration of putatively discrete categories, thus confounding the orderly principles of differentiation purchased through a reduction of traits and/or qualities inscribed in mimesis. In other words, the dissemblance of parts combined in, for example, the doorway image creates a kind of amalgamation that bursts and dissolves 'natures' as it instead combines different natures according to conventions or norms of possibility that exist beyond those inscribed in the conventional mimetic project. By thus dissolving the structural integrity of 'natures', these descriptions force different parts into combinations whereby our desire for consistency and proximity is thwarted, as is our desire to form a continuity, for forming a relation and thus gaining a sense of completion. For example, in this image, by suspending or temporarily negating the presumed inviolable integrity of the human and the presumed inviolable integrity of the inhuman or inanimate, Bowen's representation suggests that the concept of identity through differentiation is a tenuous and fragile one, and points to complicated engagements among the concepts of self and other, natural and unnatural. In a metaphysical sense, you could say that these descriptions attack nature in its very forms, which it mocks and deforms, while they scramble the hierarchical order that separates and puts humans on top, thus cancelling the linear process of their relationship. By so doing, these images contradict the absoluteness of nature's order and categorical structures, and suggest instead their instability and arbitrariness. Even where a choice between two meanings might finally be made, the sustained alternative has, by its very existence, asserted a threat to resolution; consequently, the various possibilities posed disconcert while at the same time, they enrich our sense of possibility.

By showing what is not, by sundering the expected relationship between the sign and the signified and deforming the form that contains the subject (indeed, as mentioned, there is a way in which the landscape's or object's structure as an object capable of representation is itself sometimes called into question by Bowen's transgressions; you could say that some of the objects described want a certain imaginary solidity and integrity), Bowen's excrescent imagery suggests the uncertainty of representation and its limitations, while at the same time, by replacing the descriptive apparatus of the classical model of the theory of categories and undermining its philosophical underpinnings, Bowen's representation suggests the possibility of different theories of meaning, truth, reason, knowledge and understanding than those encoded in conventional mimetic representation.

Yet while these descriptions interrupt our attempts to consistently progress towards and secure determinate meaning, it is important to note that it is, by and large, the conventional rhythm and syntactical regularity of these strange passages that keeps them from meaninglessness. Indeed, the incongruity between realistic and patently unreal formulations often goes unnoticed. Were they written completely in solecisms, we would feel at a loss, our proximity to meaning so great that it would feel untransversible, and we might choose instead of reading these descriptions just to ignore them. But as it is, even completely nonsensical phrases such as 'in their heart like a dropped pin the grey glazed roof reflecting the sky lightly glinted' sound so much as if they make sense that we experience the pull of the onomatopoeia of meaning suggested by the smooth rhythms and expected movement of sounds while at the same time we are obstructed and ultimately unable to form paraphrasable meaning. One of the great merits of these descriptions, then, derives from the reader's fluctuating cognitive affirmation and questioning of the representation.

The infiltration of transcategorical (i.e. monstrous) beings into the domestic world of tea parties and tennis matches represented in *The Last September* suggests that Danielstown and its surroundings are places in which monstrosity is neither excluded nor put on the periphery, but are instead places where the monstrous and the ordinary are unpredictably and inexplicably interdigitated. Until recently, it has been those commonplace narrative elements that represent the manifest plot in Bowen's fiction that have constituted the mainstay of critical scrutiny. But the infiltration of the monstrous discomfits the absoluteness of the natural order represented in the manifest plot and of most historical and thematic interpretations of *The Last September*, exposing them as uneasy intellectual impositions. In addition, the escape of matter from form described in many of these descriptions, the moments when things (humans, lawns, skylines) become or are represented as 'blotting out' or when they 'melt' into or out of shape, portends a return to chaos that is only insecurely and erratically stabilized by matter's resumption of coherent, recognizable form in other parts of the descriptions. In other words, the shape-shifting quality of these descriptions suggests that the boundaries of natural forms are insecure, that it is somehow possible for natural objects (trees, lawns, grass) to slip out of the clothing that declares their identities and to move in and out of shapes that confuse and may misrepresent them. As a result, these shape-shifting landscape descriptions often declare an unstable and inconstant independence from the natural, material world. As mentioned, by underscoring the variable and irregularly pressured contingency of the formed and unformed and emphasizing the instability of their relationship, Bowen creates in places a kind of monster of signification that deforms the commonly theorized relationship of sign and signified. This erratically represented deformation and defamiliarization of the relationship between formed and unformed, sign and signified, parodies the intellectual vulgarity of materialism which underlies the privileging of sign over signified; at the same time, it also rejects any definitive (spiritual or ideal) conception of the precedence of signified over sign. The erratic contraventions that take place in these descriptions, especially when form and nature are seen paralleled by sign and signified, serve to discomfit the mimetic project, as generally understood, and suggest that the comprehension of meaning is dependent on an understanding of a provisional and unsettled relation between the congruous and the incongruous.

As is generally assumed, in a conventional work of literary mimesis, the hypostatized representing subject is presumed to be a unified and homogenizing agent who provides an essential guarantee of the security of the representational space she commands. Yet the major symptoms of unease in *The Last September* and those which have provoked most derision in Bowen's work generally are those in which mimesis runs counter to its socially sanctioned forms. Because the 'mimesis' produced by *The Last September* takes the form of a series of strangely connected referential (i.e. 'realistic') and unexampled elements in which apparently disconnected parts are connected syntactically and are constantly likened to parts within a textual whole which itself as whole erratically suspends the possibility of a direct 'referential' passage to the known world beyond the text, interpretation itself must run counter to its socially sanctioned forms. 'Excessiveness' or bad execution is the term that has most often been used to recuperate Bowen's transgressions of consensual codes of recognition. However, the chief virtue of *The Last September* lies precisely in the ways that it will not allow us to take for granted the meaning of excessive as construed by consensus, just as, in the opposite emphasis, it will not allow us simply to invert that meaning. Where there is a departure from the commonplace, the site of agreed upon meanings, there is certainly a problem, and much of the interest of *The Last*

September and Bowen's fictional narratives generally lies in the way they acknowledge these problems, not in terms of reductive psychological categories, but by estranging commonly conceived and represented relations among the 'realistic' and the 'fictional', the phenomenal and the noumenal, and by Bowen's idiosyncratic disconnection of the irregular from the social context of practical knowledge. In fact, you could say that the most compelling psychological and affective drama of *The Last September* is an epistemological one, for it performs a series of epistemological suspensions whereby both the knowing subject and the objects of knowledge remain uncertain entities, the charting of the map of the relations between the self and the world blurred by the representation. In short, far from being disentangled from the question of the economy of mimesis, as some have averred, *The Last September* engages with it in provocative and important ways. Our appreciation and understanding of Bowen's work will continue to be enhanced as our susceptibility to her provocative and disarming challenges increases in depth and variety.

3

Dead letters and living things:
historical ethics in *The House in Paris*
and *The Death of the Heart*

ELUNED SUMMERS-BREMNER

Critics seem to agree that Elizabeth Bowen's novels have a peculiar relation to history. At the same time they provide uncommon challenges to the reader. As Susan Osborn notes, William Heath's book on Bowen, the first full-length study of her work, identifies her protagonists as ill-suited to the world in which they find themselves, while later critics, in a laudable effort to reaccommodate Bowen within the canon of worthy writers, impute some of that strangeness to the complexity of her historical worlds.[1] Either way, Osborn concludes, Bowen's critics 'contract the area of the unknown that exists in and around [her] narratives',[2] perhaps inevitably renovating the troubling scene of reading. This essay does not claim to have solved this critical problem, but rather comes at it from another angle. I want to see how the novel/reader relationship looks if we regard the experience of reading a Bowen novel not as an occasion for linguistic mastery over a textual object but as a rendition of human beings as objects ourselves.

I will pursue this reading in relation to two Bowen novels, *The House in Paris* (1935) and *The Death of the Heart* (1938), with the aim of discovering what the human object relation brings to our understanding, not only of Bowen, but of history. For it seems to me that it is the deadening, not the enlivening, function of reading and the obstructive, not the malleable, nature of objects as carriers of historical meaning that Bowen's novels disturbingly chart. If undead meaning can travel across generations by means of objects no letters can circumscribe, and if the meanings of letters reside in the traces they carry of readers as but one object among others – as, I suggest, occurs within these novels – then history, far from becoming legible as fiction from a distant point of vantage, becomes obstinately and obscurely pressing from within the present moment. It presses on us, too, as readers, from the very place where we would stand to get a view on it. The prescience of Bowen's fictions is, in my reading, linked to exactly this kind of transmission of historical truth.

To make a claim about truth requires some glossing at the outset. I draw here on two thinkers, Alain Badiou and Jacques Lacan, both of whom regard truth as the emergence of the human subject's relation to its history. For Badiou, as explained in his *Ethics: An Essay on the Understanding of Evil* (2001), truth is created by an event, and an event is a kind of rupture within history, if by history we assume, common-sensically, either a self-contained past world outside of which or a continuous narrative within which the human subject might be placed. A truth is not a given, therefore, but is laboriously constructed by what Badiou calls 'fidelity' to an originating event, this event being characterized by its 'bringing to pass "something other" than the situation, opinions, [and] instituted knowledges' that surround it. The event is 'a hazardous [*hasardeux*], unpredictable supplement, which vanishes as soon as it appears'.[3] Sigi Jöttkandt glosses Badiou's truth as 'the way an "event" is imbued with historical content'.[4]

From the Lacanian point of view, historical truth has a further, clinical aspect, attested to both in Lacan's teaching seminars and in the analytic practice in which they are situated.[5] Lacanian analysts treat people suffering from the damaging effects of the signifier – derived from words, letters and language – which has an irreducible material dimension, upon the human body.[6] For Lacan, as for Freud, human beings are exiled from the animal world where instincts create a form of liveable relation to birth, death and history or sexual (re)generation, a kind of closed circle which places the animal world within nature. In human beings an instinctual relation to history, to the world that produced us and to whose body we will return, is replaced by language, which performs a quasi-originating role. Functioning as a stand-in for the broken relation to our origins and ends at the same time as it institutes the break constitutive of human nature that makes us exiles from the land of instincts, language works on us opaquely, and, often, damagingly, in ways we cannot readily perceive.

Lacan's understanding of human subjectivity is close to the logic of trauma, itself a material excess within history not far from Badiou's truth-event, and, as I hope to show, also operative as a logic of historical registration in Bowen. Writing of trauma and the 'material signifier' in Lacan, Linda Belau uses a phrase that is very close to a phrase of Bowen's concerning, not the vexed origin of human being, but the vexed origin of fiction (and it is worth bearing in mind that for Lacan our most cherished beliefs about ourselves are fictions, a view with which Bowen concurs in the essay from which her own phrase comes). Noting that trauma is an event producing suffering in which neither can be understood, Belau claims that '[t]he signifier is nothing if not inadequate', and that this human encounter with an absence of meaning at the point of greatest suffering is itself 'the meaning of the materiality of the signifier'.[7]

The signifier's meaning is that of an abyssal event without salvation, then, as this event is registered by the human body. In the singular way in which it fails to save us from the consequences of our all too human desire for meaning, and in the form this absence of salvation takes within the subject's material being, the signifier writes our relation to history as one of a traumatic – that is, impossible to accommodate – negation. Bowen, in her own figuring of the exile produced in the human being by fiction, the essay 'Out of a Book', on childhood reading, says the following: 'The aesthetic is nothing but a return to images that will allow nothing to take their place.'[8] It is part of my argument here that, through this process of being driven back to particular images for which no others will suffice, the novel reproduces the structure of human subjectivity. We, no less than novelists, are driven to find images with which to screen ourselves from the unavoidable yet ultimately unknowable desires of others.

We are stopped from coinciding with our fantasy of ourselves when we read Bowen's novels by the obtrusion within her narratives of an affective surplus that belongs not to our fantasies of readerly subjectivity, that is, to mastery, which itself requires an off-stage form of material support, but to the experience of repetition, which, each time, fails to deliver complete understanding. Paradoxically, this repetitious encounter with an object that refuses to yield its meaning – Bowen's text itself in its twists of disorienting syntax, the unnerving life force shown by its *things* (telephones, houses, rooms) – is the process that returns us to our object status. Yet it is this process of returning us to our object status repeatedly – by requiring our identification with a protagonist whose vivacity is unexpectedly paralleled by the startling into life of material objects, or syntactically ousting us from a readerly subject position, where we would be safely beyond the grasp of, and so free to move invisibly within, the narrative – that makes possible an ethics of reading. Without the familiar comforts of realism in its erasure of the traces of construction, we are instead thrown upon a world where objects feel things, and, in doing so, shock us into bizarre acts of feeling recognition. The event of not coinciding with ourselves, and the felt frustration to which this non-coincidence gives rise, eventually reveals itself as the only thing, if there is anything, that it might be possible to share with others. And it is on this non-coincidence with ourselves, as well, that our historical belonging is also ultimately seen to rest.[9]

Because, as will be apparent from the above attempt at a brief glossing, trauma in its relation to historical truth is complex, I will attempt to elaborate Bowen's rendition of this relationship by focusing primarily on only one of its dimensions in each of the aforementioned texts. Trauma specialists and theorists note that, since trauma shatters the very frameworks through which we comprehend and locate ourselves in the world, namely those unremarked patternings of space and time that accord us an imagined centrality, recovery from trauma involves the gradual reconstruction of spatial and temporal bonds. *The House in Paris* is the novel that most clearly privileges temporal dislocation, as figured in its three chronologically disjunctive sections: The Present, The Past, and The Present, although, as in trauma, time and space are inextricably intertwined in Bowen's work.

The Death of the Heart, for my purposes, can be seen to similarly complicate a sense of spatial homogeneity. Its three sections, The World, The Flesh, and The Devil, ostensibly figure three sources of human temptation, while the novel itself complicates the spatial integrity of the human being suggested by these three externalizations of evil. *The Death of the Heart* ultimately locates human evil at the heart of social being, and shows what happens when loneliness, having served as a paradoxical form of unconscious belonging for the protagonist, Portia Quayne, is inevitably transformed by its move to the 'fallen', communicative and social medium of writing. There, it becomes subject to reading and so to the merely human longing to belong that drives reading, whether of books or other people. While shared, this longing to belong in a world transected by others' longings causes people to put up barriers against the implications that might follow from the fact of their sharing such displacing feelings. And it can also lead, as Portia discovers, to something worse: a cruelty that drives people to consume others' longings simply because their own have not been met.

But to come back to letters, and to *The House in Paris*. Here letters feature as overdetermined truth transmitters, and, initially, as matters for contestation. As such, they are troubling to their readers, but even more troubling to those who are excluded from reading them. In this respect the novel, which evokes the anxieties and perceptive shocks of childhood, is perhaps closest to Bowen's own childhood experience (although letters, read and unread, perform important functions throughout her *oeuvre*, as Neil Corcoran reminds us[10].) Because of family fears that Bowen might have inherited the cause of her father's nervous breakdown, she was not allowed to read until the age of seven.[11] Reading was perhaps always a conflicted experience for her, and may explain why, throughout her life, she read places with an heightened intensity: she was forced to read them first. Certainly in Bowen, an act of reading is seldom neutral.

A crucial reading scene in the novel occurs early. The child Leopold, who has been sent to stay with a Madame Fisher in Paris while he waits for his mother to join him – a mother he has never seen, for he has been brought up in Italy by guardians – has appropriated *The Strand Magazine* from Henrietta, also in the house *en route* to her grandmother in Mentone. Finding this reading matter perplexing, Leopold spies the handbag belonging to Miss Fisher, Madame Fisher's daughter Naomi, and is struck by the 'thought that inside there might be letters about him'.[12] Leopold finds three envelopes, the first containing a letter from Mentone concerning Henrietta, the second from his Aunt Marian, his guardian, to Miss Fisher, and the third, significantly, containing no letter but addressed in the hand he has only recently learned to recognize as his mother's. Reading Aunt Marian's letter is for Leopold a shocking experience, but also a deadening one. He begins it by imagining his mother about to open the door of the room he is in to meet him, as he expects to occur in the imminent future in a place given meaning only by their connection: 'That very door will open before it's dark . . . *Then* when it opens there will be her face. I shall see what I cannot imagine now. Now she's in Paris somewhere because of me . . .' (40).

This is an exemplary scene of forward-looking fantasy as a defence against loss – the absence of Leopold's mother and her letter – in which Leopold himself is both the author and the imagined centre. The correlative of this scene, however, is that Leopold is also the physical prop or reason for being of his mother's longed-for appearance. This, his object function within the imagined scene – a scene the purpose of which is to enable a reparative sense of imaginary mastery and offset Leopold's anxiety – is necessarily invisible to him. This invisibility of the object function within a process habitually supporting subjectivity, that is, vision and imagining, is similar to the function of the optic nerve within the human eye, which blindly makes it possible to see things, or the pre-digital era photographic negative that materially enables the emergence of a captured image.[13] The horror of Aunt Marian's letter for Leopold is that it forcibly collapses him into the very place the fantasy of reconciliation allows him to avoid. He is confronted with an image of himself as the sustaining object of the Grant Moodys' prurient curiosity and concern, the support of their fantasy about his life. This fantasy in turn supports that of their own importance as his foster-parents.

The Grant Moodys' interest in Leopold is derived from the question of his origins and is oriented towards his imagined end. His conception was a misconception, his guardians feel, an event that should not have taken place. Much more harshly and unequivocally than the scene of reconciliation Leopold is playing, the letter *places* him in a supercharged historical present, caught between the assumed facts of his dangerous heredity – his predetermining by the act of his conception – and his guardians' future-oriented fears. To Naomi, Marian Grant Moody writes:

> We know of your tender feeling for Leopold, which your tie in the past with his unfortunate father will always renew. How undying friendship is! We feel that, apart from the circumstance of his birth, Leopold's heredity (instability on the father's side, lack of control on the mother's) may make conduct difficult for him, and are attempting to both guard and guide him accordingly. (41)

Encountering himself in this way as the impossible point of his own origin, Leopold sees himself 'from the outside', and is threatened by a feeling that both originates in him yet threatens with external force: revulsion, a revolt from within against something felt to be alien to the self. He quickly reads the letter from Mrs Arbuthnot, Henrietta's aunt, 'as though to clap something on to the gash in his mind' (42). And yet, naturally, his thoughts return to Spezia and the Grant Moodys.

The effect of the collapse of Leopold's fantasy about his mother is deadening to him in two ways, the second of which is the more troubling. The first kind of death is the horror of finding himself the mere object of the Grant Moodys' childrearing ambitions. This rendition of himself being unrecognizable to Leopold, it occasions a self-splitting. The second result is more complex. A fantasy makes it possible for loss or anxiety – a primary affect at the heart of human subjectivity – to achieve compensatory form, yet its building and habitation is the work of that same unconscious affect and helps to stay its potentially destructive force. Discovering that what he had thought was his home is a kind of alienating prison, where he has been an object of interest and educative experiment ('[w]e do not consider him ripe for direct sex-instruction yet, though my husband is working towards this through botany and mythology', writes Aunt Marian (41)), Leopold's fearful unbelonging takes the form of avenging weather destroying the Grant Moodys' home:

'If he could have been re-embodied, at that moment a black wind would have rushed through the Villa Fioretta, wrenching the shutters off and tearing the pictures down, or an earthquake cracked the floors, or the olivey hill above the villa erupted, showering hot choking ash . . . '(45).

Writing of the commonality between physicists' theories about the origin of the universe at an unlocatable point of past time and the destructive drive energy integral to the work of Melanie Klein, Jacqueline Rose makes an observation relevant to Leopold's experience at this point:

> The advantage of theories like that of the black hole or the Big Bang [is] that they are so apocalyptic. The drama of their imagining compensates for what scares. The idea of something negative as explosion or pure inexplicable force seems oddly to be more manageable or acceptable than the idea of something negative which is at once less certain and which seems to wipe out the conditions through which it can, or should, be known . . . The concept of negativity will not provide us with a clear account of origins (even if it affects the way that the idea of origins can be thought); nor can we place it at the distance from which it could conceptually be controlled.[14]

It is the concept of negativity that Leopold is, at this moment, being forced to entertain. His real point of origin – real in Lacanian terms, which means pertaining to the body at the point of its exceeding of a culture's or an individual's framing fantasy – in an unknowable, absent person, his mother Karen, has been brought home to him only recently. Encountering himself externalized, split off from himself by the Grant Moodys' abhorrent fantasy of him but finding that that fantasy itself is grounded in the real of his unencounterable origins (and in his mother's 'lack of control', his 'father's instability'), Leopold enacts what Rose details. That is, he seeks to go further back than his own point of origin to an apocalyptic, unauthored moment, a point in space and time which might be described as *prehistoric*: where humans build shelters that are continually vulnerable to external force. Yet this force, like Leopold's own suffering, is internal, too, for houses only shelter human beings to the extent that they contain weather as well as forestall it. This is most notable in one of civilization's founding moments, the building of a frame around a hearth fire and the construction of a channel to the outside, which allows that fire to be maintained. A hearth fire is not only the heart of a home; moreover, it is also where resides the origin of repeated stories, an atmospheric guardian of history.

The volatile relation of houses as frames to the matter and meaning they enclose is always prominent in Bowen, and might be described as her own historical cause or reason for being. As her parents' only child, Bowen inherited the family's seat, Bowen's Court in County Cork, a Big House of the kind belonging to many Anglo-Irish families. Such houses had their own fraught relation to the past. Many were established in the eighteenth century, when the English imagined a hopeful future for themselves in Ireland, a hope that was soon to be disappointed. Bowen wrote a history of her family's house during the Second World War Blitz on London, and in a sense this was a return to the living past for her, as Anglo-Irish Big Houses were torched in considerable numbers during the Troubles of the 1920s.

Leopold, of course, cannot himself go back to his unknown past in order to accommodate his present and imagine a future, as we have seen. Instead, contained between two sections both named 'The Present', Bowen constructs a significant intervention in the novel containing Leopold's story. In this middle section, named 'The Past', we are introduced to Leopold's mother Karen, and to the love affair from which Leopold was produced. It is a doomed affair, and it is fitting, thus, that in this section of the novel Karen visits the Anglo-Irish Big House belonging to her Uncle Bill and Aunt Violet, where she discovers that Aunt Violet will soon die. Karen visits Rushbrook at a crucial point in her life story. Ray Forrestier has just proposed marriage to her, and it is in order to examine her own feelings about this, and thus her feelings about her future, that Karen goes away.

'We know of your tender feeling for Leopold', writes Marian Grant Moody to Naomi in the present, 'which your tie in the past with his unfortunate father will always renew. How undying friendship is!' (41). As is revealed in 'The Past', Naomi was engaged to marry Max at the time when Max and Karen had the love affair that resulted in Leopold. This love affair, and its exploitation by the sinister Madame Fisher, also resulted in Max's death. In this section of the novel we find that love, as Karen says at one point, 'is obtuse and reckless; it interferes' (174). It also causes people to go back to their beginnings, not as they might imagine them but as they were at one time placed, both hopeful and defenceless, at the mercy of others' desires.

Houses are fantasy structures as well as buildings, and it is in this section that their efficacy at sustaining desire is tested. When Henrietta arrives at Madame Fisher's house in section one of the novel, she perceives that the house is opaque with contested meanings, with unhappy history:

The inside of this house . . . was antagonistic [to Henrietta], as though it had been invented to put her out. She felt the house was acting, nothing seemed to be natural; objects did not wait to be seen but came crowding in on her, each with what amounted to its aggressive cry. (24)[15]

In 'The Past', however, the past itself is seen to undergo a test of ownership both by Karen's mother, Mrs Michaelis, and by Madame Fisher. In this section of the novel, people are frequently unreadable, while objects and natural phenomena are possessed of an unnatural kind of life. These objects stand in for human beings at key moments when they wish to avoid their object status, their ultimate unknowability within others' lives. Yet it is also in 'The Past' that the object function is isolated in one of its most crucial human operations, that of love. This is the process through which, in taking another human being as a love object, we give our own being into their trust. Or, to put it slightly differently, in love we accede to our status as a cherished object, an object found inexplicably desirable in the loving subject's eyes.

Karen goes to Ireland to escape her family, specifically the way its hold on the past would seal her into a relationship with Ray that disables her from accessing desirous feeling: 'It was natural that she should feel that everybody knew everything: she had been born and was making her marriage inside the class that in England changes least of all. The Michaelis [sic] lived like a family in a pre-war novel' (70). While for Karen's family, 'change looked like catastrophe' and 'meant nothing but loss', so that 'you lived to govern the future, bending events your way' (124); when Karen is in Ireland, as she writes in a letter to Ray, 'something . . . bends one back on oneself . . . it upsets one' (89). Karen has previously known Max in childhood, but after she meets him again, through Naomi, 'her thoughts . . . ben[d] strongly to whatever in marriage stays unmapped and dark, with a kind of willing alarm' (124). Figuring unmappability and darkness, Max is represented as extrinsic to narrative. His Jewishness is regarded by others as a working contradiction: he is a man whose historical continuity – his racial heritage – is never to quite belong. This mix of assumed natural inheritance and prejudicial construction, a mix that does not make sense of Max but only places him in relation to the fantasies of belonging held by others, is figured by Karen's observing that '[w]hat Mrs Michaelis said about Max', his finding in Naomi a similar unbelonging as his reason for marrying her, 'would be . . . true—if you pressed him flat like a flower in a book. But he . . . could not be pressed flat without losing form' (119).

Mrs Michaelis wishes only that real change should not happen. She refuses to see anything she has not imagined into existence: 'Like the classic camera, she was blind to those accidents that make a face that face, a scene that scene, and float the object, alive, in your desire and ignorance' (118). Of course, it is just this awakening of 'desire and ignorance' by the love object, Max, that Karen wishes to experience. Mrs Michaelis outlaws the longing within belonging that Max awakens in Karen, but, because her vision of changelessness masks this excluding, lawlike function, she does not see it as her own construction but imputes it to Max: '[H]e is a man who would quickly outlaw himself', she says (117). In fact, as Jean Radford points out, in the year of the novel's publication the Nazi government passed the Nuremberg laws, which deprived Jews of citizenship within the German homeland and, accordingly, led them in greater numbers to countries such as France.[16] Mrs Michaelis's act of projection differs from this self-fulfilling act only by degree.

When Karen returns home from the hotel in Hythe where she has been with Max and where she has also conceived Leopold, people are made to participate like objects in Mrs Michaelis's changeless fantasy, which now emerges in full force: 'Unconscious things – the doors, the curtains, guests, Mr Michaelis – lent themselves to this savage battle for peace' (173). People are also, like objects, rendered silent, seemingly by the force of Mrs Michaelis's will: 'Not a word from Max, not a cry from Naomi' (173). This 'battle for peace' begins with an unread note, a repetition of an event at Hythe, when Max wrote to Naomi and Karen ripped up the letter without reading it (164), wishing to deny the fact that love is never completely separable from the desires of others. When Karen returns from Hythe, she avoids the hall chest because it has a letter from Ray on it, as well as a message on the telephone pad. She tells her mother that she has been with her friend Evelyn Derrick. When Karen goes downstairs later to collect Ray's letter, the message is gone, but Karen can read the traces: 'Evelyn Derrick rang . . . to talk plans for next week-end' (171).

The silent 'battle for peace' in the Michaelis household is bisected by another battle, between Madame Fisher and Naomi, with Max the object of each mother's desire to assert her view of history. That Max is functioning here as an object whose force derives from a time before words - the time love takes us back to - is made evident by the way the run of undisclosed missives now builds in importance: increased significance is borne by what is not said and explanations for events have to be accordingly filled in later. What Karen in particular will have to reconstruct are the circumstances leading to Max's death.

A telegram from Naomi arrives at the Michaelis household in which an inquest and police investigations are mentioned. Karen buys French newspapers in which Max is not given 'much space' (178). From Naomi, Karen eventually learns what happened. Naomi, having received Max's letter breaking off the engagement – presumably the second version of the one Karen destroyed in Hythe – did not wish to see Max but he was commanded to visit in a letter from Madame Fisher. Max's next letter to Naomi was intercepted by her mother and used to force Naomi to meet Max at the house. At this meeting, Max 'spoke of a dread of being fatal to [Karen]', and after further elaboration discovered Madame Fisher listening at the door. Max, then, had admitted to his uncertain place in life, an uncertainty bound up with others' perceptions of his Jewishness. Madame Fisher is able to exploit Max's love for Karen, which leaves him unable to measure, as no lover *can* measure, the future outcome of their love, and his desire not to make things worse for Karen.

Love is able to author change in us precisely to the extent that it reduces us to the status of an object, the object that sustains the loving partner's fantasy, and, in turn, allows our own, as though these are but one fantasy opening onto but one kind of future. But love only achieves its power to change the future in this way because it takes us back to a prehistoric time when we were nothing but the object of others' fantasies – for example, those of our parents – when we were as yet unpeopled spaces marked by others' desires. Love is thus outside time, but not in the way we prefer to imagine, the way that Leopold initially imagines Karen, 'in heaven or art, in that nowhere' (67), transcendent, invisibly supported and supportive. Love is outside time in a manner closer to the way that death and birth are, truth events within history that threaten the very fantasies they give rise to and sustain. It is the racist fantasy of Jewishness as unbelonging that Max fears he will not be able to keep from affecting Karen and from destroying their love. Because of this uncertainty, further worked upon by Madame Fisher, Max kills himself by cutting his wrists, in a foreshadowing of Leopold's traumatic discovery of his lost beginnings, his clapping a replacement letter onto 'the thought gash in his mind' (42).

The trauma of Leopold's lost origins is signalled by a linguistic repetition that also signals the way to recover from the trauma. The phrase occurs at the close of the first section of the novel, the first 'Present', and is repeated at the opening of the third, the new 'Present'. It thus binds and limits the past in its influence on the present, even as it marks that present's past as the fleshing out of an unbearable negation. Arriving in the form of a message from Miss

Fisher – and we have seen how messages carry the potential to wreck the fantasies for which houses stand in this novel – the phrase is simple, signalling an event that words must reckon with yet cannot contain, an event, moreover, that has already happened to Leopold back beyond memory and is now happening again: 'Your mother is not coming; she cannot come' (66, 191).

This message of negation, however, unbeknown to Leopold, is the first step towards his regaining of his mother and their elaboration of a new, future-oriented fantasy together. In the relationship of Karen and Ray, whom Karen has gone on to marry, Leopold has sustained his true historical status in a beginning that was outlawed twice over: once by his father's death, and again by his mother's family's refusal to acknowledge the love that led to it. This double outlawing, this over-laying of the fact of Leopold with other absences – that of Karen's and Max's love, that of Max – makes Leopold, in Karen's mind, 'the mark our hands did not leave on the grass . . . He would be the Max I heard talking when I stood outside the salon, the Max I rang up', in a telling moment in the past when Karen knows the telephone will ring before it does and picks it up to hear Max, the objects of love they are for each other transferring their historical priority to the telephone, 'that other we were both looking for . . . He would be disaster' (153–4).

But because Leopold's absence in Karen's life is a truth of history, that is, the outcome of a shattering event that is not yet over – indeed, disaster – this absence re-emerges in Karen's new relationship with Ray as the object representative of Karen's and Max's cut-off future, the fantasy they could not sustain: 'When, travelling', Karen and Ray

> might have been most together objects would clash meaningly upon those open senses one has abroad. That third chair left pushed in at a table set for a couple. After-dark fountains playing in coloured light, for no grown-up eye . . . The third bed in their room at the simple inn . . . When they made love she thought: We are not alone. (219–20)

When Leopold learns that Karen cannot come to meet him, it is this same historical function of absence he encounters; that is, an absence he cannot command:

> He had cast her, but she refused her part. She was not, then, the creature of thought . . . Her refusal became *her*, became her coming in suddenly, breaking down, by this one act of being herself only, his imagination in which he had bound her up. So she lived outside himself; she was alive truly. She set up that oppo-sition that is love. (193–4)

Finally, it is Ray's decision to take Leopold away to live with himself and Karen that gives a future to this past and a future present to this absence. It occurs in a present moment in which Leopold witnesses his possible place in Ray's and Karen's lives: '[T]his present decision being come at was vital. This man affects me; I cannot affect him. He is he, but not his, hers' (223). Leopold is able to withstand this witnessing, as he was not able to withstand the rendition of his place in the lives of the Grant Moodys, because he has realized that his mother can only be his once he loses her. But this realization has itself been enabled by Henrietta's standing with Leopold, as, his body racked with sobs, he takes on the realization of his status as an object, not, this time, defensively and volcanically as though to annihilate his belonging to time and to others, but grounded in history like a tree, opaque with meaning, visited by rain and sorrow (197).

And so it is Henrietta, the historically incidental object of exchange in the events of the novel – for she accidentally crosses paths with Leopold in Madame Fisher's house *en route* from relative to relative through Paris – who is able to perform the analyst's role for Leopold when the walls of the fantasy that has hitherto sustained him in relation to his suffering break down. Leopold weeps 'because this is the end of imagination', yet this very destitution, witnessed by Henrietta, makes it possible for her to serve as a supportive object, to stand in as Leopold's reason for being at this crucial moment of a shift in his relation to his history.[17] Leopold's

> solitary despair made Henrietta no more than the walls or table. This was not contempt for her presence: no one was there. Being not there disembodied her, so she fearlessly crossed the parquet to stand beside him . . . Finally, she leant her body against his, pressing her ribs to his elbow so that his sobs began to go through her too . . . After a minute like this, his elbow undoubled itself against her and his left arm went round her with unfeeling tightness, as though he were gripping the bole of a tree. Held close like this to the mantelpiece he leant on, Henrietta let her forehead rest on the marble too: her face bent forward, so that the tears she began shedding fell on the front of her dress. An angel stood up inside her with its hands to its lips, and Henrietta did not attempt to speak. (197)

The Death of the Heart's Portia Quayne is also an object of exchange between relatives. Portia's mother having recently died, she finds herself, at sixteen, an orphan, visited by a written wish of her father's upon his son Thomas and Thomas's wife Anna for the term of a year.

Thomas Quayne is the elder Mr Quayne's son from his marriage, whereas Portia is the child of a love affair with a woman named Irene who he meets in London and with whom he is sent to live abroad by his wife once Portia is expected. We first meet Portia through the description offered by Anna, as she walks with her novelist friend St Quentin around an icy Regent's Park. This is significant, because the role of writing, in the novel, is to unsettle the relations people have with houses. As we learn, Anna is putting off going back inside her house because she has only just discovered that Portia keeps a diary, and, worse, has read it. This has not only altered Anna's view of herself and of Portia, but has denaturalized her relation to her home. It may be why Anna describes Portia's beginning as a 'bomb' going off,[18] for the diary reveals that Portia, whose previous life meets no criteria for belonging recognizable to Anna, has her own perspective on the Quaynes and their household, born of the history that has brought her there. And Anna's discovery of Portia's diary does indeed eventually shatter the fragile basis of civility in her home.

Portia's father has died some years earlier, so his daughter has come to Anna and Thomas only after her mother Irene's death, at which point the letter from the elder Thomas came to light. Anna and Thomas have taken Portia in in response to Portia's father's feeling that, 'because of being his daughter (and from becoming his daughter in the way that she had) Portia had grown up exiled not only from her own country but from *normal, cheerful* family life' (15). This is a recognizable fantasy, but one that depends on Anna's position, as a quasi-maternal figure for Portia, being both invisible and displaced, since while in the 1930s '*normal, cheerful* family life' is the work of women – based on the assumption that Anna's desire and her home life are one – it is not Anna but the housekeeper Matchett who sustains the household and who welcomes Portia into it.

The novel's structuring in three sections, The World, The Flesh, and The Devil, could suggest that we are being taken from the external to the internal cause of Portia's story. We will isolate the evil element, then go back out into the world again. However, the opposite occurs. We find that Portia's historical cause, her rootless but cherished upbringing, has the power to highlight the cause of the wish for belonging in others, making it impossible for the dynamics of others' relations with the world to go unnoticed. Yet in so far as this wish to belong is naturalized in terms of the very fantasy sustained by Portia's father, which brings Portia to live with Anna, Anna feels powerless to respond to the Portia effect. Disabled from dismantling the very fantasy she stands for as a woman with a home, a husband, and the wish for children, and unable, too, to heal from her former relationship with the damaging, and damaged, Robert Pidgeon, Portia's diary is perhaps the only route Anna feels she can take to isolate the power source of Portia's innocent gaze. I am not suggesting, however, that this strategy is a conscious one, and, of course, reading the diary does not help Anna's own cause at all.

When Anna introduces us to Portia through her conversation with St Quentin she describes her as being like an animal, which establishes her in a place that is pre-social, a world not made, as Anna's world is made, by a sophisticated relation to words. Anna is also unsettled by Portia's relation to objects: 'Nothing that's hers ever seems . . . to belong to her' (9), but it is her own rendition by Portia's writing, found 'distorted and distorting', that unsettles most (10). That Portia's gaze is found distorting by others is something Portia herself recognizes: 'She has those eyes that seem to be welcome nowhere . . . their homeless intentness makes them appear fanatical', since other people's eyes are customarily more guarded. Like windows, eyes make it possible to imagine a world without barriers, a world of belonging, yet to achieve it must also keep the need for belonging close. Human eyes must shield as well as reveal things.[19]

Portia's eyes, however, 'may move, they may affront, but they cannot communicate' (49). It is as though what is missing from Portia is that unconsciously learned rendition of human beings as houses: eyes the windows, the heart the hearth, and the objects within taking on the object function, for a house is not a home without objects, but objects lack meaning without a functional place. And yet one only learns to live out this sort of fantasy and the freedom it enables by the fact of someone or something in one's world being grounded, an experience that Portia has seldom known. This is no doubt why Portia gravitates towards the housekeeper, Matchett, who identifies with the Quaynes' house and furnishings to an almost unnatural degree. Although at the other end of the scale of the human relation to objects, Matchett shares with Portia a kind of readerly intensity that Anna, her husband Thomas, St Quentin and Anna's friend Eddie more successfully disavow. Matchett assists Portia in her search for understanding of her place in the Quayne family's history by allowing her to revisit, in conversation, the scene of her own beginnings, learning of the effect of the news of her birth on the elder Mr and Mrs Quayne before Mr Quayne was sent back to Irene (74–9). Only Matchett can connect this history with Portia's present, because she has been housekeeper in both houses.

It is not surprising, given her history, that Portia attempts to make a sort of home for herself through writing. It is other people's ideas about families, after all, that have authored hers, from Mrs Quayne the elder's ejection of her husband from the family home to her own father's importuning of Thomas and Anna. Anna notes to St Quentin that Portia 'hoard[s] paper' even though 'she gets almost no letters', and when Matchett discovers under Portia's pillow a letter from Eddie, for whom Portia cherishes romantic feelings, she warns that Eddie is 'never not up to something' (86). This suggests that Eddie is always up to something and that the something is negative, but so accustomed is Portia to creating fantasies of belonging from the barest essentials (as in the memory picture she paints of a happy life with Irene in the rooms of off-season Alpine hotels (34–5)) that she equates imagining itself with happiness (85–6). And because she has so far been a child in the care of one or both of her parents, however transient their life has been, Portia has never had to see this connection tested.

While living with the Quaynes – and, in the middle section of the novel, with Anna's former governess, Mrs Heccomb and her family at Seale-on-Sea – Portia has been gradually building a new sense of people's relations with their surroundings. From soaking up Matchett's family history lessons to hazarding her own Matchett-like observations ('[Eddie] does not like his room and I'm sure it knows' (118)) or making sharper authorial insights (of Thomas and Anna: 'Then we sat in the drawing-room and they wished I was not there' (115)), Portia's own relations with these people are being altered by the fact of her observations. But she is not yet fully aware of this. A new stage is reached when, having recently arrived at Waikiki, the Heccombs' house in Seale, Portia imagines the inside of the house at Windsor Terrace and thus holds in her mind a specifically located awareness of her absence: '*I am not there*' (139). After dreaming about Anna at Waikiki, Portia even wonders if 'Anna . . . sometimes, [did] not know what to do next'; or, '[b]ecause she knew what to do next . . . did it always follow that she knew where to turn? Inside everyone, is there an anxious person who stands to hesitate in an empty room?' (141).

'Only in a house where one has learnt to be lonely does one have this solicitude for *things*', Bowen writes, as Portia imagines Windsor Terrace without her presence. 'One's relation to them, the daily seeing or touching, begins to become love, and to lay one open to pain' (139). And, of course, this is what happens, as Portia's writerly attempt to forge a relation between herself, her past life in hotels and the Windsor Terrace present is undone by Anna's unauthorized touching and seeing of her diary, thoughtlessly revealed to Portia by St Quentin. Every initial revelation about sin or the world's or the flesh's sundering is a founding moment; nothing can be the same once this knowledge of the dividedness of things is found. But Portia has already been practising the art of division, and not just into twos, by the act of writing things down in her diary, since this initiates a three: writer, writing and reader, even if initially writer and reader are one. As St Quentin says to Anna in the novel's opening scene: 'Nothing arrives on paper as it started, and so much arrives that never started at all' (10). Writing itself, then, is an act of birth or arrival that has a prior cause, a prior start, and is itself a starter of new events.

What Anna's sinful reading reveals to Portia is the wider ramifications of the self-division Portia has been practising by writing: that all human interactions involve someone being in the position of the object, and that no human interactions can be certain to address the whole of a person (as Eddie claims: 'Darling, I don't want you . . . I don't want the whole of anyone' (214)). The world's imagined wholeness is sundered by the very desire for wholeness the divided flesh gives rise to, just as the flesh cannot be read exclusive of the world. The very ideas of sin, of flesh and of worldliness are curiously interdependent upon each other. It is not where the sin began, after all, that upsets Portia but the revelation it provides of Anna's and Eddie's intimacy, for it is as though Portia has been unable to conceive of interconnected relationships but has pictured each person as a world that exists around her.

Portia now feels as Matchett felt when she found Portia's letter from Eddie: excluded by having her presence included, but in a taken for granted way (293). But Portia cannot begin to learn that her homelessness unsettles the naturalized desires for belonging held by others until Anna does read her diary, which means that, despite the pain this causes, she is at last accorded the power of the negative that Eddie (negatively) represents. It is Anna's 'sin' that releases Portia into the world as an apprentice adult, and possibly as an apprentice writer. Anna's act of devilish disruption of Portia's world also ironically provides her with her first real sense of continuity, of history, not simply as that which surrounds her, but as a structure in which she, as well as others, have a function. She begins to see the world not as a fullness or an absence but as a set of interlocking, overlapping spaces, obscuring and implicating each other: 'I see now that my father wanted me to belong somewhere, because he did not' (292). Similarly, when Portia tells St Quentin that her diary is 'simply a thing of mine', he counters: 'No . . . Nothing like that stops with oneself . . . All the time, you go making connexions' (249).

This inter-implication of zones and spaces that might customarily be found exclusive also emerges in the animated view of history held by Matchett, for whom household objects, particularly furniture, are the repositories of family knowledge:

> Furniture's knowing all right. Not much gets past the things in a room, I daresay . . . Every time I take the soft cloth to that stuff in the drawing-room, I could say, 'Well, you know a bit more'. My goodness, when I got here and saw all Mrs Quayne's stuff where Mrs Thomas had put it—if I'd have been a silly, I should have said it gave me quite a look. Well, it didn't speak, and I didn't. (81)

Significantly, however, Matchett also describes the house's furniture as a historical obstruction or impasse in the younger Quaynes' lives, claiming that '[u]nnatural living runs in a family, and the furniture knows it . . . Oh, furniture like we've got is too much for some that would rather not have the past' (81). And Matchett's insights have some truth: furniture objects fill out the space between people and the outside world, granting flesh the freedom to not matter, its constant, demanding presence being the lot of the truly homeless. This freedom to not matter, to feel alive in a background sort of way, occurs only when someone or something else is treated as an object, and these object connections, these relations between three where the third person or thing is always being used for something, are a deadening effect without which an impression of life's continuity or completeness could not exist.

When Portia flees Windsor Terrace for the Karachi Hotel and the Quaynes' regular visitor Major Brutt, she brings him the same truth she has just discovered: 'You are the other person that Anna laughs at . . . You and I are the same' (288). And Anna has indeed previously thought this:

> In fact, he constituted . . . the same . . . undermining approach as Portia. He was not near enough their hearth, or long enough at it, to take back to Kensington with him any suspicion that the warmth he had found could be illusory. His unfulfilled wishes continued to flock and settle where the Quaynes were . . . No doubt he stayed himself on the idea of them when one more thing fell through, when something else came to nothing, when one more of his hopeful letters was unanswered . . . when he faced that the money was running out. (260)

Portia's revelation is an act of cruelty, of course, conscious or not, and as Major Brutt goes downstairs to ring the Quaynes he knows '[h]is home ha[s] come down; he must no longer envisage Windsor Terrace' (298).

And yet, before Portia's revelation, Major Brutt's compact with Anna was not entirely as she surmises. While '[t]he policy of pity might keep [her] from ever pointblank disappointing him', he is also 'the appendix to the finished story of Robert', and Robert has certainly hurt Anna. '[W]as it', Anna wonders, 'that she felt she found in him the last of Robert's hurting, hurting because never completely bitter . . . one of those hurting exposures of her limitations . . .?' (261). Major Brutt having been in the war with Robert Pidgeon, and Pidgeon having been wounded, and then in turn having emotionally wounded Anna, Major Brutt is a connector between Anna's unhappy present and her past. And Anna certainly feels that the emptiness of her present has been born of her relationship with Robert: 'Robert thought nothing of me', she tells Major Brutt in frustration, 'nothing at all. Nothing really happened; I did not break his heart' (263).

There is something in Anna's past that obeys the logic of trauma, and it is this something that is unsettled by the encounter with herself that occurs when she reads Portia's diary. There, she sees herself as other than she imagines and, while she naturally knows this to be the case, the outward fiction of her home life has previously functioned as a protection from this knowledge. Portia, too, knows that in the Quaynes' home there is an act of negation that belongs neither in the present nor obviously to the past. When at Waikiki, she discerns that:

> [T]he absence, the utter dissolution, in space of Thomas and Anna should have been against nature: they were her Everyday . . . Thomas and Anna, by opening their door to her (by having been by blood obliged to open their door) became Irene's successors in all natural things . . . They had all three worked at their parts of the same necessary pattern. They had passed on the same stairs, grasped the same door handles, listened to the strokes of the same clocks . . . To the outside world, she smelled of Thomas and Anna.
>
> But something that should have been going on had not gone on: something had not happened. They had sat round a painted, not a burning, fire, at which you tried in vain to warm your hands. (149)

For Anna, the fantasy of a home is the only acceptable way to cover over what happened with Robert Pidgeon. Robert, himself traumatized by the war, shares with Major Brutt this historical encounter with an abyssal event, and it appears that Anna has also become subject to the effects of this trauma through her love relationship, if such it was, with Robert. Anna's relationship with Major Brutt is actually one way by which she can safely stay in touch with this trauma, although it is not a happy way and it is a distanced visitation. It may be that in seeking refuge from this overdetermined 'nothing' Anna still needs to feel connected to it, and in this she and Major Brutt are more alike than they seem.

However, Anna and Matchett also have a compact, for each holds a bit of the history of the Quayne household that the other cannot see. Anna has founded a home on 'nothing', although it is a nothing that haunts and distresses her, and Matchett has founded hers on going where the objects go, the tables and chairs and the hearth screens. What these objects 'know' or perform, as Matchett surmises, is not stories but function. They are the dead matter or dumb objects marking Anna's non-engagement with an abyssal event in the past. And they stand, too, for another deadness, possibly the same kind that led Mr Quayne the elder to have an affair with Irene and that in turn gave rise to Portia: the non-presence of love and trust in her home. The objects anchor Anna's household in history because for Anna that history is too painful to be encountered: '[F]urniture like we've got is too much for some that would rather not have the past' (81).

Portia goes to Major Brutt at the Karachi Hotel, then, and transfers to him the truth of the insight she has gained about her position, that she is not the heart of anyone's world, since people use intimate knowledge of others as objects of exchange in conversation. In doing this she brings down his fantasy of home, but she also embodies the basic conditions of the human desire for home and family: 'Stripped of that pleasant home that had seemed part of her figure, stripped too, of his own wishes and hopes, she looked at once harsh and beaten, a refugee' (293). Portia's actions, although Portia does not know it, are the first step towards the possibility of a new kind of family, because a desire for belonging that could be a universal desire, and thus requiring of a genuinely singular, unforeseeable response, has shown itself. The shattering of fantasy Portia's actions have given rise to is an unconsciously wrought truth and so cannot dissimulate, something as nearly primal as it is possible to find.

Meanwhile, back at Windsor Terrace, Thomas and Anna debate the implications of Portia's absence with St Quentin, and, more importantly, what they are ethically bound to do about it:

> 'You say, he says she'll come home if we do the right thing?'
> 'Do we know what the right thing is?'
> . . .
> 'We shall know if we don't do it . . . Portia will simply stay there with Major Brutt . . . But it hasn't simply been me—you know, we

are all in it. We know what we think we've done, but we still don't know what we did . . . It's not simply a question of getting her home this evening; it's a question of all three going on living here.' (307–8)

And so Thomas and Anna send Matchett to the hotel for Portia, and in the process make another distant three of displaced persons.

The object of Portia's changing fantasy about the world has been her writing, through which she has given form, for the first time it seems, to her own absence and exchangeability, her entry into the world of adulthood where people are the exchangeable objects of others' desires. We begin the novel with the knowledge that Portia keeps a diary before we meet her. And we read that diary, like Anna, before Portia discovers it has been read. These two 'sins', or acts of voyeurism, that are built into the structure of the novel for the reader, and which have a deadening as well as an awakening effect on Portia, now become subject to a third act whose nature and outcome are unknown. As Matchett stands on the doorstep of the Karachi Hotel, pressing 'the brass knob with an air of authority' (318), two truths – Portia's and Major Brutt's – now sheltering in a makeshift home are about to encounter a third truth, although this is a truth of a different kind, and this encounter will not provide the grounds for reconstruction of a home-like fantasy. Or, it may provide such reconstructive ground, eventually, but will not do so until a fundamental historical obstruction, for which Matchett stands, has been accepted.

What is going to happen in the future is that Portia will have to perform an ethical act. It will not be ethical because of how she or anyone else sees it, however, but because it will be an act in response to an intimate non-coincidence, the opposite of fantasies of intimacy which require a third object or at least a setting. Thomas, Anna and St Quentin are waiting to learn, from Portia, not what they think they have done but what they *will* have done, what the future outcome of this past action will turn out to have been. And Portia will have to accept as the condition of what happens next that it *will have had* its origin in the worldly act of her having started to write a diary. It is a historical outcome not only because she could not foresee its end in its beginnings, but in the sense that it has intersected with the object-matter anchoring others' fantasies, fantasies that, until Portia came along, were still just able to protect those people from their history. Matchett, who anchors the heart of Thomas and Anna's house to its history, is the representative of this connection between the histories of Portia, Thomas and Anna.

Whatever Portia decides to do, it will not be an act on the basis of fantasy but an 'active engagement with that which is encountered as not being there, as absent',[20] because an active engagement with a necessarily unseen third is precisely what is involved in the act of writing. Only such an encounter will enable Portia to re-enter her history as an absence; that is, as a person who has the ability not just to repeat but also to change a pattern. It is only this kind of encounter, in other words, that can intervene from a position in the present (the what 'will have been') to alter the meaning of the past.

Bowen's next novel, *The Heat of the Day* (1948), by virtue of its backgrounding in the Second World War Blitz on London, will go on to render the spatial and temporal disjunctions animating these earlier novels at every point of the fabric of the narrative itself. It will demonstrate not only an individual but an entire culture being made subject to trauma, and will track the way the signifier – language in its ravaging by unhousable wartime affects, as it fails to compensate for the sufferings of the war-torn mind and body – is unable to protect the characters from their encounters with this event. But in these earlier works, too, we witness characters discovering how fully imbricated their material sufferings are with the structures of language, even as they must use language in the endeavour to express those sufferings. While they learn that they cannot rely on fictions about the world to save them – from others, from their own histories and attachments, often unacknowledged – they also learn that by accepting a place in another person's story it is sometimes possible to come to terms with truth.

4

Mumbo-jumbo:
the haunted world of
The Little Girls

JUNE STURROCK

A number of my stories have a supernatural element in them. I do
not make use of the supernatural as a get-out; it is inseparable
(whether or not it comes to the surface) from my sense of life. That
I feel it unethical—for some reason?—to allow the supernatural into
a novel may be one of my handicaps as a sincere novelist.[1]

Despite her disclaimer, Elizabeth Bowen's comment on the supernatural as essential to her 'sense of life' illuminates her full-length fiction
as well as her short stories. The supernatural may never play a direct
role in her novels, but, in the three that follow the end of the Second
World War, it certainly hovers in the background. In *The Heat of the
Day* (New York, 1949), the newly dead bomb victims haunt the
wartime city, making 'their anonymous presence—not as today's dead
but as yesterday's living—felt through London . . . the wall between the
living and the dead thinned' (99-100).[2] In *A World of Love* (1955)
again, the war dead haunt the survivors, though the war in question
here is the earlier, 1914-18 conflict, and the dead feature not as an
anonymous mass but as one man, Guy, whose newly discovered letters
revive his disturbing presence.[3]

The Little Girls (1964), a novel just as deeply concerned with the
devastations of war as its two predecessors, operates rather differently
from them. Here the supernatural is continually evoked through the
novel's language: in the characters' references to themselves and
others as ghosts, witches, spell-binders, revenants or enchanters, who
are haunted or possessed; in the repeated allusions to the literature of
the supernatural, from *Macbeth* and *The Tempest* to John Wyndham's
The Midwich Cuckoos; in the frequent descriptions of accumulations of
totemic objects.[4] The language of haunting and enchantment speaks

83

to the novel's insistence on the fears and uncertainties arising from
the upheavals suffered by Bowen's generation, which is also the generation of the three 'little girls' of the title, the 'weird sisters', Dicey,
Mumbo and Sheikie. This language also intensifies the sense of the
insubstantiality and vulnerability of the material world, including the
human body, which pervades a novel in which Bowen blurs the
boundaries of conventional fiction, challenging realist art both explicitly and implicitly.[5] *The Little Girls* explores how people understand
themselves and their world in time, communicating a sense of uneasy
apprehension of their position in the present in relation to a threat-
ening future and a violent past, an unease characteristic of the Cold
War years when Bowen was at work on this novel.

The Little Girls begins with a man and a woman, first in a cave, then in
a garden rich with flowers, fruit and vegetables. Both Frank and
Dinah are ageing – sixtyish – but they have retained a 'random
beauty', so that they seem 'a pair of ageless delinquents' engaged in 'a
cheating of Time'.[6] This latter-day Adam and Eve (in the garden of a
house called Applegate) are indeed cheating time, not only uninten-
tionally, through their ageless beauty, but also quite intentionally,
through the sort of time capsule they are preparing within the cave, so
as "'to leave posterity some clues'", as Dinah says. Dinah's project provokes two similar responses: "'should there be any posterity'" (14) and
"'we may all go up with the same bang'" (16). Neither response is surprising, given that this novel is set in the early 1960s, a period of
especially acute anxiety about nuclear war, nuclear winter, and the
future of the planet.[7] As Patricia Juliana Smith observes:

> the motivation for this strange activity [creating the time capsule]
> ostensibly lies in a fear of war, that most frequent force of destabi-
> lization in Bowen's works. Here, however, this anxiety takes on
> configurations peculiar to the historic moment, as the gesture is
> one of defiance and preservation in the face of the Cold War
> threat of nuclear annihilation. (103)

Various war-related anxieties about the future and about 'posterity'
run through the novel. Frank is uneasy about the approaching birth of
his first grandchild, not for the sake of his 'tough as a rhinoceros'
daughter (21), but because, as Dinah explains, "'he's terrified that
some terrible Hostile Race, which will go on to drive everyone else
out, is at any moment going to begin to be born'" (196–7) – a less
crazy fear than it may seem decades later. During the Cold War
period, fears about the effects of nuclear fallout on the coming

generations darkened all modes of fiction. Science-fiction writing, such as John Wyndham's 1957 *The Midwich Cuckoos* – to which Dinah is alluding here – was obviously affected, but so was more mainstream fiction. Doris Lessing's *The Four-Gated City* (1969), for instance, includes a conversation among students, 'discussing their children and how they might be geniuses or idiots; that they would certainly be mutants of some kind . . . What kinds of mutant might be expected? How would one recognize one?' (429).[8] Though the dread of what is to come continues to colour the novel, the focus of *The Little Girls* soon shifts from anxieties about the future to fears concerning the past, from the heterosexual plot to the relations of three ageing women, and from an Edenic garden to a notably fallen world. A chance word, a chance sign, reminds Dinah that she has, in fact, prepared a time capsule long before, as an eleven-year-old schoolgirl, with her two friends and conspirators, Clare and Sheila, though in those days the three knew each other as Dicey, Mumbo and Sheikie. The time capsule intended for the future in fact carries her back into her own distant past.

'When shall we three meet again / In thunder, lightning, or in rain? . . . Where the place? / Upon the heath.' These are the first words of *Macbeth*, the words of the three witches. As Dinah's – and the novel's – focus shifts from future to past, the allusions to the literature of the supernatural move from the future-concerned science fiction to older fantasies. Dinah carefully arranges that the three former 'little girls' should meet again on the nearest equivalent of a 'blasted heath', a setting that Clare instantly recognizes. '"This"', she says, '"could be quite a Macbeth meeting place, could it not?"' And Dinah responds instantly and appropriately '"Bubble-bubble . . . Not quite a heath, this, or exactly the weather, but near enough"' (47).[9] And she continues to speak of the three of them as *Macbeth*'s witches, greeting Clare at a later meeting, in the gift shop that Clare runs, '"My Weird Sister, you *have* got a kitchen here! . . . Trade terms for your weirder sister, I do hope? Anything in *my* line, have you, this morning? Any wombats' wombs or anything—powdered, naturally?"' (139; Bowen's emphasis). She is drawn to an odd-shaped butter knife in Clare's 'witch's kitchen' (152), realizing later the attraction is its imagined resemblance to 'a pilot's thumb, wreck'd as homeward he did come' (180), one of the Shakespearean witches' trophies (I.iii.28–9). Like Margaret Atwood's *Cat's Eye*, a later novel concerned with the enduring power of childhood relations among girls, the whole narrative is heavy with references to *Macbeth*.[10] In both cases, the strange power of the witch-children works, not on other people, but on the

girls themselves, both as children and as adults. Again, Bowen's supernatural diction communicates this mutual power. Clare, Sheila and
Dinah talk competitively of falling under each other's spell (38, 59).
Clare addresses Dinah both as an "'enchantress's child'" and as
"'Circe'" (198). (The determinedly unliterary Sheila comments, on
hearing this last, "'She always did swear like a trooper'" [223].) Frank,
now relegated to the role of outsider, resentfully recognizes Clare/
Mumbo's power over Dinah before he ever speaks to her, thinking of
her, as he glimpses her on the stairs, as an 'apparition', as a 'non-
ghost' who is 'in possession of this place' – "'Mumbo-jumbo!" he
shouted to himself, internally, silently and violently' (55).

As Patricia Coughlan remarks, 'the manipulators in Bowen's fictions are usually women, and so are most, though not all, of those
they work upon' (Coughlan, 1997, 104). Coughlan here is mainly concerned with the destructive power of older women over younger
women – with, for instance, Sidney's obsession with Mrs Kerr, in *The
Hotel* (1927), or the more obviously malevolent Mme Fisher's power
over Karen and Naomi in *The House in Paris* (New York, Avon, 1979) –
she is 'a woman who sells girls, she is a witch', thinks Karen (155).[11]
Coughlan goes on to question, 'what are we to make of this intense
consciousness of female power, albeit darkly used? How may we dis-
tinguish it from the stereotype of the Destroying Mother or witch?'
(106). Yet arguably, Bowen's sense of the power women exert over each
other gradually became more complex, less negative. In *The Little Girls*,
Bowen's penultimate novel, no one character can be regarded as
either destroying mother or malevolent witch. The power of woman
over woman that is established through the supernatural references in
The Little Girls is shared, and is neither hierarchical nor destructive.
Though Phyllis Lassner writes of 'the malice and envy that holds their
relationship together' (*Elizabeth Bowen*, 1990, 24), in fact the three
women show little malice and their only approach to envy is the child-
less Sheila's natural envy of Dinah's children and grandchildren.[12] All
the same, the former 'little girls' sense the force of their power over
each other and fear its consequences. Sheila feels 'blown upon' by
Dinah's summons through the personal columns of the newspapers
(35). Clare, who is probably lesbian, continually resists Dinah's
approaches, continually tries to refuse further contact, for fear that
Dinah might "'rock the boat. Unsettle me'" (145), and that she, Clare,
might be driven to "'make *me* a willow cabin at your gate'", out of love
for Dinah, as she believes Frank has done (194; Bowen's emphasis).[13]
Clare's fear of this love is an acknowledgement of the disturbing
potential of the relationship among the women. Dinah in turn will

eventually become seriously ill through her fear of rejection from Clare. The power of this three-way relationship is all the greater because it was established just before the great divide that tore up all their lives, 'the gap' as Dinah calls it (139).

This gap, which separates the friends for nearly fifty years, is marked physically by a graphic at the novel's mid-point.[14] It shows the top of the birthday cake of a schoolfriend of the three little girls, which reads, ironically, 'Very many happy returns of the day OLIVE, July 23, 1914'. Throughout her brilliant – both touching and very funny – account of the birthday picnic on the sea-shore, Bowen emphasizes the ominous implications of that date. The children begin to sing, 'a terrible wolf-like ululation with a spectre of tune in it', with a crescendo for the chorus: '"A-all the WO-O-Orld is sad A-AND drearee, / Ev'ry-WHERE I roam"' (124-5). Meanwhile the adults' thoughts turn to the coming war; Clare, the precociously intelligent soldier's daughter, well aware of their fears, turns in fury on Dicey, who has asked about the assassination at Sarajevo of the '"Australian Archbishop"'; and the tide continues to ebb. At the end of the picnic Clare's father comes to say goodbye to Dinah's mother, whom he loves. The muted poignancy of this scene is intensified by the reader's awareness that it will be their last goodbye: Bowen has already established that he is killed exactly a month later at the battle of Mons (33); and he has already appeared as a possible ghost in Dicey's mother's garden: 'happy this garden would be to have such a revenant, were he ever dead. Though who would be there to see, were they all gone?' (85). Dicey/Dinah's last sight of Mumbo/Clare is of her angry refusal to say goodbye: 'The rough child, up there against the unkind sky, on the rough grass, glanced at and over the sands once. She threw a hand up into a rough general wave. Then she leaped down on the land side of the sea wall. She had disappeared' (133).

These words, 'she had disappeared', end Part Two of this tripartite novel, in which the past, the summer of 1914, is sandwiched between two sections of the present, the autumn of 1963.[15] Part One ends on a similar note of loss, as Clare exclaims, learning of the destruction of their old school, '"Into thin air"' (63). Clare's allusion is to *The Tempest* (IV.i.148-58):

> Our revels now are ended. These our actors,
> As I foretold you, were all spirits, and
> Are melted into air, into thin air:
> And, like the baseless fabric of this vision,
> The cloud-capped tow'rs, the gorgeous palaces,
> The solemn temples, the great globe itself,

Yea, all which it inherit, shall dissolve;
And, like this insubstantial pageant faded,
Leave not a rack behind. We are such stuff
As dreams are made on, and our little life
Is rounded with a sleep.

The spectral nature of human life and human culture that Pros-
pero's words suggest is something the former little girls, like the rest of
their generation, might well ponder. This novel, though it may indeed
be Bowen's 'wittiest and funniest', as Edwin Kenney suggests (86), is
also full of a muffled tragedy, mostly resulting from war and its aftermath.[16] A *World of Love*, according to Corcoran, is 'a work of profound
personal and cultural mourning' (72). *The Little Girls* seems to me a
complex comedy of mourning.[17] As Dinah comments, after the children were separated in July 1914, '"the war came, showing one
nothing was too bad to be true"' (222). The novel's tragedies, though,
like those of Greek drama, happen off-stage, rather than in the central
narrative. By the time the women are reunited they have survived two
wars. As already noted, Clare's father is killed, and the ensuing break-
up of her family means that she is never properly educated, that her
'great ability' is wasted (146); her brief marriage is to a man she names
only as 'Mr. Wrong' (32). Dinah's father had committed suicide
before her birth, but her mother '"went down in that plague at the
end of the war. The Spanish 'flu, that was like a war more"' (182);
Dinah herself was widowed early. Sheila's lover, she says bitterly,
'"always was all shot up, at the best of times. He'd been through that
war. One lung left, coughing his guts out"' (229). He dies never
knowing she loved him: '"all gone for nothing, those years"', is her
verdict. After his death she marries a dull man and never has the children she longs for, and, like Clare, her talent – she was a brilliant
child dancer – is wasted.[18]

In this novel, Bowen emphasizes the ways in which not only
human lives but also material objects are distorted and destroyed by
war and the other devastations of time. As I mentioned earlier, the
seaside school the little girls attended was destroyed by a German shell
some time after 1940, as was the local High Street where they did their
shopping (a coffer, fetters, rich jewels) for the original time capsule.[19]
And, when the three women dig up their time capsule fifty years later,
the coffer is indeed there, but it is empty. This final disappearance
shakes Dinah so intensely that she feels that '"nothing's real any
more"', except for Clare: '"but *you're* real, Mumbo"' (163). In the
serious illness that follows, she cries out, '"It's all gone, was it ever

there? No, never there. Nothing. No, no, no . . ." And so on. Terrible to hear her' (239). The natural instinct to rely on the endurance of solid material things is continually shaken throughout this narrative. *The Little Girls* is, significantly, the first novel Bowen wrote after the sale of Bowen's Court, an event that would surely have strengthened the sense of the transience and instability of the material world already instilled by the London Blitz, and especially the near-destruction of her house in Clarence Terrace. She wrote to her friend Virginia Woolf, on 5 January 1941, after bombs had destroyed both Woolf's London flats, 'all my life I have said, "whatever happens there will always be tables and chairs"—and what a mistake' (*Mulberry Tree*, New York, 1986, 216).[20] *The Little Girls* expresses both that natural expectation and the knowledge that it is quite mistaken.

Bowen's treatment of the accumulations of totemic objects in this text expresses the same sense of the uncertainty of the material world. These accumulations include the contents of the two time capsules: the bones, the letter, written in blood and in a secret language, the chains ('fetters'), and the 'jewels' in the coffer buried by the little girls; the more pedestrian collection of toothbrushes, nail scissors and strings of fake pearls in Dinah's later time capsule. Besides these, there are the hoards in Clare's chain of gift shops – from personalized dog dishes to witch balls and eventually a series of masks made by Dinah's 'local witch' (41, 191). Then there are the collection of minia-ture free samples in Sheikie's childhood bedroom, the china collection of Dinah's mother and the contents of the various High Street shops where the little girls acquire their stores. There are so many of these hoards of totemic objects, in fact, that Bennett and Royle lay out one page of their study of *The Little Girls* as what they call a 'Novel Shopping List' of these collections (131). They describe it as 'ephemeral bric-a-brac' and interpret this phenomenon in terms of 'the sheer transience of the objects of mass culture to which it refers' (123). Yet in some ways, many of these totemic objects, not all of which are 'the objects of mass culture', reach across time. By defini-tion, the time capsules do this – or, rather, are intended to do so. But more certainly, other collections of objects survive the years. Dicey's mother has a large collection of presumably valuable porcelain: 'Pre-cious it must be—why else should it have been mended with such care? Delicate metal stitchery underran dishes and saucers and held lids together; tiny alloy claws enabled handles to keep their grip on cups; cemented cracks formed networks cradling fine bowls' (76). The child Clare, looking at the landscapes depicted on this porcelain, experi-ences them as if 'she had lived within them. That she knew each landscape, to her a planet, to be linked in destructibility with the cup, bowl, or plate upon which it was, added peril to love. One saw, here, how china could break. One saw also how one day or another it must do so beyond repair' (76-7). Yet the china survives to be inherited by Dinah, along with other possessions of her mother's – her embroidered footstools, an ivory Chinese puzzle, the French clock that finds its way into Dinah's drawing-room. These fragile, damaged things survive and continue to make a meaning for Clare as well as for Dicey. Survival is possible, valuable, but terrifyingly uncertain.

'All is the fear and nothing is the love'; the psychological damage and material loss suffered by the fictional protagonists of this novel, like most of their historical contemporaries, leave them profoundly afraid under their various façades as competent middle-aged women. Dinah quotes the above line from *Macbeth* (IV.ii.12) as she lies ill and in shock. Like Lady Macduff, who speaks these words, she feels abandoned and betrayed, and Clare, who has indeed temporarily deserted her, has left out of fear – fear of love. But Dinah herself has a long-standing and unarticulated fear. Clare, in a self-protective fury, accuses her of having spent her life running for cover (198); she acknowledges that in Frank's cottage she feels 'safe again' after 'a long, long time' (187); her own house, Applegate, seems to be chosen for its remarkable solidity and sturdiness. Sheila, in her turn, whom Dinah describes as '"barnacled over . . . thickly covered with *some* deposit"' (146-7; Bowen's emphasis), wears this protective carapace of conventionality and normality to keep from alerting the world to her pain. It is entirely characteristic that as a child she should have chosen to bury her witch-like sixth toe in the coffer, thinking of it as '"my deformity"', and therefore something that must be hidden (235). In an unusual moment of confidence, she tells Clare that when her lover was dying, and terrified, he kept telling her 'You never loved me . . . you never loved me', as she had presumably never felt able to tell him of her love. Meanwhile Clare has come to see all human relationships in terms of danger, of a supernatural threat, quoting to Sheila, in relation to Dicey's life, the beginning of George Meredith's strange and beautiful poem, 'The Woods of Westermain':

> Enter these enchanted woods,
> > You who dare.
> Each has business of his own;
> But should you distrust a tone,
> > Then beware.
> Shudder all the haunted roods,

All the eyeballs under hoods
Shroud you in their glare.
Enter these enchanted woods
You who dare (228)

Significantly, Meredith's Westermain is beautiful and desirable; its
enchantments are dangerous only to those who 'distrust a tone' or
who feel 'a dread of dark': 'in yourself may lurk the trap' (Meredith,
1912, 204). The poet here is concerned with the dangers of fear in
itself. Again, Bowen uses the literature of the supernatural to suggest
the paralysing fears haunting a generation blasted by two wars and
threatened by a third, a generation that has come to sense that
nothing and no one can be trusted. As we have seen, Clare tries to
protect herself from these 'haunted roods' by steering clear of love and
apparently avoiding any personal life, to the extent that she identifies
herself by the name of her chain of gift shops, proclaiming proudly:
'"I am MOPSIE PYE"' (41).

The spectral language and supernatural allusions of *The Little Girls*
blur the boundaries of realist fiction, in which category it might otherwise seem to belong. As Lassner notes, 'Bowen's themes and
subjects are usually placed in the English realist tradition of Jane
Austen, George Eliot, E.M. Forster and Henry James' (141–2). Yet
this novel challenges the tradition explicitly as well as implicitly.
Dinah, looking at a conventional painting of the Old High Street in
Southstone where they went to school (Sheikie's wedding present),
dismisses it as '"this lie"', although to Clare it appears '"correct in
every detail"' (166). Dinah goes on to argue that '"if it were slightly
better it would be very likely to be a still worse lie"', because it would
be trading on what she calls '"prefabricated emotions"' (166–7).
Through Dinah's words, Bowen challenges, as in one way or another
she had throughout her career, the ideal of art as exact representation.
Nearly thirty years previously, in *A House in Paris*, she had suggested
that, in life as in art, a view that is 'correct in every detail' is essentially distorted. In that novel, Karen thinks of her mother's view of
life as reductive: 'her well-lit explanations of people were like photographs taken when the camera could not lie; they stunned your
imagination by *being* exact . . . Without their indistinctness things do
not exist; you cannot desire them . . . [her mother], like the camera of
her day, denied. She saw what she knew was there' (117).[21] Understanding, that is, requires imagination rather than preconception, and
good art recognizes this requirement. *The Little Girls* provides the

necessary 'indistinctness' partly through its various hauntings, which imply that there are no clear boundaries between present and past, natural and supernatural, real and imagined. In *Afterthoughts*, a collection of essays and reviews that Bowen was working on at the same time as *The Little Girls*, she establishes the grounds of her suspicions about realism, talking of 'a distinction between truth and so-called reality'. She adds, 'the novelist's imagination has a power of its own. It does not merely invent, it perceives. It intensifies, therefore it gives power, extra importance, greater truth, and greater inner reality to what may well be ordinary and everyday things' (1962, 114). At the same period, according to Victoria Glendinning, Bowen was reading with admiration the fiction both of her good friend Iris Murdoch and of Muriel Spark. She especially admired the way these two younger writers combined (at least in their works of this decade) 'myth and nightmare and fantasy' with middle-class characters; 'any resulting inverisimilitude was not important' (*Biography*, 1979, 248). This admiration seems to affect both Bowen's last novels, *The Little Girls* and *Eva Trout*, in their different ways, and perhaps accounts in part for their signal difference from her earlier writings. According to Patricia Juliana Smith the last two works are a 'revolutionary accomplishment' (Smith, 1997, 102), while Wyatt-Brown in her turn writes of them as 'the last two experimental novels' (Wyatt-Brown, 1993, 164).

Part of *The Little Girls*' experimental quality arises from Bowen's deliberate decision to let the characters' words and actions speak for themselves. According to Spencer Curtis Brown, whom Bowen frequently consulted about the progress of her novels, 'in *The Little Girls*, she for the first time deliberately tried, as she said, when discussing with me the writing of it, to present characters entirely from the outside. She determined never to tell the reader what her characters were thinking or feeling' ('Foreword', 1974, xxxviii).[22] Sandra Kemp alludes to that decision and elaborates on it, commenting that in *The Little Girls* Bowen is engaged in 'a search for a new language where people and objects are not contaminated by a vocabulary of feeling and by the kinds of significance that plots usually rely on' (137). Bowen's 'new language' indirectly communicates feeling and thought, not just through action and dialogue, though this novel is exceptional among Bowen's novels in its dependence on dialogue. It communicates also through such devices as, for instance, nomenclature: in the first recorded conversation between Sheila and Clare, at various points and with various implications, the two are named as Pink Roses and Black Turban (after their hats), as Sheila and Clare, as Sheikie and Mumbo, as 'the daughter of Beaker and the wife of

Artworth, of Beaker and Artworth' and MOPSIE PYE, as Mrs Artworth and Miss Burkin-Jones, and as 'the big woman and the pretty
one'. In one sentence Sheila has three distinct identities, to correspond with her complex reactions: 'though the prospect of being quit
of things . . . should have been grateful to Mrs Artworth, it dissatisfied
Sheila, and thwarted Sheikie' (43). Identity shifts with circumstances.
It is as unstable as all other aspects of human experience. A related
aspect of this disturbing 'new language,' undoubtedly, is the diction of
the uncanny, including the allusions to the literature of the supernatural, which also suggest, without explicitly naming, the unstable
emotional states of the characters.

Bowen's 'new language', as well as her avoidance of conventional
heterosexual plotting, may well account in part for the general critical
unease with *The Little Girls*, an unease felt even by some of her most
intelligent critics. Hermione Lee, for instance, speaks of her disappointment and discontent with this novel and its 'clumsy procedures'
(*Estimation*, 1981, 205-6).[23] Neil Corcoran, too, dislikes it, repelled by
what he sees as 'the restless flurry of plotting, both busy and banal',
which 'seems almost haplessly out of key with the haunting desolation
of its theme' (Corcoran, 2004, 8). For her part, Deirdre Toomey, in
her *Oxford Dictionary of National Biography* article on Bowen's life,
simply ignores *The Little Girls* altogether. Patricia Juliana Smith finds
the narrative pace 'less than compelling' and speaks of the 'critical
dismay' with this novel (Smith, 1997, 112). Patricia Coughlan damns
both the last two novels with what seems to be faint praise, for their
'poignant awkwardness' (Coughlan, 1997, 105).[24]

I cannot share this distaste: I first read *The Little Girls* soon after it
was first published and, throughout the forty-odd years since then,
have felt compelled to reread it at intervals, either because of remembered discomfort or remembered pleasure. Despite this pleasure, I
understand the unease of these writers. The motives of the narrative
are often obscure: we can never know just why Dinah suddenly needs
so urgently to meet her old friends again; we cannot know why the
three decide to dig up the coffer; nor do we know entirely why Dinah
becomes so ill, or why the huge bruise appears on her forehead.[25]
When Clare scolds Dinah, '"don't be a fey bore"' (165), when Frank
warns her, '"Dinah, don't be fey"' (24), we accept that, while Dinah
may not be a bore, she can indeed be fey. This feyness, these obscuri-
ties, interact with the disruptions, both historical and fictional, and
with the shifts between different layers of reality that are suggested by
the supernatural allusions and diction, to suggest the terrors and
uncertainties suffered by those who have survived two devastating wars

and are faced with the possibility of a worse one.[26] The little girls, like Stella Rodney in *The Heat of the Day*, 'had grown up just after the first world war with a generation which *as* a generation was to come to be made to feel it had muffed the catch' (24). In her non-fiction, too, Bowen makes a similar observation: 'confidence was broken by 1914; from then on, decline of love for the present went with the loss of faith in it' (*Mulberry Tree*, 1986, 54). The unease that this novel has provoked arises at least in part from the success with which it communicates the lack of faith and confidence of the generation of its central characters.

In a perceptive footnote, Marian Kelly comments, 'one can only speculate that Bowen receives negative criticism because her novels initially appear more accessible than those of her contemporaries, so that when her readers encounter difficulties she is viewed as inept, while other writers who flout convention more exuberantly are viewed as brilliantly innovative' (Kelly, 2002, 10). Certainly her critics have been far more comfortable with the central, 1914, part of *The Little Girls*, in which the narration is straightforward, than with the surrounding parts set in the 1960s, when the certainties of childhood have become the anxieties of late middle age. While readers of fiction are familiar enough with narratives of childhood, from *Jane Eyre* and *David Copperfield* to *The Lord of the Flies*, a novel based on the interaction of three middle-aged women is inevitably stranger and more disconcerting.

The whole concept of *The Little Girls* – the relations between three women in 'the days before love' and 'the days after' (56) – indeed flouts novelistic convention. As Maud Ellmann says in relation to *The Little Girls*, 'novels run on sex, their plot lines driven by desire' (*Elizabeth Bowen*, 1202, 191). Here, though, Bowen avoids what Dinah calls, in her attack on realist art '"prefabricated emotions"', amongst which she includes 'love, or even sex' (168). The ending matches the rest of the novel in unconventionality. Like the conclusion of Bowen's previous novel, *A World of Love* – 'they no sooner met but they loved' (149) – it both provides some token closure, and compels a reading beyond the text. In the last few lines of the novel, Dinah wakes up and responds to Clare's identifying herself as 'Mumbo': '"Not Mumbo, Clare. Clare, where have you been?"' While this gives some kind of sense of closure, in that Dinah accepts at last Clare's adult identity, it also drives the reader into considering this relationship both in the past and in the future, beyond the ending. Smith comments, 'by ending her narrative with this exchange, Bowen stops short of a state of quiescence. More *must* transpire between the characters after this interlude, but the plotting of further interaction, not to mention the judgment as to whether or not this is a "happy" or even satisfactory ending, is thrown back upon the reader. Therein, no doubt, lies much of the critical dismay with this text' (Smith, 1997, 112).

The novel ends as it began, with Dinah's attempts to deal with time, with present and future, with present and past.[27] Throughout the novel there is a sense almost of *déjà vu*, of slipping between one period and another. Dinah is involved in the creation of two time capsules. She speaks with her dead mother's voice and has her mother's mannerisms. Like her mother, she is loved by an army officer haunted by the fear of the immediate future. The little girls as ageing women immediately drop back into their old relationship after a fifty-year gap: Sheila's first words to Clare, who has dropped a glove, is '"there you go again"' (30). Yet for all these shifts between the layers of time, the novel is never nostalgic. The child Clare gloomily recites in a poetry class the beginning of Wordsworth's 'Ode: Intimations of Immortality':

> There was a time when meadow grove and stream
> The earth and every common sight
> To me did seem
> Apparelled in celestial light
> The glory and the freshness of a dream (67–8;
> Bowen's emphases removed)

While the novel communicates the poem's sense of mourning for a lost past, it romanticizes the past no more than it does the present or the future. The children, as children do, quarrel, bully and perpetually criticize each other.[28] The narrative perpetually insists that, like those birthday wishes for 'Many Happy Returns' in July 1914, hopes and promises are never or rarely fulfilled The relations between past, present and future often involve the '"deluded expectations, harmless things coming to dreadful ends"' that Dinah talks about in relation to *Macbeth* (209). When unliterary Sheila responds, '"isn't it about witches"', Dinah answers, '"Not altogether"' (209). No more is *The Little Girls* altogether about witches. But its language of witches and of hauntings expresses the sense of discomfort and insecurity of human beings living in time, as well as the intensified insecurities of a particular generation living at a particular time. Bowen once observed, 'the universal battiness of our [twentieth] century', with its devastating wars and other horrors, was to provide ghosts 'with a propitious climate' (*Afterthoughts*, 1962, 101). This novel, concerned with, and produced during, a period of exceptional 'battiness', is especially haunted. Perhaps the equally batty century in which Bowen's readers now find themselves will foster just as many ghosts, literary and otherwise.

5

'*She*-ward bound':
Elizabeth Bowen as a
sensationalist writer

SHANNON WELLS-LASSAGNE

In his book-length study of Elizabeth Bowen, Neil Corcoran speaks of the author's 'literary bricollage'(sic) (2004, 152) as one of the wellsprings of her fiction. Indeed, studies of Bowen have emphasized her debts to Shakespeare, Dickens, Proust, Woolf and Forster, among many others, in an attempt to define her style and themes. Bowen seems to encourage this type of 'Where's Waldo?' reading, particularly in her later novels, where the three women of *The Little Girls* explicitly identify with the three witches of *Macbeth*, and where two of the characters in *Eva Trout* meet in Dickens's former home of Fort House, i.e. 'Bleak House'. This palimpsestic quality could be a second interpretation of Victoria Glendinning's famous comment that Bowen is 'the link that connects Virginia Woolf with Iris Murdoch and Muriel Spark') (*Portrait*, 1977, 1). However, for the most part the aspects of her fiction that take their cue from more popular sources have been glossed over until very recently (perhaps because critics wished to assure Bowen's place as a serious writer, something that no longer seems to be such a pressing need). However, two important nonfiction texts – the preface to Sheridan Le Fanu's *Uncle Silas* and a piece on Rider Haggard's *She* – point to the presence of popular fiction in her work, something that is now coming to light. Thus it seems particularly relevant to explore its use in Bowen's work, and its significance in terms of genre: does this mixture of high- and lowbrow references make her more palatably modernist, or even postmodernist, or instead does it brand her as a 'middlebrow writer', as Nicola Humble (2001) has termed her?

Thus, taking my cue from major studies of Bowen that mention these influences, I will be examining in more detail exactly how it is that popular fiction traditions function in what is generally considered 'highbrow' prose.[1] The initial exploration of popular, or what I will call 'sensationalist', fiction will demonstrate the omnipresence of these genres, which include the Gothic, the sensation novel, the Victorian quest romance, and the detective novel. Associating all of these genres may appear surprising, especially the sensation novel, which many consider as a proto-feminist genre, and the Victorian quest romance which originated in the refusal of a realist novel deemed too feminine, and which was often characterized by its exclusion of female characters (Showalter, 76-9). However, I would argue that these genres are similar in their emphasis on the extraordinary or the marvellous, and thus in contrast to the realist tradition of the nineteenth century. We will see that in her fiction, Bowen alternates between paying tribute and subverting their tropes. The ambivalence that this suggests will be examined, allowing us to better understand the problematic link between what we have termed sensationalism and its underlying context. This use of popular fiction, we will see, is in fact a means for Bowen to insist on her prose as 'readerly'. By accentuating textuality through the prism of sensationalism, Bowen forces reader participation while undermining the mimetic dimension of what has often been thought of as conventionally domestic realism.

'Disguise and glorify': homage and pastiche

In her essay 'Out of a Book', Bowen clearly links the artistic imagination to readings of the past:

> The imagination, which may appear to bear such individual fruit, is rooted in a compost of forgotten books. The apparent choices of art are nothing but addictions, pre-dispositions . . . The aesthetic is nothing but a return to images that will allow nothing to take their place; the aesthetic is nothing but an attempt to disguise and glorify the enforced return. (*The Mulberry Tree*,[2] 53)

If such is the case, and if Bowen's first powerful impression of literature was received from Rider Haggard's *She*, as she states in her essay of the same name, it is unsurprising that sensationalist fiction should play a significant part in her fiction.

Perhaps the most obvious texts using tropes from popular fiction are the short stories, which to her mind 'allow . . . for what is crazy about humanity' ('Preface to *Stories by Elizabeth Bowen*', MT, 130); thus, for example, murders and their portrayal in newspaper articles, typical of the sensation novel, appear in several short stories ('Recent

Photograph', 'The Disinherited', 'Reduced', 'The Cat Jumps' and 'The Apple Tree'), while Gothic ghosts appear in several others, to such an extent that they have been published in a separate collection, *Elizabeth Bowen's Ghost Stories* (including stories like 'The Shadowy Third', 'The Cheery Soul', 'Foothold', 'The Demon Lover' and 'Green Holly'). However, upon closer inspection, even the novel, which contains 'such taste as I have for rational behaviour and social portraiture' (MT, 130), shows repeated allusions to the Gothic in particular: in *The Little Girls*, for example, the three children bury a coffer with fetters and a gun, while Julian Moynahan's study of Bowen's *The Last September* insists that '[a] sense of being spied on, secretly watched, is as constant and nearly as paranoid in *The Last September* as it was in the Gothic tales of Le Fanu', and sees one of the characters as a vampire figure (Moynahan, 1995, 242, 244).

In all of these texts, the homage may be sincere, but is certainly not pure: on the contrary, it is adulterated with pastiche, even with comedy, showing that Bowen is not content to simply mimic authors of the past, but is rather seeking to rework the tropes of previous traditions and push them to their logical conclusions. This is true even in the constrained space of the short story: a choice example is that of 'The Return'. We are first introduced to Lydia, the paid companion of the horrid Tottenhams, who is dreading their return and the effect that it will have on her self-esteem. Upon their arrival, Mrs Tottenham receives a letter from a former lover who wants to see her again: in her reflection on her marriage, and her final decision not to jeopardize the relationship she once had by facing the former lover as an older woman, we are told that humanity comes back into the house. This short story uses several themes typical of the Gothic and sensation novels: Lydia is seen as being at odds with herself, and feeling the house itself turn against her, suggesting the theme of the double as well as the idea of the young girl being imprisoned in a hostile house, both of which are dear to the Gothic and sensation genres. Later, in deliberating on her reaction to the Tottenhams' humiliations, she considers murder and imagines the headlines in the newspapers, once again suggesting the link between yellow journalism and the sensation novel. Likewise, the Tottenhams, it is suggested, are a couple typical of a sensation novel, but depicted *after* the imposed happy end: though they both cheated on one another and lived in 'drab wickedness' (*The Collected Stories of Elizabeth Bowen*, 29)[3] elsewhere; when her lover leaves her, and he comes into an inheritance, they reunite. This seems to be a quick summary of a certain number of sensation novels, where initial disorder to the moral status quo is eventually rectified at the end of the novel. In this case, Bowen's short story is not so much writing in the tradition of these popular genres as it is *re*writing those traditions: what happens after the happy end? Obviously the pattern of the sensation novel repeats itself from one text to the next, but, in Bowen's version of a sensationalist narrative, though the status quo is maintained, the normative morality typical of past narratives is turned on its head. When asked why she would consider 'falling back into sin', as it were, Mrs Tottenham's reply is not one to be found in a sensation novel: 'Because it *was* wrong. It's this awful rightness that's killing me. My husband's been a bad man too, but here we both are, smirking and grinning at each other, just to keep hold of something we neither of us want' (CS, 34). The 'happily ever after' has become 'smirking and grinning', and it is by the sacrifice of Mrs Tottenham's feelings to the ideal of her former affair, rather than to the sanctity of her marriage, that the character regains dignity. To the extent to which the sensation novel itself probed the weaknesses in the established order and played upon middle-class anxieties, here we could say that Bowen's work is a logical extension of the genre that inspired it.

However, Bowen often goes one step farther, and not only reworks the popular tradition whose tropes she is exploiting, but subverts them in order to create a comic or ironic collision of genres. In 'The Shadowy Third', the reader slowly comes to realize that the happy couple depicted in the story is in fact a threesome, with the unloved dead first wife a constant companion in their lives and their home, always felt but never to be referred to except by euphemism: '"I wonder you never thought of having a sundial before," she insisted. "Did Anybody ever think of it?"' (CS, 77). Of course this short story is working within the tradition of the Victorian ghost story (to the extent that it refers not to an exotic locale, but to a new house in a familiar and contemporary setting), but in its use of capitalized pronouns as an indirect reference to the previous wife whose existence they ostensibly ignore, it also suggests another of Bowen's influences: Rider Haggard's Ayesha, She-Who-Must-Be-Obeyed. The contrast between the two characters is what initially seems most striking: the characters of Haggard's novel are unable to tear their eyes off Ayesha, whereas the unnamed wife apparently never managed to get a glance from her husband, and Ayesha incites love at first sight, whereas the first wife is haunting the house because no one has ever cared for her; likewise, while Ayesha lives in a city immemorial, the unnamed wife's dwelling-place is so freshly built that it still smells of plaster. However, in both cases these residences are places of death, where the supernatural women hold the ultimate power, acknowledged or not.

Likewise, in both cases, their desires are rewarded through a form of reincarnation (the new wife, Pussy, is a new and beloved version of the old, and her pregnancy echoes that of her predecessor; Ayesha's long wait for her lover's reincarnation comes to pass in the course of the novel): this of course bodes ill for both Haggard and Bowen's 'happy couples'. Thus the 'straight' homage to the Gothic story in 'The Shadowy Third' is doubled with the reference to Haggard's quest romance, and this incongruous addition to both the domestic setting and the seemingly innocuous plot add irony and a form of black humour to the short story.

Thus far I have spoken essentially about the short stories; given their shorter length, their tone is more coherent than that of the novels, in which the tropes of popular fiction often coexist with a more realist and often comic tone typical of drawing-room comedy. An example of the extended use of sensationalist tropes in Bowen's novel-length prose is that of *The House in Paris*.[4] The novel tells the story of a young Englishwoman, Karen Michaelis, trying to resign herself to an acceptable relationship within her upper-class society while still in love with a Frenchman, Max Ebhart, her friend Naomi Fisher's fiancé. They end up having an affair, and Karen becomes pregnant, eventually abandoning the child when Max commits suicide (as becomes obvious from the summary, melodrama has its part to play in the novel . . .). This narrative is circumscribed by the first and third part of the novel, both entitled 'The Present', where Karen and Max's child Leopold, now a nine-year-old boy, awaits his first meeting with his mother at the Fishers' home, accompanied by Henrietta, a young girl who happens to be staying at the house on her way to rejoin her grandmother in the south of France. Both children meet Madame Fisher, Naomi's mother, whose possessive relationship with Max proved disastrous to him, and when Karen fails to come and her husband Ray replaces her, Leopold's reaction is marked by this conversation. *The House in Paris* clearly is meant to be taken as a Gothic rendering: Paris is first presented through the eyes of a young English girl as a place of violence and unrest, a French setting worthy of an eighteenth-century Gothic novel: 'Windows with strong grilles looked ready for an immediate attack (Henrietta had heard how much blood had been shed in Paris); doors had grim iron patterns across their glass; dust-grey shutters were almost all bolted fast . . . ' (*HiP*, 22). This menace implicit in the exotic locale is confirmed by the particularly Gothic figure of Madame Fisher, who resides in the house of the title and manipulates all around her.[5] In fact, Madame Fisher is particularly interesting in relation to the influence of the Gothic and the

quest romance on Bowen's work because she personifies the two
novels of those traditions in which the author seemed particularly
interested, namely Sheridan LeFanu's *Uncle Silas* and Rider Haggard's
She. The relation to *Uncle Silas* is episodic: it is when the young Henrietta meets the bedridden Madame Fisher for the first time that
Bowen uses various allusions to Maud Ruthyn meeting the terrifying
Uncle Silas: in both cases, the long-dreaded meeting with the recluse
takes place in a bedroom described as a sombre-hued painting with a
strong chiaroscuro effect:

> The dark wainscoting behind him, and the vastness of the room,
> in the remoter parts of which the light which fell strongly upon his
> face and figure expended itself with hardly any effect, exhibited
> him with the forcible and strange relief of a finely painted Dutch
> portrait. (LeFanu, 192)

> . . . daylight fell cold white on the honeycomb quilt rolled back.
> Round the curtained bedhead, Pompeian red walls drank objects
> into their shadow: picture-frames, armies of bottles, boxes, an
> ornate clock showed without glinting, as though not quite painted
> out by some dark transparent wash. (*HiP*, 46)

The topics of conversation are also similar: the invalid comments
ironically both on the girl's friendly but inadequate companion to
the meeting (Milly and Naomi Fisher, respectively) as well as the
girl's guardian (Maud's father, Henrietta's grandmother) and his/her
own illness.

However, in the novel as a whole Madame Fisher is similar to
Haggard's *She*.[6] Thus, like the sensationalist heroine, Madame Fisher
fascinates through the gaze, an attraction that is described in very
similar terms in both novels:

> The sweep of dark curtains framed only her eyes, a magnet to him.
> (*HiP*, 208)

> Drawn by some magnetic force which I could not resist, I let my
> eyes rest upon her shining orbs, and felt a current pass from them
> to me that bewildered and half-blinded me. (*She*, 117)

> Transfixed half-way between the door and the window, Henrietta
> felt that pillow was all eyes. Mme Fisher's unmoved regard was a
> battery: with an unconscious quiver Henrietta drew in her chin.
> (*HiP*, 47)

> . . . presently I felt clearly that somebody was looking at me from
> behind the curtains. I could not see the person, but I could

> distinctly feel his or her gaze, and what is more, it produced a very
> odd effect upon my nerves. (*She*, 105)

Her motives are also similar to Haggard's heroine, as the climax of her
role in *The House in Paris* is her meeting with Max's son Leopold,
whom she perceives as being the reincarnation of his father,[7] much
like Ayesha awaits a similarly named Leo, the reincarnation of his
Greek ancestor Kallikrates, while the complicated quadrangle of
romantic entanglements between Leo/Kallikrates, Ustane, Ame-
nartas, and Ayesha is similar to the one between Max/Leopold,
Karen, Naomi and Madame Fisher. Examining the sequel to *She*,
Ayesha: The Return of She, makes the similarities even more striking:
there, as in the present of the narration of *The House in Paris*, She is a
mummified figure, who wants her lover to be more interested in
power than sex, and whose influence is finally fatal to him. In *The
House in Paris*, Madame Fisher is much older than Max and, though
she is in love with him, her plans are mostly for his material success,
even pushing him to pursue his affair with Karen while engaged to
her daughter because Karen comes from a wealthier family. Max comments that "'Her sex is all in her head, but she is not a woman for
nothing'" (*HiP*, 138). Ayesha is not only older (2,000 years older, in
fact), but immortal, something that makes a physical relationship with
Leo impossible:

> All she would tell me . . . was that between them rose the barrier of
> Leo's mortality, and that until his physical being had been impreg-
> nated with the mysterious virtue of the Vapour of Life, it was not
> wise that she should take him as a husband. (*Return of She*, 141)

She therefore spends her time trying to convince Leo to turn to
worldly ambition instead and plans global domination, while Leo
becomes wan and listless in the face of her refusals:

> Oh! divest thyself of all these wrappings of thy power – that power
> which strews thy path with dead and keeps me apart from thee. If
> only for one short night forget the ambition that gnaws unceasingly
> at thy soul . . . and be a woman and – my wife. (*Return of She*, 178)

Both characters precipitate the death of their loved ones: when Max
realizes that he is unable to extricate himself from Madame Fisher's
influence, he kills himself; Leo obtains his wish – a kiss from Ayesha
– and is struck dead in consequence.

The character of Madame Fisher seems to be the locus of the sensationalist influences in *The House in Paris* – to such an extent, in fact,

that she appears to personify the genres, striking a contrast with the other characters in the novel. Sensationalism is essentially relegated to the French (and to Madame Fisher in particular); in a sense the relationship between the English and the French characters is a relationship between two different literary traditions, where the realism and drawing-room comedy[8] associated with Karen and her family (they are described as a family 'living in a pre-war novel', *HiP*, 70) clashes with the dramatic nature of the French characters. Thus Karen must defend herself from Max's accusations that she takes everything with a sense of humour, to which she responds that '"to be serious is absurd; what can one do?"'. This is a vision that Max construes as 'deadly' (*HiP*, 111). Likewise, Mrs Michaelis's vision of Max is described in literary terms, and again suggests that two traditions are in conflict here:

> How right Mother had been, how right she was always. All the same, the well-lit explanations of people . . . stunned your imagination by *being* exact . . . Without their indistinctness things do not exist . . . Nothing annoyed [Mrs Michaelis] more than to be told that the personality is mysterious; it made her think of Maeterlinck, people in green dresses winding through a blue wood. It is inexcusable not to be clear, she said . . . Karen enjoyed her mother's anti-romanticism. God forbid indeed, that one should have cloudy ideas, or impart to objects one's own shifting moodiness . . . What Mrs Michaelis said about Max and his reasons for wanting to marry Naomi would be, no doubt, true—if you pressed him flat like a flower in a book. But he had a thickness you had to recognize, and could not be pressed flat without losing form. (*HiP*, 118)

This passage clearly shows the conflict between the two traditions, and the reference to Belgian symbolist Maeterlinck implies that the rivalry is conceived in terms of language (French and English) in the novel. The effects of anti-romanticism – here to be taken in the sense of opposing the literary tradition of the romance – that Mrs Michaelis exhibits is described in violent terms: the realist tradition becomes a distortion, transforming a three-dimensional figure into two, causing him to lapse into non-entity. Without romanticism and its emotional pull, the imagination is stunned, and things no longer exist. Clearly, the narrator is implying that the refusal of romance is a grave fault in Bowen's world. This becomes particularly clear when it is criticized for 'imparting to objects one's own shifting moodiness', given that one of the most striking characteristics of Bowen's prose is her tendency to personify objects, as in the following quote from the same novel: 'She felt the house was acting, nothing seemed to be natural; objects did not wait to be seen but came crowding in on her, each with what amounted to its aggressive cry' (HiP, 24). The irony of the passage is manifest: Bowen obviously situates herself in opposition to the ideas of 'anti-romanticism', without necessarily forsaking the terms of realism, which are also 'true', 'right'. Thus the pervasive influence of Madame Fisher becomes a metaphor for the power of sensationalism, both its exaggerations and its imaginative pull. If the novel as a whole is a 'quest for self', as A.S. Byatt puts it in her introduction (HiP, 11), it is significant that both Madame Fisher and Mrs Michaelis die or are dying by the end of the novel, and the French and the English factions (represented by Ray and Leopold) reach an uneasy truce and face a world of new, if complex, possibilities. Both realism and sensationalism are essential influences in this quest for self, but both must make way for new narrative possibilities.

'Bewildered and half-blinded': revealing or concealing context

In Elizabeth Bowen's preface to Joseph LeFanu's Uncle Silas, her comments on LeFanu's plea that
seem particularly relevant to

> Sensationalism, for its ow
> repute; but sensation (of
> only not disdained, it is
> pens, the most poetic ima
> of the psychological thrill
> MT, 103)

Sensationalism's justificati
exists for its own sake, clear
only relevant if it is a means
say that Bowen's recurrent
guity: on the contrary, her
sometimes be a hindrance t
The Last September, the pro
household in the midst of
femme fatale. She craves lo
simply to be part of a patte
she belongs: 'Lois recalled
whole afternoon before th

historical novel' (*LS*, London, 1952, 75). As Neil Corcoran notes, her attempts to further the plot of her own life appear in the form of letters (Corcoran, 2004, 41) sent off to a more successful version of the *femme fatale*, her friend Viola, who intrigues all the men surrounding her. Repeatedly, Lois sends off letters that seem to be summaries of sensation novels, where she is in love with a married man, where her suitor resembles Douglas Fairbanks (*LS*, 52), and then is scandalized by the memory of her writings. The passage recounting her arrival at her own tennis party seems best to relate the contradiction between the romantic heroine Lois would like to be and the subversion of this sensationalist aspect of the text:

> 'Ah, there she is!' exclaimed several people, and all looked up the bank uncritically and kindly. The dark air of the shrubbery glittered with midges; she jerked her hands from her pockets and waved her way through . . . She had been looking down at the party, deployed in all its promise, with greed and eagerness as at a box of chocolates; eyes like a thumb and finger hovering to selection. Now, engaged by its look, she became all profile; her step flattened, she would have liked to crawl. She was, as Mr Montmorency had noticed, very self-conscious. (*LS*, 40)

The passage shows a mixture of sensational and ironically comic language; vocabulary which could initially suggest drama, like 'dark' or 'glittered', is subverted and undermined by the pointedly banal objects it modifies: 'shrubbery', 'midges'. Likewise, the response Lois originally generates, which corresponds to the stereotype of the fascinating sensation heroine – everyone taking notice of her arrival – is qualified immediately by the look that is 'uncritical and kindly', just as her own reaction to the party, an initial desire for power and manipulation, is immediately flattened into self-consciousness.

Here it is clearly the sensationalist aspirations of the heroine that come in for criticism and ironic commentary, and which are punished accordingly in the rest of the novel: when Lois finally does have the brush with real tragedy for which she has been hoping – her all-too-dependable English suitor ironically becomes worthy of her sensationalism by virtue of being killed by rebels – she reacts in a markedly non-romantic manner: '"Would you like me to—shall I just let the others know?" She nodded, wondering where to go, how long to stay there, how to come back. Her mind flooded with trivialities' (*LS*, 201). It is also in the wake of this novel's single moment of violence that Lois finally comes to a realization as to the political ramifications of their relationship and his death, which were originally failed subjects of sensation: "'I expect—I don't know—one probably gets past things." "But look here, there are things one can't—" (She meant: "He loved me, he believed in the British Empire.") "At least, I don't want to"' (*LS*, 203). It is because Lois's generic obsessions are keeping her from recognizing that she is in fact 'someone in a historical novel' – but a historical novel that has political as well as romantic or exotic possibilities – that causes the author to subject the character to such harsh treatment. Indeed, my contention is that sensationalism as it is presented in Bowen's fiction can either hinder or reveal the author's chosen subtext, according to whether or not the reader is capable of maintaining critical distance in the face of its purely emotional impact. Lois is unable to see beyond her own desire for the simple thrill of sensationalism to grasp the truth of the political situation (a civil war that will soon oust the Anglo-Irish from their position of power and privilege) until she is obliged to relinquish her romantic preconceptions. Blinding oneself to all but the overtly sensationalist aspects of a story seems more cynically deliberate, and thus more harshly condemned, in the short story 'Recent Photograph', where the journalist Lukin is too interested by the story of a local murder to be interested in the truths it might contain: 'He didn't want two stories, after all, and he knew perfectly well that Verbena was only going to contradict her mother's . . . The whole truth was, for the purposes of his profession, a thing of too various dimensions to be easily encompassed' (*CS*, 217).

However, I do not wish to call into question the importance of sensationalism to Bowen's work: both the Gothic and the sensation novel include subtexts that are very relevant to the author's concerns, and which come to the fore in her fiction. Thus, if the defining characteristics of the sensation novel include a strong heroine and the intrusion of the public into private life (Sturrock, 2004, 86), then there is no doubt that *The Heat of the Day*,[9] Bowen's novel about the London Blitz, is working in a sensationalist vein. The protagonist Stella Rodney is perceived by other characters as being a *femme fatale* because she supposedly left her husband for another man, but is in fact innocent of wrongdoing (her husband was actually the guilty party), while the public world of the war becomes intensely private when Stella is told that her lover is an enemy spy. However, these two political implications of the genre (for female stereotypes and for the ideological ramifications of the private) are taken from the original tradition and once again reworked: Stella has chosen to let the misconception about her stand ("'Who, at the age I was, would not rather sound a monster than look a fool? . . . Whoever's the story *had* been, I let it be mine. I let it ride, and more—it came to be my story, and I stuck to it. Or rather, first I stuck to it, then it went on sticking to me: it took my shape and equally I took its"', *HD*, 224). This is a vision of the character that differs markedly from that given by the narrative. By showing the distorting sensationalist vision of the character at the end of the novel when a newspaper misrepresents her, the author makes it clear that this tradition is a means by which to signal the political implications of these themes, but not a limit to their significance in this new context of her own late modernist fiction.

Likewise, to come back to *The Last September*, we can note that, though the heroine may be a failed sensationalist, the narrative tone can also occasionally be interpreted as bordering on sensationalism; indeed much has been made of its relation to the Anglo-Irish Gothic tradition, specifically as concerns the ruined mill scene in which Lois and the captivating Marda step into an abandoned mill, only to be threatened at gunpoint by the rebel hiding within. In *Heathcliff and the Great Hunger*, Terry Eagleton postulates that, if the Gothic was such a prevalent genre in Ireland, it was perhaps in part because realism, as the genre of stability and settlement, was inappropriate there (Eagleton, 1995, 147). Indeed, what is the most obviously Gothic scene in the novel ('Those dead mills—the country was full of them, never quite stripped to skeletons' decency: like corpses at their most horrible', *LS*, 123) is explicitly made into a metaphor for the state of the Irish economy by one of the Anglo-Irish characters: '"Another," Hugo declared, "of our national grievances. English law strangled the—" But Lois insisted on hurrying: she and Marda were now well ahead' (*LS*, 123). This quote seems to confirm that Lois is unwilling to listen to the subtext implicit in the Gothic, and the metaphor, while explicit, is swept aside before it is verbalized. Julian Moynahan is no doubt correct in considering that this comment attributes fault only to the English, without allotting to the Anglo-Irish their fair share of the guilt (Moynahan, 1995, 244), something that Corcoran corroborates and expands on, suggesting that 'this is precisely Bowen's point' (54) – thus perhaps implying a possible political justification for this ellipsis. However, it is indisputable that Bowen chose to foreground the political implications and ramifications for the Anglo-Irish tradition of the Gothic within the text of her novel at the same time as she shows her sensationalist heroine wilfully ignoring it. As her friend Viola tells Lois in reaction to one of her overwrought missives, 'don't lose detachment . . . do not lose distance' (*LS*, 70): the sensationalist aspects of the text, and the emotional pull they invoke, serve to draw attention to deeper meaning. In Bowen's early short story 'Daffodils', Miss Murcheson says as much when lecturing her students:

'We've all got nice, fresh, independent, outside things so smeared over with our sentimentalities and prejudices and—associations— that we can't seem to see them anyhow but as part of ourselves . . . if I could be able, I'm always trying, to make you care about the fine little things you might pass over, that have such big roots under- ground.' (CS, 26)

'The power of the pen': reading sensationalism

Thus when Bowen insists on a mixture of styles to reinvent previous tra- ditions, subverting them to comedic or political effect, she is in fact insisting on the very textual nature of her prose. Clearly, she associates the sensational and the act of writing. As the title of the last part of *Pic- tures and Conversations*, her unfinished autobiography, implies, for her the act of writing itself was intrinsically linked to the supernatural: 'Witch- craft: A Query. Is anything uncanny involved in the process of writing?' (MT, 298). Likewise in her fiction, one of the things that can be noted in the examples given above is the massive presence of language in relation to sensationalism: Lois writes and receives letters, newspapers figure prominently in short stories and novels reminiscent of sensation novels, and the Gothic opening descriptions of setting in Bowen's novels *To the North* and *The House in Paris*, for example, are described respectively as 'cardboard' (*TTN*, 6) or as 'inky buildings' (*HiP*, 21).[10] Her final com- mentary on Haggard's *She* implies that sensationalism had such an effect on the author not simply for its violent imagery, but for the realization that it afforded her of the effect of language on its readers:

This book *She* is for me historic—it stands for the first totally violent impact I ever received from print. After *She*, print was to fill me with apprehension. I was prepared to handle any book like a bomb. It was—did I realize that all the time?—Horace Holly, not ever, really She-who-must-be-obeyed, who controlled the magic. Writing—that creaking, pedantic, obtrusive, arch, prudish, opaque overworded writing . . . what it could do! That was the revelation; that was the power in the cave. The power whose inequality dear Holly laments at the opening of every passage. The power of the pen. The inventive pen. (MT, 250)

I believe that it is this same effect that Bowen wants to produce in her own readers, the same realization of the power of language and of the artistry inherent in the text. Therefore, far from 'slumming it' by using these lowbrow references in her fiction, Bowen is in fact taking advantage of the very visceral nature of the images and tropes inherent to sensationalist fiction in order to harness them to the aesthetic aims of her work. Taking my cue from Barthes's reality effect, which makes a text seem more realistic, Bowen's use of sensationalism is an *unreality effect*, which she chooses to use in order to emphasize the unreality, i.e. the textuality of the work. Indeed, if we look at the definition of the term 'uncanny' Bowen used to define her writing in her autobiography, we find not only an association with the Gothic, but also a certain philosophy of representation: 'the uncanny, a form of Gothic or fantastic effect quite central to modern fictions . . . is not one code but a kind of gap between codes, a point at which representation itself appears to fail, displace, or diffuse itself' (Sage, 1996, 2). If the uncanny is the gap between codes, between forms of representation, in that case the clash between different genres within the framework of the Bowen text becomes profoundly uncanny, and this failure of representation is in fact a means of reminding the reader that the representation was but a semblance of reality to begin with, thus pushing the reader to look more closely at the textual clues, the artifice used to accomplish this feat. By mixing her genres, and by explicitly linking these pastiches to textuality, Bowen emphasizes the literary ascendants to whom she pays homage, while calling attention to the literary nature of her own text. The reworkings of sensationalism systematically focus on language rather than the extraordinary events for which the genre is famous. The short stories dealing with murder reported in the newspapers no longer emphasize the murder, as in sensation novels, but the newspaper reporting in 'The Cat Jumps', for example, the characters read about the horrible murders that occurred in the house they are staying in, though the reader is never entirely informed of the incidents themselves, and it is the insidious impact of these descriptions that causes the characters to react as if they were part of a sensational world. In fact, it is sensationalist *language* that comes to take the centre stage rather than sensationalism itself.

In this sense the use made of Haggard's *She* in the Bowen short story 'The Mysterious Kôr' seems particularly relevant:

> 'Oh, I didn't get much from that [poem]; I just got the name. I knew that must be the right name; it's like a cry.' [...] 'But the poem begins with "Not" . . . And it goes on, as I remember, to prove Kôr's not really anywhere. When even a poem says there's no such place –' 'What it tries to say doesn't really matter: I see what it makes me see.' (CS, 730)

The poem quoted here is a sonnet written by Andrew Lang and inspired by Haggard's novel: in a sense, then, the poem functions as a parallel to the short story itself in its relation to the original. In this case, the fact that the poem is being analysed and interpreted by the characters in relation both to its predecessor and to its relevance to reality seems to be a model for the reader himself to follow, and what becomes important is less the story than the language used, and its effect on the reader. Given both its strong emotional and imaginative pull as well as its underlying political and social significance, it is a tool used to highlight how one should or should not read.

The character of the reader becomes particularly relevant in relation to a last genre that was mentioned but has remained undiscussed, the detective novel. Surprisingly, though Bowen was an avid reader of detective fiction, the character of the detective never really appears in her work. *The Heat of the Day*'s Harrison, the secret agent who has discovered Stella's lover's treasonous behaviour, is perhaps most similar, but it is her unwilling and unspoken investigation that we follow rather than his own.[11] Likewise, in *The Little Girls*, when Dinah goes in search of her long-lost childhood friends, the 'investigation' consists solely of advertisements in a newspaper to which the other characters reluctantly reply. It may be, however, that the influence of detective fiction on Bowen's work appears not in the character or the events of the narrative, but in its presentation. Thus in a BBC interview about the novel *The Little Girls*, Bowen states:

> [*The Little Girls*] should be read with that attention to detail generally accorded to a detective story. There is little explanation in *The Little Girls*, but there are many clues. Even inanimate objects can be important. And random sayings, or seemingly trivial events may acquire retrospectively a strange significance. (*Before Publication*)

I would argue that the *reader* is in fact the recurrent image of the detective in Bowen's novels, and must constantly be reading actively for clues as to the deeper meaning of her work. It could be argued that this comment should be applied only to *The Little Girls* and *Eva Trout*, given that the author made major stylistic changes in these last two novels, including the decision to no longer include an omniscient narrative voice; but if we take what is arguably the most classically domestic novel in Bowen's *oeuvre*, her third novel, *Friends and Relations*, we see that the reader's role as detective is in fact crucial to the narrative. The novel opens with Edward's marriage to Laurel, while Laurel's sister Janet will later marry Rodney. The apparent trouble begins when the characters realize that Rodney's uncle had an affair with Edward's mother, making Janet's marriage awkward for the two couples. It is not until Edward insists that his two children leave Janet and Rodney's house (upon discovering that the two former lovers are also in residence) that the reader becomes aware of the underlying problem: Edward and Janet are in love, and have been previous to the novel's incipit, despite Edward's efforts to deny it. Without paying close attention to seemingly innocuous comments earlier in the narrative – to 'trivial events', as Bowen says – and treating the narrative as an investigation, the text's mysteries will remain unsolved.

This active reading includes a refusal to limit oneself to one interpretation, or to be satisfied with the preconceptions of one genre; thus, in one of the most interesting of Bowen's ghost stories, 'The Back Drawing-Room', the traditions of the Victorian ghost story are explicitly analysed and overturned. Instead of first sensationalizing and then explaining the events, 'The Back Drawing-Room' opens with a frame story of a group of English intellectuals who philosophize about ghost stories and sightings. When one of the characters gives an example that cannot be distanced (as is traditional in Gothic stories) either by exoticism (the story takes place not abroad, but in Ireland, at a cousin's house), by time (it takes place in the very recent past), or by sensationalism (the unknown and very mundane narrator gives a very pedestrian description, where the ghost in question, it appears, is not even dead), the reader, like the listeners of the frame story, is obliged to reconsider the very basis of the genre, and the need for this distancing effect. If the story cannot be distanced from its public, however, neither can it be explained, despite the attempts of the listeners to do so. The disdain for the genre ('"Bring in the Yule log, this is a Dickens Christmas. We're going to tell ghost stories"', CS, 203) and the attempts to scale it back to a simple structure ('" . . . all ghost stories have one of three possible climaxes, A, B, or C, and every climax has its complementary explanation. Get on to the climax, and I'll guarantee you the explanation pat"', CS, 207) are definitively refuted by the open ending, where the characters are all left speechless at the outcome of the tale. The resolution of the short story, then, is quite simply that there is no resolution; rather, the expectations of the genre raised by the other characters are thwarted by the narrator, and call attention to the politicized subject matter (here the tragedy of the Anglo-Irish, both alive and ghost-like in their displacement from their homes). In its mixture of genres (Gothic subject matter and realist storytelling), as well as in its thwarting of generic expectations, the text refuses to be limited to one explanation, leaving both the political undercurrents and the storytelling itself to the reader's appreciation. Bowen seeks to provoke thought rather than limit her method of expression to 'A, B, or C'.

This emphasis on reader participation and textuality is of course typically modernist, but I would argue that the hybridity that is crucial in inspiring it is specific to Bowen, as her fiction functions simultaneously as realist, as comic and as sensationalist prose, maintaining its status as fantastic in Todorov's sense of the word.[12]

Elizabeth Bowen has often been taxed with being an élitist writer. Readers complain that the upper-class background of the vast majority of her characters, the very well-bred nature of her novels, ruins her fiction for them. There is no denying the socio-economic circles about which Bowen mostly writes, but my contention is that, far from wishing to speak only to Stendhal's 'happy few', she sought to be inclusive of as many readers as possible (something that she succeeded in doing far better in her own time than in ours), in part by including popular influences in her fiction, and then reworking these tropes to create new and more literary meaning. The mix of high and low references, is, as we have said, a modernist technique; however, the inclusive nature of her hybrid fiction, her clear desire to create a better reader rather than exclude the non-literary reader, and the way in which this 'lowbrow' literature is celebrated even while it is subverted, in fact make her impossible to successfully categorize: Elizabeth Bowen is, I would argue, in a class of her own.

6

Territory, space, modernity:
Elizabeth Bowen's *The Demon Lover and Other Stories* and wartime London

SHAFQUAT TOWHEED

Complaining about the lack of critical attention devoted to the importance of place in her fiction during her lifetime, Elizabeth Bowen pointedly asked, 'am I not manifestly a writer for whom places loom large?', adding 'as a reader, it is to the place-element that I react most strongly: for me, what gives fiction its verisimilitude is its topography' (*The Mulberry Tree*, London, 1999, 282). Academic criticism, increasingly sensitive to Bowen's valuation of her own work and her charge that 'Bowen topography has so far, so far as I know, been untouched by research' (*MT*, 282), has since risen handsomely to this challenge. Maud Ellmann has written convincingly of Bowen's 'anxious solicitude for place, hallucinatory in its intensity of focus' (*Shadow*, 2003, 7), while Hermione Lee has noted that, while her characters are continuously in 'transit', permanence is solely 'an attribute of recalled places' (Lee, *Elizabeth Bowen*, London, 1999, 81). Heather Bryant Jordan has examined the topography of (in particular) Bowen's wartime writing, while Andrew Bennett and Nicholas Royle have linked the 'radical disruption of temporality, memory and causality' in her novels with their 'fanatic immobility' (42) of place. Bowen's critics have, almost without exception, noted the centrality of place and its discontent, *displacement*, in her fiction.

Bowen's overcharged concern with place, her repeated, insistent and enforced returns in her fiction to the place of an earlier event to reinscribe the validity of a narrated event (or indeed, to challenge its veracity and our own readerly obtuseness), often through the character's interaction with material objects, verges on the obsessive and the *Unheimlich*.[1] 'The locale of the happening always colours the happening, and often, to a degree, shapes it' (*MT*, 283), Bowen asserted,

113

interweaving the conscious and the unconscious, the animate and the inanimate, and demonstrating that 'her addiction to personification creates the sense that every object has a psyche' (Ellmann, *Shadow*, 2003, 6). Bowen's specificity of place extends not just to things, but to people as well. 'What she likes best', Hermione Lee observes, 'in the stories as in the novels, is to put groups of people into the place they deserve' in order to examine the 'moral relationship between places and people' (Lee, *EB*, 1999, 130). As a member of both the Anglo-Irish Ascendancy and the London literary élite, this was a moral responsibility that Bowen could not shirk. Putting someone in their proper *place*, I would like to suggest, invariably involves more than just taxonomy, or even snobbery; it suggests occupying, inhabiting, producing and consuming a specific, sometimes proper and sometimes improper, *space*. While academic criticism has increasingly noted the importance of specific physical locations and their imaginative and psychological implications in Bowen's writing, relatively little attention has been paid to the complexities of space – physical, temporal, acoustic, emotional, social, mental and creative, to name but a few – recursively opened up and closed down in her fiction, a fiction that tends at once to both claustrophobia and agoraphobia, to both stasis and constant flux. In the first part of this essay, I want to outline some of the discussions (theoretical, linguistic, figurative and literary) about space in the decades leading up to that great definer, destroyer and creator of spaces, the Second World War. In the second part, I want to interrogate Elizabeth Bowen's wartime short stories in the collection *The Demon Lover and Other Stories* (1945) – her most immediate fictional responses to the relentless spatial flux of London life during the conflict – from the specific interpretative perspective opened up by this discussion: that of space.

I: Territory vs. space

Asked about the disjuncture between his uncertainty over spatialization and the profusion of spatial and geographical metaphors in so much of his writing, Michel Foucault responded by categorizing a range of geographical terms that he had used in an explicitly non-spatial sense:

> *Territory* is no doubt a geographical notion, but it's first of all a juridico-political one: the area controlled by a certain kind of power. *Field* is an economico-juridical notion. *Displacement*: what displaces itself is an army, a squadron, a population. *Domain* is a

juridico-political notion. *Soil* is a historico-geological notion. *Region* is a fiscal, administrative, military notion. *Horizon* is a pictorial, but also a strategic notion. There is only one notion here that is truly geographical, that of an *archipelago*. (Foucault, 1980, 68)

Dismissing the spatial element in all but one of these terms, archipelago, Foucault admitted the political bias of his rejection of space: 'the use of spatial terms seems to have the air of an anti-history', he declared; 'to talk in terms of space . . . meant that one was hostile to time' (1980, 70). For Foucault, 'the devaluation of space that has prevailed for generations' and that had started with Bergson and continued throughout the twentieth century had resulted in space being 'treated as the dead, the fixed, the undialectical, the immobile', thereby representing a transformation of discourses 'through and on the basis of relations of power' (1980, 70). Admitting his own complicity in the marginalization of space as a critical concept despite his use of many seemingly spatial terms, Foucault admitted that '*space* is reactionary and capitalist but *history* and *becoming* are revolutionary' (1980, 70; Foucault's emphases).

Unlike 'territory', a word that is both concrete and demarcated, or in Foucault's words 'juridico-political', 'space' has always posed both theoretical and practical problems, not least for philosophers and literary critics. For example, the leading contemporary theoretician of space, Henri Lefebvre, has cogently noted the lack of a clear definition of the term 'mental space' in his Marxist critique *The Production of Space*:

No limits at all have been set on the generalization of the concept of *mental space*: no clear account of it is ever given and, depending on the author one happens to be reading, it may connote logical coherence, practical consistency, self-regulation and the relations of the parts to the whole, the engendering of like by like in a set of places, the logic of container *versus* contents, and so on. (Lefebvre, 1991, 3)

In its polysemic slipperiness, space has evaded the hegemonic codes of time, power and knowledge, something that both Foucault and Lefebvre accept, and has even, as Coroneos concedes, 'eluded the comforting anthropomorphisms' (Coroneos, 2002, 5) of time. Lefebvre's project, 'spatiology', writes Andy Merrifield, attempts 'a rapprochement between *physical* space (nature), *mental* space (formal abstractions about space) and *social* space (the space of human interactions)' by integrating these seemingly separate fields (104). '*The Production of Space*', Merrifield writes, 'seeks to "detonate" everything, for Lefebvre considers 'fragmentation and conceptual dislocation as serving distinctly ideological ends' (104). In fact, Lefebvre's analysis, based on the idea that capitalism produces spaces which become central sites and definers of mass consumption and individual alienation, frequently draws upon the idea of the explosion of space, or even the explosive space. 'The form and content of *The Production of Space*', Merrifield reminds us, 'unfolds *eruptively* and *disruptively*' (117); Lefebvre's earlier work on the student revolution of 1968 was aptly titled *The Explosion*.

But how ubiquitous was thinking about space, its conceptual and interpretative value, its potential to detonate and explode, in the years between Europe's two great cataclysms, and before both Foucault and Lefebvre published their thoughts on the matter? The decades leading up to the Second World War saw perhaps the greatest rise in spatial thinking – and theorizing – in the twentieth century; this was prompted largely by developments in a range of widely differing fields such as sociology, particle physics, developmental psychology, cellular biology, architecture, aesthetics, acoustics, optics, evolutionary genetics, philosophy and even linguistics. Both proponents and detractors of the importance of space proliferated in this period: Adorno, Bergson, De Chirico, de Saussure, Einstein, Le Corbusier, McTaggart, Minkowski, Poincaré, Russell, Schütz, Simmel, Worringer, to name but a few, and of course the young Lefebvre, who would not publish *The Production of Space* until 1974 but had already become in the inter-war period both a committed Communist and a surrealist.

Ferdinand de Saussure's clear distinction in *Cours de linguistique générale* (1916) between the abstract *langue* and the spatial-temporal and diachronic *parole* heralded the increasingly heated contest between space and time in the next thirty years – one in which space would almost always come off second best. Henri Poincaré's geometric conventionalism had convincingly rejected Newtonian notions of absolute space, and Euclidian geometry had itself been bypassed by Einstein's espousal of relativity in 1915. Minkowski's postulation of 'spacetime' consisting of four vectors (time and the three dimensions) in a unified field theory would by his own admission lead to the fading away of space and time as separate and potentially opposed conceptual categories. Ever since Bergson, the depreciation – if not the actual death – of space had been repeatedly stated, and yet philosophers, social scientists, linguists and psychologists continued to use the idea of space metaphorically as well as theoretically. The social scientist Alfred Schütz, for example, in *The Phenomenology of the Social World* (1932) proposed a *lebenswelt* determined by the spatial proximity of the subject and its referents (consociates share the same spatial access to one another). Modernist experimentation in architecture (Le Corbusier) and music (Webern) championed space rather than structure, the rest rather than the note, with a conscious sense of the elevation of positive negative space; as Stephen Kern has suggested, 'the affirmation of positive negative space rejected the conventional view of space as less important than the objects contained in it' (Kern, 1983, 315).

The traffic in this period between different disciplines over the conflicting ideas of space and time (or, indeed, space and territory) is registered in their rhetorical flowering. Attempting to explain the relevance of Leibniz in the context of emerging (and competing) field theories, Bertrand Russell coined the term 'spatio-temporal' in 1900, seemingly anticipating Einstein and Minkowski's conflation, space-time. By 1934, 'spatialist' was already in use as a noun, appearing in both Wisdom's *Problems of Mind and Matter* and James Joyce's letters; decades later it would be adopted by the French poet Pierre Garnier to name his radical school of poetry.

Even in cartography, spatial thinking was revolutionizing map-making, and from the least likely of sources. Phyllis Pearsall's heroic *A–Z: Atlas and Guide to London and Suburbs* (1936), the work of one exceptionally determined amateur, offered not only the first comprehensive atlas of the city, but also biased its distortions in favour of the pedestrian and the driver. It was, in effect, the first street map that privileged the spatial over the mathematical, and user orientation over precise measurement, and it reciprocated Harry Beck's revolutionary London Underground map of 1933, whose clarity is based entirely on the proportionate spatial relationship *between* stations rather than the actual distance separating them.[2] Pearsall's A–Z rapidly became a best-seller, but its very ubiquity and utility inevitably resulted in its being banned during the war; the Control of Maps order prohibited the sale and distribution of the A–Z from 4 July 1940 until the flood of increasingly disorientated Allied troops arriving in London forced the rescinding of the order on 13 January 1944. No sooner had London been effectively mapped in favour of the spatial movement of both the pedestrian and the motorist rather than the cartographer than this was taken away; the catastrophic effects of the Blitz meant that Pearsall's pre-war effort had already become a historically inaccurate artefact.

This flux in the demarcation of space, its causes and consequences and, above all, its effect on human temperament is evident in the literature of the inter-war period. The earliest recorded uses of the word 'claustrophobic' as an adjective in English fiction are suitably in

Elizabeth Bowen's spatially obsessed novel *To the North* (London, 1932), where the travel-agent heroine (another first in English fiction) and demon driver of an open-top car, Emmeline Summers, describe herself as 'claustrophobic' (167).[3] Bowen would reprise these ideas again with Kathleen Drover in her story of the uncanny set in the London Blitz, 'The Demon Lover'; while Emmeline's driving in an open-top car is seen as an escape from her claustrophobia, Kathleen's being driven in a closed taxi precipitates a claustrophobic attack. Her use of the term 'claustrophobic' in fiction preceded Alix Strachey's use of the term 'agoraphobic', its conceptual and clinical twin, by several years and registers the widespread clinical and popular interest in the anxieties caused by new technology; the fact that Bowen uses this term before Strachey, who was both a translator of Freud and a subject of his analysis, suggests her intense and lifelong interest in mental responses to space.[4] Bowen's depiction of Emmeline's conflicted spatial state was prescient, for claustrophobia had indeed entered the public consciousness; a flurry of letters to the editor of *The Times* followed the death in custody of Thomas Parker, a confirmed claustrophobic, in June 1933.[5] Bowen's work alludes repeatedly and insistently to the spatial and temporal conditions that both cause and define claustrophobia and agoraphobia, namely the unexpected constriction or expansion of space. Emmeline Summers, like Bowen herself, permanently shuttling between her two homes, is continuously on the move.

The burgeoning clinical interest in the psychopathology of space and its discontents found new areas of research with the outbreak of the war. Attempting to explain the rise in claustrophobic and agoraphobic symptoms among her existing patients after the start of the bombing campaign, the Hampstead clinical psychologist Melitta Schmideberg noted the enormous spatial change in London as a result of the Blitz: 'At dusk some of the big streets looked almost like a village street: at night they were dark and deserted. One became district and even street conscious. What happened in one's own street was of vital importance, whilst other districts seemed very remote' (158). The physical contraction of each individual's orbit, the fact that London was becoming (in Foucault's term) an archipelago, provoked renewed anxiety among the mentally (and spatially) disturbed, as the psychologist E. Stengel noted: 'the town appears as a single unit which closes down round the patient' (Schmideberg, 167). Stengel was one of the leading observers and interpreters of wartime psychological phenomena; noting the immediate effect of the Blitz on the well-being of his patients, he coined the term 'air-raid phobia' (Stengel, 135) to explain the exaggerated fear of many patients that the air raids were specifically and personally targeted at them, and linked this to existing symptoms of both claustrophobia and agoraphobia. An individual suffering from 'air-raid phobia', Stengel surmised, could not feel secure crammed into a subterranean bomb shelter, or evacuated into the wide-open space of the countryside; both the constriction and the relaxation of space would provoke an anxiety attack. In his work with Mass-Observation, which the clinical psychologist Edward Glover noted was the only 'anthropological analysis' (Glover, 1942, 17) of the psychological effects of the Blitz, Tom Harrisson disputed the claims of psychologists that it was only 'overanxious superstitious people who imagine every bomb is aimed personally at them' (Harrisson, 1976, 77). 'There is no factual support for this Harley Street view', he observed from his reading of the diaries of participant observers; 'people of all sorts and temperaments . . . were liable to describe their first experience in these terms' (77). The spatial dislocation of Londoners living through the Blitz, and the fear, anxiety, or even feelings of euphoria that the destruction of space produced, was not therefore confined to the sufferers of claustrophobia or agoraphobia; it was ubiquitous.

In her wartime writing, Bowen concurred with the idea of London as a spatially dislocated archipelago, separated by the explosive spaces blasted into the fabric of a city that had only just been comprehensively mapped; 'entire districts, because of the time-bombs, become enislanded' (Glendinning, *Portrait*, 1977, 129), turning London into 'a city of villages—almost of village communes' (MT, 23-4), she observed. The destruction and reshaping of space in London during the Blitz, the fact that it turned privacy into 'a thing of the past' (129), almost certainly caused the change in reading habits that Rod Mengham notes; wartime readers, he claims, evidently preferred writers with a unity of space and time, such as Tolstoy and Trollope, to modernist experiments in narratives ridden with lacunae. And yet, it was undoubtedly writers such as Elizabeth Bowen who directly addressed the radical disjuncture *between* space and time, and indeed the relentless challenge to spatial certainty during and immediately after the conflict, who best capture the increasing interdisciplinary awareness about space, time and the individual in the period. Glossing both Foucault's idea of territory and Lefebvre's theory of spatialogy, Bowen's fictional terrain, by her own admission 'cannot be demarcated on any existing map' for it is 'unspecific' (MT, 282). 'There is no particular locality I have staked a claim on or identified with', she added, because the 'scenes of my stories are scattered', like an archipelago; 'nothing (at least on the surface) connects them' (MT,

282). Bowen's fictional terrain is both utopia and heterotopia, both nowhere and everywhere, and, like London during the Blitz, is composed of archipelagic patches both separated and connected by the explosive spaces blasted between them.

II: Bowen's 'explosive' spaces

'An explosion is the most lasting thing in the universe', wrote Joseph Conrad to his friend Edward Garnett, decades before either of Europe's self-inflicted cataclysms; '[i]t leaves disorder, remembrance, room to move, a clear space.'[6] Unlike Conrad, Bowen's experience of the lasting impact of high explosives, temporal, psychological and otherwise, their ability to *fill* as well as *clear* space, was first hand. She spent the war years shuttling between her two nations, England and Ireland, working to defend both from the direct and indirect consequences of fascism; as an Air Raid Precautions (ARP) warden in Regent's Park, she helped enforce the nightly London blackouts, while, in her intelligence work for the Ministry of Information, she passionately defended Ireland's neutrality.[7] Bowen's defence, as I intend to show, was as much spatial as it was territorial, for the front line in this conflict was not in essence a geographical demarcation, but an experiential one.

'These are all war-time, none of them *war*, stories', Bowen wrote in her postscript to *The Demon Lover and Other Stories*, 'there are no accounts of war action . . . for instance, air raids' (*DL*, 217). In a literal sense this is, of course, true; and yet every story in the collection, I would suggest, attempts to shape, resolve or represent a spatial-temporal dilemma: space created (emptied or filled in) by an 'explosion' (past, current or anticipated) of one sort or another. In the first story in the collection, 'In the Square', the spatial and psychological effects of an earlier bomb blast touch all the inhabitants, both recent and established, of a house in a London square. On a 'Hot bright July evening' lengthened by the rays of light from the sun 'too low to enter normally' but 'able to enter brilliantly at a point where three of the houses had been bombed away' (*DL*, 9), Rupert visits his married lover Magdela, who is sharing her absent husband Anthony's house with his mistress Gina, who has now taken up with a 'regular' (18); other occupants include an 'independent' couple 'down in the basement' who are 'supposed to be caretakers' (13–14) and have a 'son who is a policeman' and a 'schoolgirl daughter' (14); in addition, and apparently for one night only, Magdela's precocious nephew Bennet has come to stay.

The unexpected light flooding across the square through the immediate site of the blast – the three-house gap – captures and frames its lingering defenestration; some of 'the glassless windows' continue to frame 'hollow inside dark' (9). The impact of the bomb and its displacement of material continues to be felt by the inhabitants. The blast that created this 'dazzling breach' has enforced a democratization of space – 'the house seems to belong to everyone now' (15) – despite leaving the soundscape unchanged: 'the square's acoustics had altered very little' (9). Magdela's 16-year-old nephew Bennet, noticing the pairs of lovers standing in the square waiting for the enveloping privacy of darkness, asks Gina whether 'they go into the empty houses?' (17), to which she replies 'they're all locked up . . . they're property' (17). Even during the Blitz, the propriety of London property owners (even *in absentia*) seemingly outweighs the physical and emotional needs of the city's beleaguered inhabitants.

The searing light, the 'ghost of the glare of midday' (9) introduced into the square by the space created (destroyed? liberated?) by the bombing, has the effect of arresting the mobility and agency of the pairs of lovers, inside the house and in the square, simultaneously trapped by its interrogating, illuminating gaze and enislanded by the 'dusk of the square, that lay at the foot of the steps like water' (18). Far from producing room to move, the lingering effects of the blast have instead enforced a physical *cordon sanitaire* disruptively at odds with the hothouse emotions of the house's besieged inhabitants. A surplus of space has upset the symmetry (if not the acoustics) of the square and its inhabitants; the characters, caught in the surplus light of a 'virtual eight o'clock', are as effectively immobilized as figures in a still life.[8] The repercussions of Bowen's explosive space work both literally and metaphorically; glancing at the beautifully mutilated Georgian square – another Euclidian *gnomon* in Bowen's geometrically obsessed writing – Magdela's words to Rupert are deliberately functionally ambiguous and pregnant with possibilities for the future as well as the freight of the past: 'who would have thought this could really happen? The last time we—how long was that? Two years ago?' (12).[9] Her eyes transfixed by the 'dazzling breach' of the square, Magdela's words raise the possibility of sexual consummation, even at the point of forestalling it; once again the agencies of the actors are shaped by their response to the changing, elastic nature of space in wartime London.

Blasted out of their emotionally unfulfilled complacency, yet blasted into the merciless gaze of renewed (self-)scrutiny, Magdela and Rupert, continuously looking out of the first-floor windows on to the light flooding in from the exploded space left in the west side of the square, have already witnessed a 'great change' (19): the recognition of the contingency of their happiness. The square itself reaffirms the importance of positive negative space and demonstrates the emotional and psychological challenge faced by Londoners during the Blitz.

The randomness of the bombing during the Blitz stands in stark contrast to Bowen's famous dictum on the importance of place in fiction – 'nothing can happen nowhere' (*MT*, 283) – by showing that the 'nothing' created and enforced by the explosive blast could happen anywhere, or indeed, everywhere. Ronald Cuffe in 'Sunday Afternoon' insists upon the irrelevance of the Blitz to literature. 'This outrage is *not* important', he avers, 'there is no place for it in human experience; it apparently cannot make a place of its own. It will have no literature' (23), and yet, of course, the stories gathered together in *The Demon Lover* – and indeed, Henry Russel's own 'story' in 'Sunday Afternoon' – emerge from the space (temporal, physical and emotional) created precisely by the blast of the explosion. Denied a legitimate (or legitimizing) 'place' by Ronald Cuffe, Bowen's explosive spaces act in all sorts of ways, fictionally glossing, for example, neologisms such as the 'blast wave', defined in 1939 as a 'non-translational shock wave that is transmitted through the air to considerable distances from an exploding bomb'.[10] The ripples of the 'blast wave' that have completed destroyed Henry's London flat in his absence and, with it, the material evidence of his forty-three years of life, reach all the way across the Irish Sea and lap Mrs Vesey's seemingly tranquil Sunday afternoon Dublin tea party; Bowen herself registered the same sense of wartime news transmitted spatially in blast waves across to (and spilling over) Bowen's Court years later.[11] Henry's new existence *in vacuo* is one that his Irish relatives cannot place, largely because it no longer occupies a specific domestic space: 'You live with nothing, forever . . . I wonder how much of you *has* been blown to blazes' (25, 26), Ria insensitively asks him, a question that he cannot answer directly: 'I still want the past' (28), he concedes to Mrs Vesey's niece, Maria, implicitly defining himself through the space filled with his lifelong material possessions that has been blasted out of existence. Henry's horror of the depersonalizing void is telling, nor is this the only example of the vacuum as a source of fear in Bowen's stories; the absent, unreclaimable father – the paternal void in 'Songs My Father Sang Me' – is, rather aptly, a vacuum cleaner salesman.

Just such a 'blast wave' is central to the plot of 'The Inherited Clock', the story of Clara and the disturbing implications of her inheritance – a skeleton grandfather clock – from her elderly cousin, Rosanna. Cousin Rosanna's south-coast residence, Sandyhill, the locus of several of Clara's most potent childhood memories (and some which have been repressed, if not erased), is now in an 'officially dangerous position' (36) facing the Channel, and has already taken a solitary hit from seemingly random German aerial bombing; the effect of the blast wave is more destructive than that of the impact itself. The bomb, 'so far Sandyhill's only bomb', despite having fallen in a 'small lake, sunless most of the day' in the grounds, had, 'by a freak of travel, obliterated the glass winter-garden projecting west of the house' (36–7). The blast wave's 'freak of travel' has effectively amputated the west wing of Sandyhill from the rest of the house and, with it, has seemingly severed Clara's missing limb of memory – her sadistic bullying at the hands of her second cousin Paul in the library room – by locating it in the space dominated by the imperturbable clock.

By (re)tracing her childhood steps 'straight to the door where the house had been forced by the war to stop' (37), Clara is lured into the library room by the clock 'expectantly ticking' (38), where she can remember everything – 'which picture used to hang in each oblong' and 'the names of the books in the bookcase under the sheet' (39) – except the clock itself and the particularly traumatic events associated with it. Clara's memory is undeniably visual, aural and, above all, spatial: 'every glade, every seat, every vista at the turn of a path' (40) in the winter garden outside the library 'drew out' her precise recollection of the past – 'there was nothing, no single thing, in the history of Clara at Sandyhill that she could not remember' (41) – except, of course, a specific event when she was six. Her inability to remember exactly what Paul had done to her and their shared past in Sandyhill, the 'crevasse in her memory' (41), is in fact based not so much on place, as space.

Cousin Rosanna's death results in Clara's inheritance of the skeleton clock, carried bodily – 'embraced inside her exhausted arms' (41) – by Aunt Addie to Clara's St John's Wood flat. Attempting to claim it for himself, Paul comments that the clock is a 'little large for the room' (47) and notices Clara's increasingly haggard and disturbed appearance since the arrival of her inheritance, the inheritance that she hoped would set her both materially and emotionally free. The clock's physical domination of Clara's flat and its incessant, bomb-like ticking reprises and amplifies the effects of the 'blast wave' on Sandyhill's west wing. Blasted by the waves of repressed memory of her involvement with Paul and inexorably aurally reminded of her waste of the last nine years waiting for Henry to divorce his wife, Clara is forced into the streets of blackout London by the oppressive occupied space of the 'inherited clock':

> Brought to a halt for breath, she began to spy with her torch at the
> things round her—a post-box, a corner with no railing, the white
> plate of a street name. Nothing told her anything, except one
> thing—unless she had lost her memory, she had lost her way. (45)

Physically displaced from her home by the clock, Clara is forced to
confront the erased darkness of a sign-less, un-signified London, *sans*
Phyllis Pearsall's temporarily prohibited A–Z: a spatial realm which
exists only through the material sense of touch and the immaterial
recall of memory (Pearsall herself had noted with interest the disappearance of signage across the country, forcing people to resort to
their instinctive spatial sense).[12] Clara has lost her way, because she
has indeed lost her memory; the enforced claustrophobic trauma of
another night with the 'inherited clock' has led to insomnia, aphasia,
spatiation and disorientation.

At the end of the story, Paul re-enacts the original trauma in
Clara's flat by forcing her now adult finger into the skeleton clock's
mechanism, reprising the wound he inflicted upon his cousin as a six-
year-old and stopping the clock once again, just as he had done
twenty-four years earlier. Clara finally recalls all of the events between
them at Sandyhill, and this is brought about by a spatial action
(inserting her finger into the site of the original trauma, stopping the
movement of the minute hand and filling the gap between the cogs of
the skeleton clock) and not by an enforced return to a physical place
(the library room in Sandyhill). The locus of Clara's repressed childhood trauma proves to be not a place, but an object in a perpetual
spatial and temporal movement. Bowen's psychologically accurate
(even, perhaps, pseudo-clinical) fictional handling of a case of
repressed trauma and its condensation is all the more important when
we consider the paucity of systematic analysis of the psychological
effects of the Blitz; as Edward Glover noted, 'for practically all psychological research purposes, the blitz went unobserved . . . there has
been little or no immediate psycho-analytical investigation of cases'
(Glover, 1942, 17).

The blast at Sandyhill prefigures the arrival of the skeleton clock,
itself a ticking time bomb from the past, and precipitates in Clara the
release and acknowledgement of a previously repressed childhood
memory, her sadistic abuse at the hands of Paul. The *heimlich*, corpo-
real space around the skeleton clock in cousin Rosanna's library,
becomes *unheimlich*, agonizingly (and agonistic) claustrophobic space
in the living room of Clara's St John's Wood flat; a spatial dislocation
caused by a blast wave in Sandyhill results in an answering spatial,

temporal, psychological and emotional disorientation in wartime London, cured only by revisiting the original trauma. 'The Inherited Clock' is not just a tale about Clara's enforced return to a specific *place*, but the recursive return of a specific *space* occupied and encap-sulated by the clock (the locus of her trauma), at a time when the spatial sense of Londoners was inexorably heightened by the flux and trauma of wartime. Bowen's wartime short fiction repeatedly captures the constricting elasticity of space (mental, aural, visual and physical) through the effects and possibilities of the explosive blast, even when the physical place of the explosion is only glanced at (and perhaps not even directly experienced) by her fictional protagonists.

The relentless destruction of productive space in wartime London – by May 1941 over a million homes in the city and its suburbs had been damaged – and the claustrophobia that it compelled is ubiquitous in Bowen's short stories.[13] In 'Careless Talk', space – physical, emotional and imaginative, and not just elbow room in a crowded restaurant – is at a premium, while words are cheap; Mary's observation that 'this table's going to be terribly small for four' (100) sets the tone for the discussion that follows: the restaurant is so full that 'the waiters had to melt to get past the backs of the chairs' (100); Eric, who works at the War Office, observes that 'everywhere outside London seemed to me very full' while he 'unlocked his chair from the chair behind him' (103) before tackling his grouse; and Mary pointedly observes to Joanna, her visitor for the day from Shepton Mallett, 'I expect you see how crowded everywhere is?' (100).

Close proximity in wartime London extended beyond the physical – the cheek-by-jowl seating in restaurants, the attempt to keep three fresh eggs unbroken – and into the emotional and the imaginative. Joanna has been bombed out of town, her house in 'Belmont Square' (103) – another mutilated Georgian square – having been completely destroyed, which prompts Eric to declare 'you don't want a house, you know. None of us live in houses' (104). What he means is that none of them live in private houses of their own choice, houses having been transformed into shared dwellings, like Anthony and Magdela's former marital home in 'In the Square'; the paucity of spare rooms and constant pressure on privacy was noted by Mass-Observation in their study of housing.[14] His advice to Joanna is telling: 'You could move in on someone. Sylvia has moved in on Mona', which prompts a strong rebuke from Mary: 'that's not a good example' (104). Mary's objection is fleshed out with the implications of these enforced reori-entations: 'Mona moved out almost at once and moved in on Isobel, but the worst of that is that Isobel wants her husband back, and meanwhile Sylvia's taken up with a young man, so Mona can't move back to her own flat' (104).

There is a curiously deliberate semantic slippage here from the occupation of a physical place to the incursion into emotional space, from the hospitable to the predatory, from social solidarity to sexual competition, from 'moving in *with*' to 'moving in *on*'. In a metropolis whose population had become increasingly transient and contingent, 'moving in with' often resulted in 'moving in on'; Bowen's wartime writing is replete with snatched, illicit affairs, reconstituted relationships and their ramifications. The geometric love plot (or, perhaps, love chain) glanced at in 'Careless Talk' (Mona, Sylvia, Sylvia's 'young man', Isobel, Isobel's husband) is relentlessly iterative, or as Maud Ellmann observes, always 'one-too-many' and therefore essentially a movement in space; love in much of Bowen's fiction is 'constantly in transport rather than at rest' (Ellmann, *Shadow*, 2003, 93) and it rarely follows a simple, linear trajectory.

Territoriality, Foucault's 'juridico-political' definition of a demarcated, even arrested, place is infringed upon (and displaced by) the spatial trajectories of transgressive, potentially libidinous wartime bodies, cutting across boundaries of propriety, linking and de-linking according to time and opportunity. Bowen herself was forced to move in with Clarissa Churchill (Lady Eden) in July 1944, after 2 Clarence Terrace took a direct hit from a V1, and stayed with her until October; famously her longest and most fully developed sexual relationship (with the Canadian diplomat Charles Ritchie) flourished in the 'one-too-many' domestic arrangements of wartime London, despite their never living under the same roof (emotionally at any rate, he had 'moved in on' her – nominally, at least, a married woman).

Curiously, while Bowen was prepared to acknowledge (and even to accept) the enforced proximity and breakdown in spatial (and sexual) domestic order during wartime, she had been far less tolerant of such transgressions in peacetime. Goronwy Rees's indiscretion with Rosamond Lehmann while staying at Bowen's Court had earned nothing but her scorn: writing to Isaiah Berlin, she condemned their 'ruthless incontinence' and accused Rees of defiling her hospitality, a breach that she could not easily forgive.[15] She was similarly scornful of voluntary claustrophilia in peacetime; visiting T. S. Eliot in the two-roomed flat he shared with his wife, and immediately noting her profound mental disquiet, she observed 'two highly nervous people shut up together in grinding proximity' (Glendinning, *Portrait*, 1977, 80). The flux in the rules governing domestic space, the possibility of 'moving in on' someone, or of being 'moved in on' during the conflict, provided Bowen's writing with more than geometric plot material; it allowed her to explore the electrifying emotional possibilities opened up (and perhaps not always fulfilled) by the war. Hemmed in by explosive spaces beyond their walls that constantly threatened to eliminate the demarcation between private and public, houses themselves become emotionally and sexually charged spaces; Bowen's fictional characters are forced to traverse this new, potentially hostile terrain.

Nowhere in *The Demon Lover* is the spatial aspect of Elizabeth Bowen's wartime writing more evident than in 'Mysterious Kôr', the last story in the collection. Reciprocating the blinding fixity of the unexpected evening sun of 'In the Square', the full moon arrests, and even dissolves like 'some white acid' (197), human participation in London's public spaces; the homeless lovers Arthur and Pepita stand 'outside the now gateless gates' (197) of Bowen's beloved Regent's Park, but, like the self-conscious lovers of 'In the Square', it is an unsignified Rubicon that they do not (and cannot) cross. London's open spaces are filled to overflowing with moonlight, 'which drenched the city', and have left 'not a niche' to 'stand in' (196). The haunting desolation of the open spaces of the metropolis under a full moon enforces the claustrophobia of its closed and densely packed spaces during the Blitz. 'People stayed indoors with a fervour that could be felt', the narrator tells us, like a ship in a storm, 'the buildings strained with a battened-down human life, but not a beam, not a voice, not a note from a radio escaped' (196).

Arthur and Pepita look up at the surreal sight of a seemingly deserted, moon-drenched London and their response is simultaneous, and imaginative: both see Rider Haggard's abandoned and fantastical city of Kôr, and quote lines from Andrew Lang's sonnet, 'She', written for the novel: '*Mysterious Kôr thy walls forsaken stand/Thy lonely towers beneath a lonely moon*' (198). Rider Haggard's ersatz orthography at once mimics authenticity and inscribes difference by introducing an explicitly spatial diacritical mark (the circumflex, ˆ), alien to English and used to represent a contracted or lengthened vowel in non-tonal languages, or a rising and falling (or, more typically, just falling) pitch in tonal languages. Both Arthur and Pepita comment on the appealing aural and spatial estrangement of a previously familiar vowel: 'I knew it must be the right name; it's like a cry', Pepita observes, to which Arthur replies, 'most like the cry of a crow to me' (199). But is it a cry of excitement or one of despair? Does Haggard's manufactured circumflex, displacing the native 'o', now convey the rising tide of hallucinatory euphoria among Londoners living through the Blitz, or does it serve a psychological reparative purpose, registering the visual image of a great city partially destroyed? Is it an escapist gesture, an attempt, as Gill Plain suggests, to 'spiritually abscond from the physical environment of conflict' (Plain, 1996, 122), or an aesthetic response to a new reality?

For the stranded lovers, the mental association between Haggard's topless towers and a moonlit London is instinctive, and was clearly Bowen's own; she had been deeply moved by her childhood reading of *She*, describing it as the 'first totally violent impact I received from print', after which she was 'prepared to handle any book like a bomb' (*MT*, 250). For Bowen, her shell-shocked childhood reading of *She* provoked two responses. First, the Foucauldian epistemic shift from reading temporally to reading spatially – 'I resigned from history and turned to geography' (*MT*, 246–7) – which led eventually to disappointment: 'there was no undiscovered country . . . what an absence of prospect' (*MT*, 247). Secondly, the opening up of her imagination, and its ability to shape (and even dictate) her engagement with reality: 'I saw Kôr before I saw London', Bowen wrote: 'I was inclined to see London as Kôr with the roofs still on' (*MT*, 249). For Bowen, reading *She* as a child had explosively opened up imaginative space; for her fictional protagonists, the same imaginative experience fills in the explosive spaces left behind by German bombing. Arthur notes the ambivalent nature of explosive space: 'if you can blow whole places out of existence, you can blow whole places into it', he observes, adding 'we can't say what's come out since the bombing has started' (199). Or in fact, one might want to add, what has *gone in*; Bowen's story illustrates the imaginative and emotional investment that Londoners made in keeping the illusion of their pre-war city alive through the Blitz.

While the bombing has explosively opened up Arthur and Pepita's imaginative sympathy and reinforced their emotional commitment to one another, it has also left them homeless, 'without any hope of a place of their own' (201), for Pepita shares a 'two-roomed flatlet' (201) with her girlfriend Callie: 'what was once a three-windowed Victorian drawing room had been partitioned, by very thin walls, into kitchenette, living-room, Callie's bedroom' (203). The clumsily fashioned tripartite structure where 'you could hear everything' is not room enough for the resolution (or perhaps, even, consummation) of Bowen's iterative plot: 'there was really no room for a third, and least of all for a man' (201).

The lack of private space is crushing in 'Mysterious Kôr'. It is not just the flat that is too full, as Arthur explains to Callie, but available public space in London: 'we couldn't get near any movie or any place for sitting', he observes, 'so then we took the tube to that park down there, but the place was as bad as daylight' (212). Trapped by the 'siege of light' (214) of a full moon bearing down on a cold and gateless Regent's Park more powerfully than a searchlight, Arthur and Pepita's love, a 'collision in the dark', (208) remains unconsummated: 'we hadn't the nerve' (212), he admits to Callie. Returning from active service, Arthur's own clumsiness in the darkness of Callie's flat (he bumps into things and spills cigarette ash over the bed) denotes his alienation from the changed spatial circumstances (and survival skills) of blackout London, a city whose abiding theme was a relentless and *unheimlich* de-familiarization of the known and experienced. Bowen herself observed that 'walking in the darkness of the nights for six years' had led her to develop 'new bare alert senses, with their own savage warnings and notations', each night's experience contingently reprised in daylight: 'by day one was always making one's own new maps of a landscape always convulsed by some new change' (223). For Bowen, the 'grinding impersonality' of the war was inseparable from its 'obliteration of so many tracks and landmarks' (*MT*, 56) through which Londoners had defined their sense of self.

As in 'In the Square', the heightened emotional, sexual and sensory acuity of Londoners in the Blitz is both enervated and chastened by their relentless spatial constriction in a London already 'full enough before the Americans came' (201). 'Walls went down; and we felt, if not knew, each other' (218), Bowen wrote in the postscript to *The Demon Lover*, echoing the enforced proximity of Callie and Pepita's awkwardly shared bed: 'sometimes I hardly knew where I stopped and someone else began' (218). And yet close proximity created both the possibilities of intimacy and the context for claustrophobia. Increasingly, wartime London luxuriated in unusable public space, while usable public, and, more importantly, private space seemed to be in perpetual diminuendo.

On one level, 'Mysterious Kôr' narrates what Lefebvre has called the 'overlapping claims of heterotopias, isotopias and utopias' (Lefebvre, 1991, 366), in presenting an unhistoricized, even prehistoric utopia (the moonlit vision of Kôr) fleetingly projected before a historicized, territorialized dystopia (Callie's 'flatlet'). The story epitomizes the central tension in all of Bowen's wartime short stories and many of her novels: the terrifying vertiginous difficultly of anthropomorphizing, inhabiting or even temporarily occupying space. In *The Demon Lover and Other Stories*, Bowen reminds us that, while 'place is frightfully important' (*MT*, 39), space – its presence, absence, elasticity or constriction – is potentially frightful. By her own admission, Bowen wanted to explore the 'claustrophobia of not being able to move about freely' (222) that typified life in London during the war in these stories, and she used a spatial term to explain how she came to write them: 'the stories had their own momentum . . . they were flying particles of something enormous and inchoate' (216). Bowen's 'flying particles', the 'sparks from experience—and experience not necessarily my own' (217), reprise and revise the idea of the explosive space that is ubiquitous in her writing.

Bowen's interest in the potential tyranny of space was not confined to her experience and representation of the war in her short stories, or indeed, only to the period of conflict. In *The Heat of the Day* (London, 1949), visitors to Stella's two-room flat (as well as Stella herself) are constantly in transit between the room they occupy and its 'Other' and, despite the grinding proximity of the protagonists (Stella has two rooms – and entertains two different lovers), their spatial appreciation of the flat is elastic. Distances between interlocutors and objects in Stella's two-room flat (clearly, for Bowen, an archetypal abyss – as well as a *mise-en-abyme*) expand and contract according to their perspective and their emotional state, as Maud Ellmann notes, with 'disconcerting elasticity' (154), while, outside, Bowen's narrative registers the creation of new spaces as a result of the conflict: 'there was plenty of everything in London—attention, drink, time, taxis, most of all space' (*HD*, 89).[16] Caught between the conflicting terrors of claustrophobia and agoraphobia, of grinding proximity and desolate expansiveness, Bowen's characters negotiate uncharted spaces, often without benefit of maps or signs.

In the afterword to *Bowen's Court*, written years after the demolition of her own Big House, she refused to admit that 'the space is empty' (*BC*, 458), preferring her own mental picture of the house to reality and betraying once again what Con Coroneos has termed 'an aboriginal horror of void' (Coroneos, 2002, 5). For Bowen, filled imaginative space was emotionally preferable to the cleared physical space of the *not*-Bowen's Court, subverting Worringer's idea that space is the enemy of both abstraction and its concomitant, empathy; Bowen's mental attachment to this previously concrete, now empty, space echoes Lyotard's concept of the 'immemorial' – that which can be neither forgotten nor convincingly reconstituted. Her own sense of the empty spaces in Bowen's Court while it still stood again suggests the importance of positive negative space, its filling with the accreted emotional responses of those who have occupied it, for these seeming empty spaces are in fact full: 'the empty parts of the house, piled up in the winter darkness, palpably and powerfully existed . . . with each death, the air of the place had thickened: it had been added to' (*BC*,

451). The cumulative experiences of generations of Bowens, members of a class defined by their spatial trajectory (Protestant Anglo-Irish Ascendancy) as much as by their physical possession of land, have invested the space with more imaginative value than the structure of the building could hold; the materially empty but emotionally filled space has outlasted its edifice, and the aboriginal horror of the void – a horror negotiated by generations of Bowens – has been averted, even after its disappearance. 'So great and calming was the authority of the light and quiet round Bowen's Court that it survived war-time', she wrote, 'and it did more than that, it survived the house' (*BC*, 457).

Elizabeth Bowen's fictional characters are haunted not just by material things or chronological events, but by spaces, whether occupied, emptied, displaced or imagined; the 'enforced return', the witting or unwitting trajectory of so many of her protagonists, invariably re-engages with a previous spatial experience. Nowhere is this more apparent than in her wartime stories collected in *The Demon Lover and Other Stories*, for at no time was the spatial experience of millions of fellow Londoners more acutely felt and their expectations more disruptively challenged. 'It is precisely space', Wilhelm Worringer claimed in support of Bergson's assertion of the supremacy of time over space, 'which is not susceptible of individualisation' and is 'the major enemy of all striving after abstraction, and hence is the first thing to be suppressed in representation' (Worringer, 38). Bowen, like Wyndham Lewis, believed just the opposite, by insisting on seeing the temporal in spatial terms, claiming that 'time is one kind of space; it creates distance' and that 'chafing geographical confusion' could only lead to the vertiginous 'giddiness of unfocused vision' (*A Time in Rome*, 6). Bowen's wartime fictional characters, perpetually in transit and forever forced to engage with material objects in the world around them, atavistically betray the spatial origins of both language and identity; but, more importantly, they also display the extent to which individuals have invariably defined themselves in relation to the constantly changing explosive spaces, filled as well as cleared, that they have had to negotiate, occupy and even inhabit.

7

Narrative, meaning and agency in
The Heat of the Day

BROOK MILLER, with LUKE ELWARD,
TESSA HEMPEL and PHILIP KOLLAR

> *Freedom. Freedom to be what?—the muddled, the mediocre, the damned.*
> *Good enough to die for, freedom, for the good reason that it's the very thing*
> *which has made it impossible to live, so there's no alternative.*
> Robert Kelway, in *The Heat of the Day*

Questions about the nature of freedom abound in *The Heat of the Day* (1948; New York, 2002). Whether signifying – as in the epigraph above – an empty call to patriotism or rather as a means of defining the self outside of national ideologies, freedom is treated ambivalently. From the public fictions of propaganda to stories told to others and the self, strategic fictions shape the experience of post-Blitz London in Elizabeth Bowen's war novel. There are two ways in which post-Blitz London is traumatic for the subject: first, the impact of the bombs has obliterated personal and public landmarks; second, the omnipresence of a surveillance apparatus engenders a pervasive paranoia. Being located in the bombed city, as some critics have suggested, heightens the sense of contingency, illusion and alienation that is characteristic of modern life. In addition, the novel is replete with a sense of cynicism about the very mode of identity most associated with London's response to the Blitz: popular nationalism. Just as the Blitz urges a reading of the city as a broken icon of modernity, so the failure of nationalistic rhetoric is emblematic of a general suspicion of the impersonality of modernizing narratives. The novel's focus upon the function and value of personal stories reflects a sense that identity must resist simple identification with place or ideology.

In *The Heat of the Day* the construction of personal and interpersonal narratives is ambivalent. If attempts to make stories – that is, narratives that relate the self to others, to social contexts, and that are in some fashion teleological – are at once necessary responses to conventional narratives and ways of coping with the alienation induced by the Blitz and the emergence of a culture of surveillance, they are also, inevitably, fraught with an anxious sense of their own falsity. That is, self-narration within this context either reflects contingency or a form of liberation. Here, the price of the liberation each major character discovers involves inscription of the self into a conventional type. The character's evolution is thus haunted, for the reader and perhaps for the character her- or himself, by consciousness of repressed history and personal desires.

The dynamics of war, which effectively concentrate a sense of interconnectedness in what Benedict Anderson calls the nation's 'imagined community' (Anderson, 2006) by turning the citizenry's attention to an unfolding common narrative, provided Bowen with a vehicle for developing the ongoing exploration of the dilemmas of subjectivity initiated in earlier novels. If novels like *The Last September* (1927; New York, 2000) and *The House in Paris* (1935; New York, 2002) establish and unravel an expressionistic mapping of inner experience with the history of a place, in *The Heat of the Day* that problematic mapping has been multiplied beyond all recognition. That is, in her war novel Bowen expanded the range of space and characters to whom this mapping applies so as to dissolve the reader's easy relation to it. Houses, parks, cafés, and even larger spaces like London and Ireland become problematic containers for subjects. On the one hand, they provide the grounds for inter-subjective symbolic identification and remain 'free', offering the possibility of both a plenitude of meaning and of a continued flexibility of identity. Yet these possibilities are decidedly compromised by the pervasiveness of ideology, which shapes meaning around the agency of the state, limits freedom to the recognizable and nameable, and, most significantly, operates a surveillance apparatus that, while nominally protecting citizens, deeply conditions their social experience. The war normalizes these effects, but it does not essentially change the nature of social experience.

It is this point on which this essay stakes its value, following Barbara Bellow Watson's claim that 'a conviction is established . . . by the end of the novel that the unreliability of knowledge and of people has been revealed rather than created by war' (Watson, 1981, 132). Since Watson's essay was published, critics have intervened by approaching the novel through a variety of contemporary critical lenses.[1] Yet in their work, readings of the ending locate resolutions that synchronize with their approaches and ultimately posit the passage of the war as a solution to the human crises that drive the plot.

Angela Dorenkamp rightly points out that *The Heat of the Day* deals 'with mysteries which are only apparently solved' (Dorenkamp, 1968, 13). But it is not just key questions about motivation and event in Robert Kelway's treason and its detection that remain unanswered at the end. Epistemic problems fostered by the instability of language, the unreliability of knowledge and the fragility of loyalty linger hauntingly. Further, as we will explore, the conclusion enacts a partial repression of earlier textual revelations, steeping the novel's resolution in irony.

Such a reading implicitly critiques the idea, held by numerous critics, that the war creates (rather than reveals) the epistemic and ontological crises the major characters experience. Deborah Parsons, following such a perspective, argues that we should make distinctions along gender lines about Bowen's representation of war-torn London. According to Parsons, the novel's 'men cling to, or are entrapped by, symbols of the past and view the uprootedness of the war-time urban condition with nihilistic horror. Women, by contrast, adjust to the enforced displaced and "wandering" lifestyle, and can come to experience a degree of emancipation' (Parsons, 1997, 26). Yet Parsons does not grant women unfettered freedom: 'Her heroines, attempting to express their perceptions of this world through the masculine language system, do not really fit anywhere . . . unable to correspond to the identity types available' (31). This analysis supplements Parsons' claims by noting that, while male characters' attempts to evade nihilism are fraught with irony, female characters' final fates reflect an uneasy identification with traditional identity types to which they do not entirely correspond. This notion of the incommensurability of the city with individual fulfilment thus helps us grapple with the complexities of the novel's ending, even if Parsons holds a different view of the effects of the war.

Parsons is not alone in mapping the experience of war with an unmooring of meaning. Yet when Neil Corcoran claims that meaning is contingent in wartime London – 'the meaningfulness of the days depends upon the air raids at night and London as a organic body' (Corcoran, 2004, 169) – he suggests not simply that the war heightens feeling, but that the war's destructiveness lends meaning where otherwise it is exhausted. That is, the war, above all, conditions the fictions through which people make sense of their lives. As opposed to the conventional temporality of peacetime, for Corcoran fleeting social and sexual ties assume greater meaning and greater flexibility during the war. Rather than depleting the 'meaningfulness' of social life, the war in fact seems to facilitate improved recognition of and connection to others, all the while highlighting the contingent and fleeting nature of social exchange. As the narrator puts it, 'it was characteristic of that life in the moment and for the moment's sake that one knew people well' (103). In this context conventional barriers to social congress have relaxed, and the subject appears more open to the desires, values and narratives of others. Yet, in locating her novel in this moment, Bowen discovers a context for continuing the exploration of subjectivity begun in earlier novels. That is, this apparent openness casts light upon normative choices as much as it offers Bowen's vision of differences between war- and peacetime Britain. The porousness of marginal characters, such as Stella Rodney's son Roderick, reflects a powerful human drive towards assimilation initially treated in *The Last September* and *The House in Paris*.

In *Elizabeth Bowen: The Shadow Across the Page*, Maud Ellmann describes *The Heat of the Day* as 'a novel about leaks, about the porousness of architectural and psychic space, about the failure to keep secrets in, intruders out' (Ellmann, 2003, 153). Ellmann notes that the novel's opening scene in Regent's Park is described in terms of seepage and the porous quality of the environment. Stella and Robert share a 'hermetic world' together, losing themselves in each other (97). Robert Kelway is portrayed as a human 'leak' (35). Louie penetrates Harrison's shelter of thought, distracting him from his own business. Harrison's mind has been invaded by thoughts of Stella, thoughts that lead him to invade her home. Yet in her analysis of this discourse of invasion and intrusion, Ellmann largely ignores Roderick, the centre of one of the novel's elaborate subplots. Indeed, Roderick is perhaps the most 'porous' figure in the novel, absorbing narratives of national honour, Anglo-Irish aristocracy and the secrets of his mother's sheltering familial narrative.

As a soldier, Roderick appears to embrace a sense of national duty. He inherits this role from men before him, specifically from uncles who 'had been killed fighting in Flanders' (24). Like many other young men of his generation, Roderick's options are limited by the demands of the nation; while he is not conscripted, he does not resist public pressure to engage in military service. Rather, he enters the army precisely because he lacks will and a sense of purpose: 'his ineptness to play any other part would have more distressed him had there been any other part to play' (51). Roderick's martial identity, then, is strangely passive. The army hails him into the national narrative, but Bowen depicts this identity in ambivalent terms.

In fact, Roderick's military position interferes with what had been most important to him: his relationship with his mother. Through this pair, Bowen introduces the way subjects are enmeshed in others' life-narratives, a situation both constricting and necessary to a sense of belonging. Ironically, Stella appreciates a certain distance from Roderick, whose presence previously trapped her into an uncomfortably conventional domestic existence: 'to her, the opportunity to make a break, to free herself of her house, to come to London to work had been not ungrateful' (24). Moreover, Roderick's visit foregrounds his mother's unspoken demands upon his persona:

> Months in the Army had made Roderick notice what he had taken for granted when he was more at home—the particular climate in which his mother dwelled. Of this, the temperature and the pressure were gauged by no other person, unless Robert. To re-enter this climate, to be affected by it, could have been enervating if one had not loved her. (50-1)

Stella's fears about Roderick's military service underlie the 'enervating' aspects of this environment: 'what nagged at her, what flickered into her look each time she confronted the soldier in battle dress, was the fear that the army was out to obliterate Roderick' (50). Their rather claustrophobic relationship highlights the degree to which self-definition is mediated by others' demands. In fact, Roderick responds by emulating his former self: 'His body could at least copy, if not at once regain, unsoldierly looseness and spontaneity' (50). During the visit, Roderick reshapes himself as 'the Roderick his mother remembered, the Roderick he could feel her hoping to see' (50). He transforms himself for her sake, but depends upon her cues to do so: 'He searched in Stella for some identity left by him in her keeping. It was a search undertaken principally for her sake: only she made him conscious of loss or change' (50). Her 're-redefinition' of him in response to the army's influence extends Ellmann's description of *The Heat of the Day* as 'a novel about leaks' into something larger, a meditation upon how self-definition is ambivalently forged in relation to inter-subjective and national (ideological) desire.

Interestingly, these pressures lead Roderick to value rootedness rather than freedom. In his inheritance of Mount Morris, a property he has never seen, Roderick attempts to embrace traditional familial and social forms in Ireland. Through this subplot, Bowen continues her commentary on the tenuous search for identity and authenticity implicit in Anglo-Irish experience. When an elderly distant cousin bequeaths an Anglo-Irish estate to Roderick, the will asks him to sustain the old family tradition: 'Francis left Mount Morris and the land to Roderick, "in the hope," it was written, "that he may care in his own way to carry on the old tradition"' (77). The ambiguously worded will leaves Roderick confused as to just what Francis had intended him to do with the estate. He dwells on the wording, seeking to understand exactly what Francis wanted of him: 'Does he mean, that I'm free to care in any way I like, so long as it's *the* tradition I carry on; or, that so long as I care in the same way he did, I'm free to mean by "tradition" anything I like?' (95). Roderick's questioning of the wording points to a key dilemma for the subject who attempts to embody aristocratic authority: does one locate limited freedom in the distance between self and persona that comes from consciously *performing* an identity that does not match one's desire; or rather, does identifying completely *with* the position grant one the freedom to reshape tradition, albeit at the cost of yoking oneself entirely to the dying Anglo-Irish aristocracy?

Through Roderick's preoccupation with Mount Morris, Bowen depicts this dilemma as a response to his own sense of contingency. He pesters his mother constantly for information about the estate, eagerly digesting what information she does provide. The copy of the will is described as 'a good deal thumbed' when the two meet to discuss it (95). The postscript of a letter to Stella also betrays his devotion to Mount Morris in excited questions about acreage, the presence of guns, and the like. This desire for knowledge is augmented by Roderick's defence of Francis when his mother refers to the late cousin as 'a disappointed man' (96). Even though Roderick knows very little at all about Francis and never actually met him, he is eager to jump to defend his cousin against accusations that he was a poor husband and a cowardly servant of Ireland: 'Cousin Nettie went off her chump; Ireland refused to fight. But that's not the same as to say he let himself down' (96). His desire to know all he can of Mount Morris, along with his defence of Francis, paint Roderick as a willing recipient of Francis's posthumous influence. This eagerness reflects Roderick's fundamental condition: apparently sophisticated but actually naïve, apparently heroic but actually rather feckless, Roderick seeks a habitat that secures his sense of identity and belonging.

In fact, Mount Morris initially does appear to confer authority upon Roderick. By questioning his mother, Roderick develops a sense of purpose. He takes this interest further by going against her wishes and seeking a meeting with Nettie, Francis's widow. He hopes to gain her favour and blessing in his inheritance of her former home, and fears that she will feel usurped if he does otherwise:

> 'I don't think, for instance, you yet quite grasp how much it is on
> my mind about Nettie and that I really should do something about

her. She may well feel she has had rather a bad deal . . . I really
must see her and have her good will. It would spoil everything if I
was an usurper.' (224-5)

Roderick's anxiety about 'spoil'-ing his new position reflects an idealism troubled by underlying fears about its tenuousness.

Roderick's new authority has consequences almost immediately, as
his aggressive pursuit of Nettie's blessing leads to an unwanted discovery that his father's infidelity had broken up his parents' marriage.
This development is emblematic of the subtle ways in which Bowen
problematizes the resolution of Roderick's story at the end of the
novel. If *The Heat of the Day* basks in 'the difficulties of knowing' and
'doubtfulness, ambiguity, mistake, falsity', Roderick becomes a key
figure for the difficulties of self-transformation (Watson, 1981, 132).

Ellmann points to the ironies of Roderick's credulity in his
repeated quotations of his friend Fred. The most revealing of these
quotations occurs early on: 'as Fred says, it comes to seem fishy when
one *is* told anything. Go by what you find out for yourself, he says . . .
Whereas if anybody goes out of his way to tell you something, Fred
says you can take it he's got an axe to grind' (64). Roderick's ironic,
but unwitting, refusal of Fred's advice by parroting it hints at Roderick's lack of understanding. His naïvety, oddly, enables him to
overlook the flaws in Francis's desire that he inherit Mount Morris. In
an immediate sense, the succession proceeds only because Roderick is
naïve enough to believe he can embody an authority he (wrongly) associates with his cousin, when in fact the estate will demand more of
him than he realizes. On his first night there, he finds that 'the place
had concentrated upon Roderick its being' leaving him 'possessed,
oppressed and in awe' (352). This parallel to his mother's demand
upon him is unpropitious, and the spectre of future financial burdens
seems even more ominous. Roderick decides that 'Mount Morris has
got to be my living', a prospect that Donovan the steward finds
unlikely to succeed: 'That way, you could sink a terrible lot of money'
(353). Roderick persists, leaving Donovan to reminisce about how 'Mr
Morris used to be the one for considering improvements' (354).
Despite any dreams Roderick may have of asserting 'his own way', he
appears poised to repeat the disappointments of his predecessor.

Indeed, Bowen imbues Roderick's project with a sense of fatalism
by creating a number of parallels with his cousin. They both possess a
startling naïvety about military affairs. While Roderick does not
realize the true extent of the war's danger until he visits Mount
Morris, Francis pompously and naïvely offers his aid to the British

cause. He sends letters offering unwanted help to government officials, who are relieved to be 'spared the embarrassment of replying' by Francis's sudden death (75).

Late in the novel, Bowen laces scenes in which Roderick asserts his ownership of Mount Morris with a sense of impending failure, hinting that he will in fact replace Francis's failed idealism. When Donovan greets Roderick with a welcoming speech, Roderick 'listen[s] less to the words than their echo through this house of his own' (348). In place at Mount Morris, Roderick's feckless immaturity continues. He is still quite dependent, mentally 'reproach[ing] his mother' for not reminding him to make a will (353). When Stella needs his support after her lover's death, Roderick cannot convincingly comfort his mother, instead mumbling about his inability to help. Finally, he reaches a bleak conclusion: 'if I could even only see the thing as a whole, like God!' (337). Roderick's excuse for not understanding, for not succeeding, reflects his naïve idealism. The paralysis associated with Roderick's immaturity stands in stark relief to his fantasies about becoming the master of Mount Morris. At the end of the novel, Donovan laments that Roderick 'couldn't prevail on [Stella] to wait' until a new round of bombing concludes in London (355). Roderick's response is his final speech of the novel, and as such exposes his failure to achieve the mastery and sense of rooted identity about which he has fantasized: 'Oh' (355). In this impotent response, and in the contrast with Donovan's more experienced voice, Bowen anticipates the eventual failure of his project. Just as Francis, his predecessor, has made a mess of marriage, estate management and politics, so Roderick seems poised to fail. His pursuit of a tradition to assuage the pain of his lack of a father figure works only too well; in desiring to make life meaningful by following a tradition, he unwittingly embarks upon repeating the failed narrative of his predecessor.

Roderick's quest for meaning illustrates how self-definition responds to social conventions and values; as such, narrative becomes a key site for transacting interpersonal power. This logic applies widely in Bowen's novel. Ellmann notes that in *The Heat of the Day*:

> Everyone seems trapped in someone else's story: Nettie is co-opted into Francis' fantasy of marriage, Roderick into his romance of fatherhood; Stella, misrepresented as a *femme fatale* in her in-laws' story of her marriage, is also blackmailed by Harrison into the inconclusive story of his lust; Robert is scripted into 'fictions of boyishness' cooked up by his sister and his mother; while Louie Lewis is flattered into ready-made identities spewed out by the daily press. (Ellmann, 2003, 162)

To Ellmann, notions of narration, story and fiction are not simply characteristics of the work, but exist as themes within the sequence of events depicted in the novel. She claims that specific characters have different relationships to the narration; for example, Ellmann argues that the government counter-espionage agent, Harrison, takes on the role of the narrator, while Francis's estranged wife, Nettie, and Louie, a lonely working-class Londoner married to a soldier at the front, resist being narrated. Ellmann asserts that there is a 'third presence' in the novel that intrudes into the private lives of the characters (Ellmann, 2003, 155). She frames the third presence of Bowen's novel in several ways: as the narrative, as history, as Robert's secret espionage activities and as Harrison's invisible surveillance of Stella. The surveillance motif takes many forms in the novel; however, the interrelation of narration and surveillance is more extensive than Ellmann suggests. The narrative does not simply function as a way to draw attention to the fictionality of the story, but rather the narrative is itself a spy, like Robert and Harrison, that is ever present in the characters' lives. The narrative places the reader unwittingly in a position akin to surveillance, robbing the characters of their privacy and exposing thoughts that the characters hide from each other.

Other critics treat the phenomena that Ellmann describes as a 'third presence' differently. Andrew Bennett and Nicholas Royle, for example, introduce the notion of 'sheer kink', implying that the novel's inter-textual and self-referential nature loosens the novel from verisimilitude. Whereas Ellmann's 'third presence' connotes the inevitable intervention of history in the experience of human beings, both as actors and as readers, Bennett and Royle's 'kink' identifies the text as an ephemeral, contingent site that decommissions readings even as the novel seems to evoke them.

Between these approaches, Neil Corcoran sees a middle way in which the materialist and the deconstructive merge into a politics of subjectivity:

> Woven into this central, self-reflexive, story are 'many stories' which people tell about themselves to one another, or even, more poignantly sometimes, which they tell about themselves to themselves, in order to maintain identities in peril . . . The virtually febrile self-consciousness about being narrated informs the entire narrative; and it also crosses with, just as individual stories leak into, the public narratives of wartime . . . the sense of being narrated, of being part of a discourse you cannot control, is also congruent with the wartime narratives of propaganda. (Corcoran, 2004, 169–71)

Indeed, Corcoran argues that the novel culminates Bowen's aesthetic of speech-acts: 'of no novel of [Bowen's] is it truer that, as she claimed of the novel generally, and italicized the claim, "Speech is what the characters *do to each other*"' (2004, 187).

Such a view illuminates a variety of characters in the novel, especially Robert's mother, Mrs Kelway. In fact, Corcoran's point can be extended to other acts of signification, as Mrs Kelway's arrangement of Robert's room asserts her narrative of Robert's childhood. The narrator describes Robert's room as being interspersed with 'fictions of boyishness', which Robert finds alienating and oppressive (127). The room is full of pictures of Robert at various ages, which he remarks are only imitations of real moments that make him feel like he does not exist (129).

Outside of Robert's room, Mrs Kelway is also crafting fictions. Her children subscribe to an unspoken rule that she be called 'Muttikins', despite the lack of warmth in their relationships. Indeed, everyone in Holme Dene acts and speaks based on what Mrs Kelway expects of them. Mrs Kelway never concedes to others' stories, but narrates to secure authority over the family home, Holme Dene, and the people within. In this scene, Mrs Kelway's power can be read as a more focused, personal version of the impact of place in Bowen's earlier novels. As Ellmann notes, she represents one of the environmental factors that condition Robert's existence: 'Robert's crime is imputed to his father's impotence, his mother's wickedness, his sister's brassiness, her labrador's subservience; to the unearthed materialism of the middle-class; to the Kelways' contempt for language . . . A crooked house creates a crooked mind' (160). This condition demands a reappraisal of the ways in which the suspension of conventional life leads to freedom in the novel. The power transacted through interpersonal versions of interpellation has, apparently, shaped the identity of the characters since well before the war.

This dynamic seems, however, peculiarly modern, insofar as it engenders a sense that identity is shaped by the need to perform in the interpellated (rather than the interpella*ting*) subject. As Corcoran notes, the novel's 'modes of theatricality undermine the very self-identity of character. *The Heat of the Day* is governed by an almost Berkeleian metaphysics, in which you are what you are perceived to be' (Corcoran, 2004, 188). Yet the dynamics of narration are somewhat more complicated here. The coercive power of others' stories is not distinctive from pressure to conform to the larger fictions of popular patriotic propaganda. For when characters narrate to one another, they tell stories that defend their sense of identity against, on the one hand, propaganda and, on the other, meaninglessness. Where Ellmann sees the emergence of history, Bennett and Royle see the deconstructive fascinations of textuality and Corcoran locates the quasi-Berkeleian subject as a site of contest; the play of narratives also suggests a reading of the paradoxes of ideology. That is, the subject is inevitably confronted with a coercive official story of the self, yet without that sense of citizenship one confronts an absence of meaning. Such a crisis, however, does not have liberatory potential. In *The Heat of the Day*, accepting socially constituted versions of the self is both a form of bad faith and necessary.

The test for this position comes in the form of Aunt Nettie who, by feigning madness and rejecting her position as lady of the Mount Morris estate, does seem to be moving away from the fictions into which the other characters are placed. Nettie's move, however, is not away from an entrapment in her Mount Morris role to total freedom from narration; instead, it is a substitution of one sort of story for another. By becoming, quite literally, a 'madwoman in the attic', Nettie gains a freedom she did not have at Mount Morris. Nevertheless, this involves maintaining a fiction she both accepts and performs. Nettie explains to Roderick, 'what he had wanted me to be was his wife', and she subsequently enters an asylum to escape this fate (242). When Roderick and the readers find that Nettie is quite sane, she claims that it frees her from the pressures of being narrated: 'here I am, and you can't make any more stories out of that' (240). Yet her claim is undermined by her meeting with Roderick, in which an unwillingness to look outside her window and a compulsion to shatter Roderick's false views of his father signal a deeply repressed sense of alienation. In attempting to dispense with others' stories, she has evidently done deep violence to her own identity.

To what ends, then, do individual narratives tend? Simply, they are ambivalent. In their familiarity they provide a cover for the subject, a way of hiding in convention. Yet that hiding inevitably entails violence to or degradation of the self. That is to say, if subjectivity entails a desire for recognition, the grounding of selfhood in type is inevitably fraught with a sense of failure. In adopting a role, the subjects in *The Heat of the Day* wield power in a tenuous fashion. The fate of the major characters testifies to Bowen's interest in these dynamics, and it is in this sense that *The Heat of the Day* appears to draw parallels between the pressures of generic narratives and the compromises of the social subject. Attempts to redefine the self are torn between two conflicting impulses: on the one hand, resisting definitions of the self offered by others, whether through interpersonal communication, the newspapers or other means; on the other, embodying a familiar role as a means of securing recognition and empathy from others.

To Ellmann, Louie Lewis is emblematic of the desire to resist conventional narratives: Louie 'resists narration in the sense that she has no command of words' (163). While the novel initially does suggest Louie's inability to find her own language to describe her world, this actually leaves her open to the narratives of others. She openly accepts the narrative identity the newspaper provides her:

> Dark and rare were the days when she failed to find on the inside of her paper an address to or else account of herself. Was she not a worker, a soldier's lonely wife, a war orphan, a thinking democrat, a movie-goer, a woman of Britain, a letter-writer, a fuel-saver and a housewife . . . Louie now felt bad only about any part of herself which in any way did not fit into the papers' picture. (169)

Accepting such an identity literally confers a sense of agency upon her: 'after a week or two [of reading the papers she] . . . discovered that she *had* got a point of view, and not only *a* point of view, but the right one' (168).

When such naïve identification is discredited, however, Louie latches onto Connie, the source of the critique. By accepting Connie's advice and control, Louie internalizes Connie's narrative of her situation. Nevertheless, some critics have located in Louie a form of successful resistance to ideological interpellation. Ellmann asserts that when Stella tries to 'author' Louie, the latter resists this authority 'through silence or through counter-narratives' (Ellmann, 2003, 165). Indeed, Louie does ultimately respond to Stella by maternally describing her as a 'soul astray'. This counter-narrative, however, is problematic in two ways. First, it responds to the coercive aspects of others' stories by merely offering a confining story of its own. Second, Louie's new image of Stella is grounded in Stella's own theatrical performance of an identity with which she is resisting interpellation. That is to say, Louie's description of Stella, while overtly empathetic, nevertheless obscures the complexities of her (Stella's) personal dilemma.

Neil Corcoran locates in Louie the possibility of reconciling oneself with the past and, in doing so, moving beyond the debilitating sense of panoptic scrutiny that paralyses many of the characters. By freeing herself from the guilt embodied in the condemning stare of her recently dead husband, Louie can go on to what Watson calls a generative future. Corcoran sees this possibility emerge in the following passage: Louie 'felt herself beckoned into that gaze of abstention and futurity—was she not in her own way drawing ahead of what was to be?' (325). Ironically, in embracing a vision of her future self Louie decommissions her own desire. Where Corcoran locates a liberated self, the repressive aspects of her evolution raise the question of whether Louie is in fact autonomous. For Corcoran, 'Louie's sense of a new future prompts her into a "gaze" . . . when she looks at Tom's photograph . . . [she begins] the reconciliatory and benevolent transformation of the largely negative and malevolent imagery of scrutiny elsewhere in the novel' (197). Corcoran's reading points to what many critics have oversimplified about the novel: the complexity of the ending.

In much of the criticism of the novel, the end of the war offers, through its traumatic break with the past, a history-less space afterwards characterized by new freedoms. Bowen at least gives voice to such a perspective in the prediction of the ageing Colonel Pole, who claims that the young generation will want 'to travel light': that is, free of a deep connection to tradition, and thus free from the demands of convention (89). However, Pole's fleeting appearance in the novel as an anti-sentimental, brusque persona – 'sentiment is the devil', as he puts it – stands in such stark contrast to Bowen's consistent valorization of empathetic relationships as to render it parodic (89).

Further, the novel troubles such notions of liberation by making the coherence of relationships dependent upon their appropriateness to a given historical moment. As Ellmann argues, 'in their final interview, Stella describes Harrison as . . . the shadowy third that both abetted and destroyed her trance with Robert . . . Unpinned by a third presence, twosomes fall asunder' (Ellmann, 2003, 166–7). These assertions usefully point to the interrelation of the personal and the political. Ellmann claims '*The Heat of the Day* . . . is Bowen's most strenuous attempt to show how the political is implicated in the personal; how the "third presence" of history seeds itself into the cracks of private life' (2003, 155). Yet Ellmann misrecognizes the nature of the shadow beneath each character's fate; it is in some sense a repetition, either of history or of a type. In this way the personal is more than simply penetrated by the political; rather, it is a covert form of the political. Indeed, the return to history is not ultimately just a 'third presence' or 'shadow across the page'; it is constitutive. That is, Bowen alludes to the necessary enmeshing of the subject in the bad faith of an ideological field.

While each of the characters' fates can be read as ambivalent, Louie's potential association with futurity has led to particularly optimistic critical commentary. Watson, for instance, sees hope and a sense of 'generation' in the birth of Louie's child: 'provisional yet not improvised, old platitude and fresh response to genocidal war, the hope lies in preservation and generation, specifically in the child nurtured with natural feeling, not cramped in a cage of orthodoxies or ideologies' (Watson, 1981, 132). Louie's move into motherhood and out of London lends the ending clarity rather than ambivalence, and indeed a 'clearly implied possibility of hope' (1981, 132). Here Watson locates important affinities between Louie and the other fully developed characters, Roderick and Stella. Louie and Stella 'share essentials both in their fate as women and as war victims, and in the soundness of their response' (1981, 145). Likewise, Corcoran sees a redemptive transformation occur in Louie's decommissioning of the impulse to narrate: 'it is through her attitude to Stella that Louie is saved from the propagandistic version of herself; and it is therefore the parallelism between Louie and Stella which designs one of the novel's most striking ethical effects' (Corcoran, 2004, 173). For Corcoran, the story of Louie in *The Heat of the Day* intensively 'transforms the history of a cultural moment . . . into the troubled, exacerbated, extreme story of characters caught between past and future, making their own more complicated stories in the face of the constrictingly singular narratives they are everywhere offered' (2004, 175).

Dorenkamp focuses on Louie's exodus from London, noting that she 'takes her baby to live on Seale-on-Sea where she is happy' (Dorenkamp, 1968, 14). She views Louie's son as 'fatherless, yet of noble birth', and argues that Louie 'gives posterity a future' by lifting 'the child up to observe the flight of swans not only for the pleasure of the moment, but for his own future' (1968, 20). Dorenkamp imagines the swans as 'the triumph of art, of imagination, of immortality, the future of unambiguous alliances and unqualified loyalties' (1968, 20). In this raft of optimistic assertions, however, these critics ignore the numerous ironies of Louie's fate.

As the novel comes to a close and Louie's pregnancy is revealed, Louie takes on a new inconsistency while maintaining her lack of knowledge and inability to learn. Responding to Connie's discomfiture towards Louie's announcement of her pregnancy and infidelity, Louie weakly replies that 'it's been on my mind' (364). In the early stages of the pregnancy, Louie seems completely unconcerned about the child, instead fretting with Connie over 'what's your husband going to say' (365). Louie takes almost too much solace in the idea that she is 'just one of many' lonely women to find lovers while their husbands are away, allowing it to grant her 'a sort of illumination . . . a sureness . . . a look of inward complacency, even sublimity' (365).

Yet this sublime assurance is fraught with irony, self-doubt and repression. When she recalls Stella's grace, Louie recognizes her failure to live up to her ideal vision of Stella. After her child is born, Louie attempts to free him from attempts to define his identity through the circumstances of his birth, telling Connie, 'I don't think the name would mean anything to you' (366). Yet her decision to name her son Thomas Victor bizarrely merges the absent figures of Louie's and Stella's husbands, evoking emblems of fatherhood in a manner parallel to Stella's attempt to protect Roderick's sense of his paternity.

In the final sequence, Louie deepens this sense of repression in constructing a future for her son, who has been fathered by an anonymous soldier on leave. While she had been haunted by Tom's ignorance of her betrayal, she ultimately finds herself repeating over and over, 'There's always only this: Tom not knowing', until finally Connie must take up a pen and write to Tom herself, 'owing to [Louie] not knowing quite what to say' (368, 369). Learning of Tom's death in combat brings a sense of relief; Louie in fact plans to keep the telegram announcing Tom's death 'for the kid', clearly with the intention of pretending that Tom is the child's father (370). Taking after his mother, the first thing that is said about Thomas after his birth is that 'he took no notice of anything' (371). The mother's change from naïve ignorance to wilful repression is supported by her son's own infantile naïvety and lack of curiosity. After moving to the provincial Seale-on-Sea, Louie imagines her child 'every day . . . growing more like Tom' (372). This imaginative development not only represses her son's paternity; it also secures Louie's own conventional identity as a war widow.

As the novel closes, Louie offers her son an aesthetic vision she hopes will become a fond childhood memory: 'she gathered Tom quickly out of the pram and held him up, hoping he too might see, and perhaps remember. Three swans were flying a straight flight' (372). However, the baby notices nothing, and, only moments earlier, as three war planes flew by, 'the baby had not stirred' (372). Here the novel ends, with Louie's attempt to orchestrate her son's memories further ironized by its failure. Bowen leaves her not as a liberated figure for hope, but as a subject desperately striving to maintain her own fictions by crafting an identity for her son that represses the fact of his paternity.

This final image of the novel, while most immediately pertinent to Louie, also has emblematic significance for the resolution of the plot as a whole. Corcoran most astutely notes the problems with a celebratory reading of the image:

The projected English future and the projected Irish future, both figured as pacific in the repeated figure of the three swans, are here dreamed by the novel itself into a new harmony of post-war inter-relationship, even if the figure is, in its first Irish appearance, ambivalently associated too with what is not so much peace as the absence of war, the nullity of neutrality . . . In such moments *The Heat of the Day*, a novel of great emotional and political bruise and damage, seems obliged to unsettle or distress its own potential affirmations; and there are other unsettlements too as it reaches conclusion. (197)

This is true, but all signs point to Bowen's message throughout the novel being purposefully 'unsettled', not simply something she was 'obliged' to do at the end. These final images merely serve to drive the point home.

When the swans flit past after the bombers returning home, Bowen offers an image for how the subject emerges out of the economy of narratives that link the subject to the nation. For the bombers parallel, of course, the German bombers who destroyed the symbolic referents for the self in London; in doing so, we recognize in their return a return of one's own destructive impulses. If the average British citizen is not directly responsible for bombing Dresden, his/her identity as a victim of bombings is ultimately linked to the way the economy of war is read as self-defence, as national suffering. That is, it is British bombers that are returning, highlighting the linkages between the Blitz's devastation and propagandistic reporting of the war as twinned means of orienting the subject to national identification.

Subsequently the swans, swimming aerially past, reflect a movement back into the obfuscation of conventional ideology and mythmaking. For while they may represent an escapist hope for unity and peace in response to a traumatic unhinging of meaning, in the swans we also find embedded images of a competing – Irish – nationalism. Such irony should only remind the reader of the necessity of fantasy, and of the contingency and bad faith that it betrays.

As noted earlier, Watson argues that 'a conviction is established by the end of the novel that the unreliability of knowledge and of people has been revealed rather than created by war' (132). In addition, problems regarding the instability of language, the unreliability of knowledge and the failures of loyalty remain at the end. During the war, subjects briefly confront the societal and interpersonal narratives that bind them, but ultimately they embrace conventional social roles as a defence against nihilism. With the war over, a public surveillance apparatus no longer overtly conditions social experience. But that does not mean it is no longer there; both Roderick's and Louie's attempts to start over are rife with the paradoxes and difficulties of living in a social sphere in which agency and a sense of belonging are available only through the constricting, repressive embrace of conventional self-narratives.

Notes

INTRODUCTION

1. Of all Bowen's late twentieth-century readers, hoogland has made the gamest attempt to address what she refers to as Bowen's 'unclassifiable' narrative style, which she links to currents of disruptive same-sex desire that she suggests play a prominent role in Bowen's narratives (see hoogland, p. 83 and chapter 5).

1. UNSTABLE COMPOUNDS

1. Maud Ellmann, *Elizabeth Bowen: The Shadow Across the Page* (Edinburgh: Edinburgh University Press, 2003), p. 15.
2. Neil Corcoran, *Elizabeth Bowen: The Enforced Return* (Oxford: Oxford University Press, 2004), p. 63.
3. W.J. McCormack, *Dissolute Characters: Irish Literary History through Balzac, Sheridan LeFanu, Yeats and Bowen* (Manchester and New York: Manchester University Press, 1993), p. 216.
4. Samuel Beckett, 'Dante . . . Bruno . . . Vico . . . Joyce', in *Disjecta: Miscellaneous Writings and a Dramatic Fragment*, ed. Ruby Cohn (London: John Calder, 1983), p. 19.
5. Victoria Glendinning, *Elizabeth Bowen: Portrait of a Writer* (London: Weidenfeld & Nicolson, 1977), p. 1.
6. John McCormick, *Catastrophe and Imagination* (London: Longman, 1952), p. 93.
7. Andrew Bennett and Nicholas Royle, *Elizabeth Bowen and the Dissolution of the Novel: Still Lives* (New York: Palgrave Macmillan, 1995), p. xv.
8. Harold Bloom (ed. and intro.), *Modern Critical Views: Elizabeth Bowen* (New York, New Haven, Philadelphia: Chelsea House, 1987), p. i.
9. Ellmann, *Elizabeth Bowen*, p. 70.
10 See S.E. Gontarski, *The Intent of Undoing in Samuel Beckett's Dramatic Texts* (Bloomington: Indiana University Press, 1985).
11. Elizabeth Bowen, 'Out of a Book' (1946), in *The Mulberry Tree: Writings of Elizabeth Bowen*, ed. Hermione Lee (London: Virago, 1986), p. 53.
12. Sigmund Freud, *Beyond the Pleasure Principle*, trans. James Strachey (London: Hogarth Press, 1950), pp. 36, 37.

13. Samuel Beckett, *The Complete Dramatic Works* (London: Faber, 1986), p. 83 (hereafter *CDW*).
14. Samuel Beckett, 'Three Dialogues with Georges Duthuit', collected in *Disjecta*, ed. Ruby Cohn, p. 139.
15. Elizabeth Bowen, *The Heat of the Day* (London: Jonathan Cape, 1949), pp. 140–1 (hereafter *HD*).
16. Elizabeth Bowen, *Eva Trout or Changing Scenes* (New York: Alfred A. Knopf, reprinted 1968), p. 54 (hereafter *ET*).
17. Frank Kermode, *Essays on Fiction 1971–82* (London: Routledge & Kegan Paul, 1983), p. 72.
18. Elizabeth Bowen, *The Death of the Heart* (Harmondsworth: Penguin, 1962), p. 310.
19. R.F. Foster, 'The Irishness of Elizabeth Bowen', *Paddy and Mr Punch: Connections in Irish and English History* (Harmondsworth: Penguin, 1993), p. 103.
20. Hermione Lee, Introduction to Bowen, *The Mulberry Tree*, p. 4.
21. Samuel Beckett, *Proust and Three Dialogues with Georges Duthuit* (London: John Calder, 1965), pp. 18–19.
22. Elizabeth Bowen, *The Last September* (London: Vintage, reprinted 1998), pp. 25, 45, 34, 137–8 (hereafter *LS*).
23. Sean O'Faolain, 'Elizabeth Bowen, or Romance Does Not Pay', in *The Vanishing Hero: Studies in Novelists of the Twenties* (London: Eyre and Spottiswoode, 1956), pp. 173–4.
24. For a discussion of the Nobel Prize controversy, see the Introduction to John P. Harrington, *The Irish Beckett* (Syracuse: Syracuse University Press, 1993).
25. Sean O'Faolain, 'A Reading and Remembrance of Elizabeth Bowen', *London Review of Books*, 4–17 March 1982, pp. 15–16, quoted in Foster, *Paddy and Mr Punch*, p. 122.
26. Jack Lane and Brendan Clifford (eds), *A North Cork Anthology* (Millstreet: Aubane Historical Society, 1993). See also the same editors' Introduction to *Notes on Eire: Espionage Reports to Winston Churchill 1940–2* (Millstreet: Aubane Historical Society, 1999). Foster's 'The Irishness of Elizabeth Bowen' provides a useful discussion of both texts.
27. Elizabeth Bowen, *Pictures and Conversations*, Foreword by Curtis Brown (London: Allen Lane, 1975), pp. 22–3.
28. R.F. Foster, *The Irish Story: Telling Tales and Making it Up in Ireland* (London: Allen Lane, 2001), p. 155.
29. Elizabeth Bowen, *A Time in Rome* (London: Longman, Green, 1960), p. 42.
30. Samuel Beckett, 'Homage to Jack B. Yeats', collected in *Disjecta*, ed. Ruby Cohn, p. 149.
31. Elizabeth Bowen, *The Hotel* (Harmondsworth: Penguin, reprinted 1943), p. 88 (hereafter *TH*).
32. Corcoran, *Elizabeth Bowen*, p. 75.
33. Barbara Bellow Watson, 'Variations on an Enigma: Elizabeth Bowen's War Novel', in Bloom (ed.), *Modern Critical Views*, p. 100.
34. McCormack, *Dissolute Characters*, p. 208.
35. Quoted in John Fletcher, *The Novels of Samuel Beckett* (London: Chatto & Windus, 1964), p. 59.
36. McCormack, *Dissolute Characters*, p. 219.
37. Samuel Beckett, *As the Story Was Told: Uncollected and Later Prose* (London: John Calder, 1990), p. 25.

38. 'Contemporary', *New Statesman*, 23 (23 May 1942), p. 340.

39. Ellmann, *Elizabeth Bowen*, p. 8.

40. Elizabeth Bowen, *The Collected Stories of Elizabeth Bowen*, Introduction by Angus Wilson (New York: Alfred A. Knopf, 1981), p. 683.

41. Samuel Beckett, extract from *Dream of Fair to Middling Women* and 'The Essential and the Incidental', a review of Sean O'Casey's *Windfalls*, collected in *Disjecta*, ed. Ruby Cohn, pp. 47, 82.

42. Elizabeth Bowen, postscript to *The Demon Lover*, in *The Mulberry Tree*, pp. 95, 99.

43. Review of *In My Good Books* by V. S. Pritchett; 'Sources of Influence', in Elizabeth Bowen, *Afterthought: Pieces about Writing* (London: Longman, Green, 1962), p. 209.

44. Tom Driver, 'Beckett by the Madeleine', in Raymond Federman and Lawrence Graver (eds), *Samuel Beckett: The Critical Heritage* (London: Routledge, 1979), pp. 218–19.

45. Quoted in Foster, 'The Irishness of Elizabeth Bowen', p. 103.

46. Corcoran, *Elizabeth Bowen*, pp. 4, 8.

47. Samuel Beckett, *Watt* (London: John Calder, reprinted 1976) (hereafter *W*).

48. Quoted in Ellmann, *Elizabeth Bowen*, p. 203.

49. Quoted in Ellmann, *Elizabeth Bowen*, p. 206.

50. See Leslie Hill, *Beckett's Fiction: In Different Words* (Cambridge: Cambridge University Press, 1990), p. 34.

51. Bennett and Royle, *Elizabeth Bowen*, p. 142.

52. Corcoran, *Elizabeth Bowen*, p. 200.

2. 'HOW TO MEASURE THIS UNACCOUNTABLE DARKNESS BETWEEN THE TREES'

1. I would like to thank Julian Moynahan and Guarav Majumdar for their insightful comments on earlier versions of this essay.

2 William Heath also suggests that the novel's theme involves internecine warfare and has to do with the opposition between the non-events inside the house and the war taking place outside (38). In a complementary reading, Bennett and Royle relate what they interpret as a dissolution of the boundaries of the protagonist's self to the problematic construction of political boundaries in Ireland in 1920 (14–22). Typically, even the 'love relation' in the novel is viewed as a 'microcosm' of the more elaborately discussed political conflict and generally takes one of two forms: Lois, the protagonist, is either seen as the tragic young innocent, shocked and fatally disappointed by war's realities (writes O'Faolain, Lois is a 'girl emerging, awkwardly for herself and for others into womanhood' and who dreams of romance and has a thirst for life but is 'inadequately wary of its complexities' [1957, 152]), or the aspiring young feminist who longs for something beyond the presumably claustrophobic clamp of a marital relationship and who, by virtue of war's fortunes, escapes potentially tragic unfulfilment; see, for example, Lassner (*Elizabeth Bowen*, 1989, 152–5). In a contrary reading that offers an exciting platform for greater and more complex elaboration, Jacqueline Rose suggests that the representational instability in Bowen's work, including *The Last September*, repudiates the political undercurrents in Bowen's narratives (*On Not Being Able to Sleep*, 93).

3. Other valuable feminist readings of *The Last September* include Claire Hanson's, who writes that Bowen's stories and, by implication, all of Bowen's fictional narratives, were written in 'response to problems of entrapment within the patriarchally

coded adult female body' (73), and Harriet S. Chessman's, who writes about the female characters' alienation from and identification with language (123–38).

4. This queer, 'provisional' quality of Bowen's fictional narratives ('not quite like sleep, not quite like the future', as John Bayley wrote of her short fiction [1988, 166]), the obscure, edgy indeterminacy that undoes our efforts at conceptual clarity has been noted by a few earlier readers, including William Trevor, who notes that '[t]here are echoes of mystery in many of Elizabeth Bowen's stories, like reverberations after an explosion that has not itself been heard' (1981, 131), and Harriet Blodgett, who suggests that Bowen's 'resonantly allusive' prose will not bear 'too literal reading' (1975, 24).

5. Of Bowen's past readers who have approached the troubling instability in her prose, Robert Caserio has perhaps been most astute when he describes the 'conflict of unity and disunity' (1999, 265) that he sees in her work. Bowen's stories have a 'habit of ruining or muting oppositions'; quoting Bowen, he writes that they pursue '"a thinning of the membrane between the this and the that"' (271).

6. It is worth noting, as Jocelyn Brooke has, that of the great novelists of the nineteenth and twentieth centuries, including Dickens, Hardy, Lawrence, Woolf, James and Joyce, only Bowen has not created any memorable characters. As he writes, even the characters in *The Heat of the Day*, Bowen's novel which is most often cited as being well and legibly plotted, seem to inhabit 'a kind of a limbo' (25). Think of Lois, the protagonist of *The Last September*, for example, although we might just as well be considering any of Bowen's artless and uncertain protagonists, including Jane, the unconcentrated protagonist of *A World of Love* (1955); Emmaline, the erratically recessive and prominent main character of *To the North* (1932); Callie, the undetermined main character of 'Mysterious Kôr'; or the uncondensed Tibbie of 'The Girl with the Stoop'. Although the relative vagueness of these characters is often attributed to a kind of inherent innocence, Bowen's female protagonists are more often united by a want of clearly defined qualities and especially by a want of clearly motivated actions and condensed purposes than by any moral or ethical choices that might lead one to characterize them as innocent or guilty. For more on this aspect of Bowen's strange characters, see Osborn ('Reconsidering Elizabeth Bowen', 2006, 190–2).

7. As Brooke has noted, Bowen's stories can hardly, with the possible exception of *The Heat of the Day*, be said to have plots at all (8).

8. Elizabeth Bowen, *The Last September* (1929; New York, 1979), 218. All references are to this edition and will be cited in the text.

9. She is the missing 'link', as Victoria Glendinning regrettably claims, connecting 'Virginia Woolf with Iris Murdoch and Muriel Spark' (*Biography*, New York, 1978, xv). More often, she is cited, with an undercurrent of disdainful largesse, as a 'less experimental heir to Virginia Woolf' (Kershner, 68). As Bennett and Royle have noted, this unfortunate hierarchical comparison has done much to constrain Bowen's literary reputation and to relegate her to the status of a minor novelist (xvi).

10. For a sensitive discussion of the effects of Woolf's periodicity, see McCluskey, *Reverberations*, 1986, especially 122–6.

11. In a fairly feckless if well-intentioned passage, Heath, specifically citing Bowen's penchant for double negatives, suggests that they may support, in some way he seems unsure of, Bowen's 'defiantly' avowed intentions (and here he refers to her essay 'Notes on Writing a Novel'), even as he owns that these 'tricks' form

'deliberate trials of the reader's patience' (142). More recently, Roy Foster has written that '[Bowen's] more risky and over-the-top passages do not always come off' (*Irish Story*, New York, 2002, 149), while Paul West simply dismisses her fiction, complaining that her narratives are 'too oblique, too exacting' in their demands on the reader (77). In an early and suggestively ambivalent reading, Jocelyn Brooke observed that Bowen's complex style (which he likens to a kind of 'neurotic impediment, a kind of stammer') creates a 'distorted, fragmentary effect' that, in places, 'leads to actual obscurity' (25, 26).

12. Lee is here quoting Elizabeth Hardwick, who mocks Bowen in a *Partisan Review* essay noteworthy more for its provincialism than its insight ('Elizabeth Bowen's Fiction', 1949, 1114–21), and John McCormick in his *Catastrophe and Imagination* (1952, 93).

13. Although his discussion is not lengthy, in a contrary reading, Paul Muldoon, writing specifically about 'The Tommy Crans', has noted the formal and thematic 'concomitancy' of 'discrete coexistent realms' in Bowen's work, a characteristic that he suggests ties her work to Joyce's and Beckett's and that positions her work, along with theirs, 'at some notional cutting edge' (24, 25).

14. Bowen's narratives have been called pictorial and, in some ways, her narratives are painterly. But they call to mind less the representational work of Sargent or the fragmented perspectives of Picasso than they do the epigraphic ornamentation found in Islamic art that functions simultaneously both as writing and decoration. In other words, because Bowen's strange prose possesses both decorative and representational qualities, it both shows and tells.

15. For recent examinations of some of those critiques, see Prendergast, Melberg, Potolsky and Burwick. For an excellent, wide-ranging and recent discussion of issues associated with the history and aesthetics of mimesis, see Halliwell.

16. As George Levine notes in *The Realistic Imagination*, a 'topographical survey' of novels in the realist canon would produce an 'unilluminating catalog'. As he notes, be it Dingley Dell, or Loamshire, or the Belgian lowlands, landscapes in realist novels are 'barely varied by the slightest rise' (216, 208); one thinks more of Dutch realism than Turner when reading these landscapes. Extremes such as we see in Bowen's descriptions of psychic intensity, violent behaviour or geography are generally avoided.

3. DEAD LETTERS AND LIVING THINGS

1. William Heath, *Elizabeth Bowen: An Introduction to Her Novels* (Madison: University of Wisconsin Press, 1961); Neil Corcoran, *Elizabeth Bowen: The Enforced Return* (Oxford: Clarendon Press, 2004); Maud Ellmann, *Elizabeth Bowen: The Shadow Across the Page* (Edinburgh: Edinburgh University Press, 2003), cited in Susan Osborn, 'Reconsidering Elizabeth Bowen', *Modern Fiction Studies*, 52(1), 2006, pp. 188–90.

2. Osborn, 'Reconsidering Elizabeth Bowen', p. 189.

3. Alain Badiou, *Ethics: An Essay on the Understanding of Evil* [1998], trans. Peter Hallward (London: Verso, 2001), p. 67.

4. Sigi Jöttkandt, *Acting Beautifully: Henry James and the Ethical Aesthetic* (New York: SUNY Press, 2005), p. 128.

5. Dany Nobus, *Jacques Lacan and the Freudian Practice of Psychoanalysis* (London: Routledge, 2000), pp. 135–6.

6. Jacques Lacan, *The Four Fundamental Concepts of Psycho-Analysis* [1973], trans. Alan Sheridan (London: Vintage, 1998), pp. 129, 188.
7. Linda Belau, 'Trauma and the Material Signifier', *Postmodern Culture*, 11(2), 2001, paragraph 3 (http:\\muse.jhu.edu/journals/pmc/v011/11.2belau.html).
8. Elizabeth Bowen, 'Out of a Book' [1946], in *The Mulberry Tree: Writings of Elizabeth Bowen*, ed. Hermione Lee (London: Virago, 1986), p. 53.
9. Joan Copjec, '*Gai Savoir Sera*: The Science of Love and the Insolence of Chance', in Gabriel Riera (ed.), *Alain Badiou: Philosophy and Its Conditions* (New York: SUNY Press, 2005), pp. 133–4.
10. Corcoran, *Elizabeth Bowen*, p. 3.
11. R.F. Foster, 'Prints on the Scene: Elizabeth Bowen and the Landscape of Childhood', in *The Irish Story: Telling Tales and Making it Up in Ireland* (Harmondsworth: Penguin, 2001), p. 161.
12. Elizabeth Bowen, *The House in Paris* [1935] (London: Vintage, 1998), p. 39. Further references are given in the text.
13. Lacan, *Fundamental Concepts*, p. 185.
14. Jacqueline Rose, 'Negativity in the Work of Melanie Klein', in *Why War: Psychoanalysis, Politics, and the Return to Melanie Klein* (Oxford: Blackwell, 1993), pp. 174, 176.
15. The same pre-inhabited quality is registered by Karen when she visits Rushbrook. *The House in Paris*, p. 77.
16. Geoff Layton, *Germany: The Third Reich, 1933–45* (London: Hodder & Stoughton, 1992), p. 89, cited in Jean Radford, 'Late Modernism and the Politics of History', in Maroula Joannou (ed.), *Women Writers of the 1930s: Gender, Politics and History* (Edinburgh: Edinburgh University Press, 1999), p. 42.
17. Nobus, *Jacques Lacan*, pp. 79–80.
18. Elizabeth Bowen, *The Death of the Heart* [1938] (London: Vintage, 1998), p. 18. Further references are given in the text.
19. Gérard Wajcman, 'The Birth of the Intimate', trans. Barbara P. Fulks, *lacanian ink*, 23, 2004, pp. 57–81.
20. Joan Copjec, 'The Tomb of Perseverance: On *Antigone*', in Joan Copjec and Michael Sorkin (eds), *Giving Ground: The Politics of Propinquity* (London: Verso, 1999), p. 257.

4. MUMBO-JUMBO

1. Quoted by Brown, who adds, 'she adhered to this ethic, but no one could have written her books who had not this feeling – however kept in bonds by the novelist – of the supernatural and no one can read her books without being aware of it' (Brown, 1974, xxvi). Angus Wilson writes of 'her apparent total acceptance of ghosts, of the occult' (Wilson, 1982, 10). Morris also quotes this passage (Morris, 1990, 114).
2. This passage continues, 'not knowing who the dead were you could not know which might be the staircase somebody for the first time was not mounting that morning'. As McCormack says, 'in this the conventional ghost-story attention to footsteps on the staircase is inverted and intensified' (McCormack, 1993, 224). Bowen elsewhere writes of the bombed-out, near Regent's Park: 'Illicitly, leading the existence of ghosts, we overlook the locked park' (*The Mulberry Tree*, New York, 1986, 24). See also Maud Ellmann's 'The Shadowy Fifth' (2001, 15), on the subject of the devastations of war.

3. Corcoran argues that *A World of Love* is the closest 'to the explicit supernaturalism of some of her short stories' (Corcoran, 2004, 64).

4. Christensen notes a 'word-cluster that has to do with the supernatural: Black Mass, Circe, devil, enchant, fetichism, fey, ghost, harpies, haunt, magic, mumbo-jumbo, obsession, omen, phantasmagoric, phantom, poltergeist, revenant, superstition, trance, visitant, voodoo, witch, witch-balls, etc.' (Christensen, 2001, 95).

5. Ian Watt in *The Rise of The Novel* defines realism as 'the premise or primary convention that the novel is a full and authentic report of human experience, and is therefore under an obligation to satisfy its reader with such detail of the story as the individuality of the actors concerned, the particularities of the times and places of their actions, details which are presented through a more largely referential use of language than is common in other literary forms' (1964, 32). Rosen and Zerner, basing their discussion on Flaubert's letters, think of it rather as the mode that allows 'the mediocre to retain its mediocrity', while abandoning 'grand rhetorical gestures' (Rosen and Zerner, 1984, 146).

6. *The Little Girls* (1982, 12). Unless otherwise indicated, all parenthetical references are to this novel.

7. The third Aldermaston March (against nuclear weapons), at which this conversation seems to be set, took place in 1960.

8. An 'Appendix' to *The Four-Gated City* moves into the kind of science-fiction writing that engaged Lessing for the next few years, but my quotation comes from the main body of the novel, which uses the realist mode characteristic of the rest of the *Children of Violence* series. The first chapter of Michael Innes's *Hare Sitting Up* (1959) provides an example of mystery writing with the same preoccupations.

9. Bennett and Royle describe Bowen's novels as 'demonstrably and powerfully Shakespearean' (Bennett and Royle, 1995, 84). For references to Shakespeare in *A World of Love* and *The Last September*, see Corcoran (2004, 67). Christensen notes the references to *Macbeth* in *The Little Girls*, but without interpretation (Christensen, 2001, 116).

10. The narrator, who becomes an artist, paints a picture she calls 'Three Witches', which depicts the sofas in the three girls' homes. Further *Macbeth* references may be found on pp. 262-4, 321, 357, and 368.

11. Two of Bowen's short stories, 'Charity' and 'The Jungle', deal with these power-relations as they affect little girls. Coughlan sees 'strong lesbian feeling' in the latter (120). It should be noted that Mme Fisher's power over men is just as strong and even more destructive than her power over women.

12. Glendinning's account seems more accurate: 'the three learn to attempt through kindness a synthesis between past and present, between innocence and experience' (*Biography*, 1979, 248).

13. Clare's reference, of course, is to *Twelfth Night* (I.iv.263). Dinah gets no clear answer to her question, '"Are you a Lesbian, Mumbo?"' (197), but there is a clear parallel between this question and her earlier query as to whether Sheila has ever killed anybody, the answer to which is 'not exactly' (150). Smith notes this parallel, saying that it indicates that 'Clare is in some sense a lesbian' (Smith, 1997, 110). hoogland, like Smith and Coughlan, approaches Bowen 'from a Lesbian feminist angle' (hoogland, 1994, 21); Jane Rule's earlier study takes a somewhat similar approach (Rule, 1975).

14. It is on p. 121 of 237 pages.

15. Or, at least, in one autumn during the early 1960s. For a discussion of the implications of this structure, and a comparison with the similar structure of *The House in*

Paris, see Marian Kelly's article (Kelly, 2002). In *The House in Paris* the childhood scenes surround the adult scene, whereas here the adult scenes surround the childhood scene, although in both cases the central act is chronologically earlier. Moreover, here the central childhood narrative is told directly, whereas in *The House in Paris* it is represented as a narrative that could be told 'only in Heaven' (63).

16. Corcoran writes that 'the aftermath of the first world war is as acute in Bowen as it is in Virginia Woolf' (Corcoran, 2004, 68).

17. Wyatt-Brown discusses the role of mourning in the two last novels fully (Wyatt-Brown, 1993).

18. Phyllis Lassner notes that 'Bowen . . . pays greater attention to the lack of access to self-expression for female characters than Woolf' (Lassner, 1990, 163).

19. Bowen records taking part in a similar 'burying ritual' when she was at Harpenden school, but says that it was 'less impressive, more scatterbrained, and had a tinge of facetiousness', unlike the fictional burial (*Pictures and Conversations*, 1974, 57). This 'burying ritual' happened soon after her mother's death (*Afterthoughts*, 1962, 41).

20. Her house at 2 Clarence Terrace, Regent's Park was badly bombed at the beginning of the Blitz in 1940 and then later in the V1 attacks of 1944 (Glendinning, *Biography*, 1979, 146–9).

21. Bennett and Royle draw attention to Karen's thoughts about photographs (Bennett and Royle, 1995, 59).

22. Of course she could not entirely keep to this decision. In the last pages of the novel, for instance, she does tell us what Clare is thinking and feeling.

23. Lee seems not to have read this novel with her usual care. Her description of Frank as 'a faint reworking of Major Brutt and drawn presumably from Alan Cameron' (*Estimation*, 200), distorts Bowen's presentation of this handsome, lovelorn and fantastic character, who resembles Major Brutt only in his army rank, while Francis, Dinah's 'houseboy', cannot convincingly be described as 'a faint reworking of Eddie' (*Estimation*, 200).

24. Jordan complains of 'stiff characters' and a 'narrow plot' (1992, 182). *The Little Girls* has its admirers, too. Bennett and Royle, for instance, describe it as 'Bowen's most sustained, most hilarious and devastating analysis of the work of the past on people's lives: the transition of the past into the present. But it also concerns posterity . . . and the attempt by the living to live among them' (Bennett and Royle, 1995, 121).

25. Some critics believe she hits her head on the steps to the cave; I have always understood that she hits her head against the ground, swinging with her body hanging over the swing, as she did in her childhood.

26. Corcoran sees Bowen as being 'drawn to fracture or disintegration' (Corcoran, 2004, 13).

27. Bennett and Royle's interesting observation about the careful datedness of the novel in relation to the cars of the 1960s – bubble cars, Hillmans, mini-minors, Triumph coupés – is relevant here (Bennett and Royle, 1995, 172).

28. Maud Ellmann, however, finds them 'perilously cute' (*Elizabeth Bowen*, 194).

5. 'SHE'-WARD BOUND

1. Even Nicola Humble qualifies her readings of Bowen as 'middlebrow': 'Elizabeth Bowen's work, with its writerly qualities and philosophical concerns, is located at the highbrow end of the middlebrow. Her novels nonetheless share many of the

typical preoccupations and stylistic features of the feminine middlebrow' (Humble, 2001, 78).

2. San Diego, 1986 (hereafter *MT*).

3. Hopewell, 1981 (hereafter *CS*).

4. London, 1976 (hereafter *HiP*).

5. The sardonic use of juxtaposition in the following sentences makes Mme Fisher's character painfully (and comically) clear: 'She wanted to be with some gaunt, contemptuous person who twisted life his own way . . . An hour later she went to the post again, this time with a letter to Mme Fisher [asking to be able to visit]' (*HiP*, 79).

6. Indeed one could argue that all of the mesmerizing older women who inevitably prove detrimental to their young protégées are in fact versions of Ayesha.

7. '[In Leopold, s]he reread a known map of thought and passion in miniature' (*HiP*, 202); '"If you were less a child, I could enjoy more thoroughly my short time of being alive again"' (*HiP*, 204).

8. Of course the association of realism and drawing-room comedy is not immediate; however, in Bowen's fiction I suggest that both traditions share a tendency to disavow the extraordinary typical of sensationalist genres, thus making them antagonistic forces.

9. London, 1976 (hereafter *HD*).

10. Indeed, given the purple prose obvious in the quotes from Haggard's novels, and Valerie Pedlar's affirmation that sensation novels' subject matter – 'extreme situations' – causes 'rhetoric veer[ing] towards exaggeration' (Pedlar, 2001, 50), one may argue that the very fraught nature of Bowen's style is itself proof of sensationalist influence.

11. This could perhaps be associated with *The Moonstone*, for example, where the detective's investigation is finally undertaken and resolved by private individuals.

12. 'An inexplicable phenomenon takes place; to give in to his deterministic spirit, the reader must choose between two solutions: either the phenomenon must be explained by common causes . . . making the extraordinary facts into works of imagination; or it must be labelled as supernatural . . . The fantastic lasts as long as this uncertainty lasts; once the reader opts for one solution or the other, he moves towards the uncanny or the marvellous' (Todorov, 1971, 186, my translation).

6. TERRITORY, SPACE, MODERNITY

1. A classic example of this is in the story 'The Inherited Clock', which I discuss later in the essay.

2. Pearsall's A–Z was based on twelve hardback notebooks filled with sketches, house numbers and street names that constituted her research; her method was to walk radially from a central point (Charing Cross) – spatiation in its most literal sense.

3. *OED*, 'claustrophobic'.

4. *OED*, 'agoraphobic', Alix Strachey's translation of Freud's *Inhibitions, Symptoms and Anxieties* in *The Collected Works*, 1936.

5. See *The Times*, 2 June 1933; 12 July 1933; 15 July 1933.

6. Joseph Conrad to Edward Garnett, 12 March 1897.

7. For Bowen's wartime work, see Victoria Glendinning, *Elizabeth Bowen: Portrait of a Writer* (London: Weidenfeld & Nicolson, 1977), Heather Bryant Jordan, *How Will the Heart Endure: Elizabeth Bowen and the Landscape of War* (Ann Arbor: University of Michigan Press, 1992), and Hermione Lee, *Elizabeth Bowen* (London: Vintage, 1999).

8. For Bowen's interest in stillness (to the point of catatonia), see Andrew Bennett and Nicholas Royle, *Elizabeth Bowen and the Dissolution of the Novel* (Basingstoke: Palgrave Macmillan, 1995).

9. For a compelling reading of Bowen's interest in Euclidian geometrical forms, see Maud Ellmann, *Elizabeth Bowen: The Shadow Across the Page* (Edinburgh: Edinburgh University Press, 2003). To further Ellmann's brilliant analysis of Bowen's geometric love-plots, 'In the Square' features a square with a missing corner: Magdela, Rupert, Gina, her 'regular' and, of course, the missing corner, the owner of the house in the square, Anthony.

10. Definition of a 'blast wave' from *OED*, 1939.

11. 'Only the wireless in the library conducted the world's urgency to the place. Wave after wave of war news broke upon the quiet air of the room and, in the daytime when the windows were open, passed out on to the sunny or overcast lawns' (*BC*, 457).

12. See Phyllis Pearsall, *Women at War: Drawn and Overheard by Phyllis Pearsall* (Aldershot: Ashgate, 1990), p. 11.

13. See *Front Line 1940–1: The Official Story of the Civil Defence of Britain* (London: HMSO, 1942), p. 73.

14. See 'Bedroom Problems in Wartime', in Anon., *An Enquiry into People's Homes: A Report Prepared by Mass-Observation for the Advertising Service Guild* (London: John Murray, 1943), pp. 76–7. Mass-Observation's survey of a C-class housing area in a small town found that 'in 1942, eight out of every ten houses were full compared with five out of ten in 1939, while the proportion of empty bedrooms fell from one-fifth to one-twentieth'. The situation in London, even in Bowen's own rarefied milieu, with one in five houses destroyed or damaged, was much more acute.

15. Elizabeth Bowen to Isaiah Berlin, 23 September 1936: MS, Berlin Archive, Wolfson College, Oxford.

16. For a bravura reading of spaces in *The Heat of the Day*, see Ellmann, *Shadow*, 2003, pp. 151–64.

7. NARRATIVE, MEANING AND AGENCY IN *THE HEAT OF THE DAY*

1. In addition to the critics cited in this article, many others, including Barbara Brothers, Robert L. Caserio, John Coates, Thomas Dukes, Phyllis Lassner, Kristine Miller, Petra Rau and Shannon Wells-Lassagne have written insightful commentary on *The Heat of the Day*.

Bibliography

Works by Elizabeth Bowen

Afterthoughts: Pieces about Writing, London: Longman, Green, 1962.

Bowen's Court, Introduction by Hermione Lee, London: Vintage, 1999.

The Collected Stories of Elizabeth Bowen, Introduction by Angus Wilson, Hopewell, NJ: Ecco Press, 1981.

The Collected Stories of Elizabeth Bowen, Introduction by Angus Wilson, New York: Alfred A. Knopf, 1981.

The Death of the Heart, London: Vintage, 1998.

The Death of the Heart, Harmondsworth: Penguin, 1962.

The Death of the Heart, New York: Vintage, 1955.

The Demon Lover and Other Stories, London: Jonathan Cape, 1945.

'Elizabeth Bowen: *The Little Girls*', in *Before Publication*, BBC, 16 February 1964, transcript.

Eva Trout or Changing Scenes, London: Penguin, 1968.

Eva Trout or Changing Scenes, New York: Alfred A Knopf, 1968.

Friends and Relations, London: Penguin, 1959.

Friends and Relations, Harmondsworth: Penguin, 1943.

The Heat of the Day, New York: Anchor Books, 2002.

The Heat of the Day, London: Penguin, 1976.

The Heat of the Day, London: Jonathan Cape, 1949.

The Heat of the Day, New York: Alfred Knopf, 1949.

The Hotel, Harmondsworth: Penguin, 1943.

The House in Paris, New York: Anchor Books, 2002.

The House in Paris, London: Vintage, 1998.

The House in Paris, New York: Avon Books, 1979.

The House in Paris, Introduction by A. S. Byatt, London: Penguin, 1976.

The Last September, New York: Anchor Books, 2000.

The Last September, London: Vintage, 1998.

The Last September, New York: Avon, 1979.

The Last September, London: Penguin, 1952.

The Little Girls, Harmondsworth: Penguin, 1982.

The Mulberry Tree: Writings of Elizabeth Bowen, selected and introduced by Hermione Lee, London: Vintage, 1999.

The Mulberry Tree: Writings of Elizabeth Bowen, ed. Hermione Lee, London: Virago, 1986.

The Mulberry Tree: Writings of Elizabeth Bowen, ed. Hermione Lee, New York: Harcourt Brace Jovanovich, 1986.

The Mulberry Tree: Writings of Elizabeth Bowen, ed. Hermione Lee, San Diego: Harcourt Brace Jovanovich, 1986.

'Out of a Book', in *The Mulberry Tree: Writings of Elizabeth Bowen*, ed. Hermione Lee, London: Virago, 1986.

Pictures and Conversations, Foreword by Curtis Brown, London: Allen Lane, 1975.

Pictures and Conversations, New York: Alfred A. Knopf, 1974.

A Time in Rome, London: Longman, Green, 1960.

To the North, London: Penguin, 1960.

To the North, London: Victor Gollancz, 1932.

Why Do I Write? An Exchange of Views between Elizabeth Bowen, Graham Greene & V. S. Pritchett, London: Percival Marshall, 1948.

A World of Love, Harmondsworth: Penguin, 1987.

Secondary works

Anderson, Benedict, *Imagined Communities: Reflections on the Origin and Spread of Nationalism*, New York: Verso, 2006.

Anon., *An Enquiry into People's Homes: A Report Prepared by Mass-Observation for the Advertising Service Guild*, London: John Murray, 1943.

Atwood, Margaret, *Cat's Eye*, Toronto: Seal Books, 1989.

Badiou, Alain, *Ethics: An Essay on the Understanding of Evil* [1998], trans. Peter Hallward, London: Verso, 2001.

Barthes, Roland, 'L'effet de réel', in *Littérature et réalité*, Paris: Seuil, 1981, pp. 81–90.

— 'L'effet de réel', *Communications*, 11, 1968.

— *S/Z*, Paris: Seuil, 1970.

Bayley, John, *The Short Story: Henry James to Elizabeth Bowen*, New York: St Martin's Press, 1988.

Beckett, Samuel, *As the Story Was Told: Uncollected and Later Prose*, London: John Calder, 1990.

—*The Complete Dramatic Works*, London: Faber, 1986.

— *Disjecta: Miscellaneous Writings and a Dramatic Fragment*, ed. Ruby Cohn, London: John Calder, 1983.

— *Murphy*, London: Picador, 1973 edn.

— *Proust and Three Dialogues with Georges Duthuit*, London: John Calder, 1965.

— *Watt*, London: John Calder, 1976 rpt.

Belau, Linda, 'Trauma and the Material Signifier', *Postmodern Culture*, 11(2), 2001 (available at: http://muse.jhu.edu/journals/pmc/v011/11.2belau.html).

Bennett, Andrew, and Nicholas Royle, *Elizabeth Bowen and the Dissolution of the Novel: Still Lives*, Basingstoke: Palgrave Macmillan, and New York: St Martin's Press, 1995.

Blackmur, R.P., 'Examples of Wallace Stevens', *Selected Essays of R. P. Blackmur*, New York: Ecco, 1986.

Blodgett, Harriet, *Patterns of Reality: Elizabeth Bowen's Novels*, The Hague: Mouton, 1975.

Bloom, Harold (ed. and intro), *Modern Critical Views: Elizabeth Bowen*, New York, New Haven, Philadelphia: Chelsea House, 1987.

Brooke, Jocelyn, *Elizabeth Bowen*, London: Longman, Green, 1952.

Brown, Spencer Curtis, 'Foreword', in Elizabeth Bowen, *Pictures and Conversations*, New York: Alfred A. Knopf, 1974, pp. vii–xlii.

Burwick, Frederick, *Mimesis and its Romantic Reflections*, University Park, PA: Pennsylvania State University Press, 2001.

Caserio, Robert L., *The Novel in England 1900–1950: History and Theory*, New York: Twayne, 1999.

Chessman, Harriet S., 'Women and Language in the Fiction of Elizabeth Bowen', in Harold Bloom (ed.), *Modern Critical Views: Elizabeth Bowen*, New York, New Haven, Philadelphia: Chelsea House, 1987, pp. 123–38.

Christensen, Lis, *Elizabeth Bowen: The Later Fiction*, University of Copenhagen: Museum Tusculanum Press, 2001.

Collins, Wilkie, *The Moonstone* [1868], London: Penguin, 1994.

Conrad, Joseph, *The Collected Letters of Joseph Conrad*, ed. Frederick R. Karl and Laurence Davies, vol. I, Cambridge: Cambridge University Press, 1983.

Copjec, Joan, '*Gai Savoir Sera*: The Science of Love and the Insolence of Chance', in Gabriel Riera (ed.), *Alain Badiou: Philosophy and Its Conditions*, New York: SUNY Press, 2005.

— 'The Tomb of Perseverance: On *Antigone*', in Joan Copjec and Michael Sorkin (eds), *Giving Ground: The Politics of Propinquity*, London: Verso, 1999.

Corcoran, Neil, *Elizabeth Bowen: The Enforced Return*, Oxford: Oxford University Press, 2004.

Coroneos, Con, *Space, Conrad and Modernity*, Oxford: Oxford University Press, 2002.

Coughlan, Patricia, 'Women and Desire in the Work of Elizabeth Bowen', in Eibhear Walshe (ed.), *Sex, Nation and Dissent in Irish Writing*, Cork: Cork University Press, 1997, pp. 103–34.

Dorenkamp, Angela, 'Fall or Leap: Bowen's *The Heat of the Day*', *Critique: Studies in Modern Fiction*, 10(3), 1968: 13–21.

Eagleton, Terry, 'Form and Ideology in the Anglo-Irish Novel', in *Heathcliff and the Great Hunger: Studies in Irish Culture*, London: Verso, 1995, pp. 145–225.

Eco, Umberto, *A Theory of Semiotics*, Bloomington: Indiana University Press, 1976.

Ellmann, Maud, *Elizabeth Bowen: The Shadow Across the Page*, Edinburgh: Edinburgh University Press, 2003.

—'Elizabeth Bowen: The Shadowy Fifth', in Rod Mengham and N.H. Reeve (eds), *The Fiction of the 1940s: Stories of Survival*, Basingstoke: Palgrave Macmillan, 2001, pp. 1–26.

Ermarth, Elizabeth Deeds, *Notes from Realism and Consensus in the English Novel*, Princeton: Princeton University Press, 1983.

Federman, Raymond, and Lawrence Graver (eds), *Samuel Beckett: The Critical Heritage*, London: Routledge, 1979.

Fletcher, John, *The Novels of Samuel Beckett*, London: Chatto & Windus, 1964.

Foster, R.F., *The Irish Story: Telling Tales and Making It Up in Ireland*, New York and Oxford: Oxford University Press, 2002; London: Allen Lane, 2001.

– *Paddy and Mr Punch: Connections in Irish and English History*, Harmondsworth: Penguin, 1993.

– 'Prints on the Scene: Elizabeth Bowen and the Landscape of Childhood', in *The Irish Story: Telling Tales and Making It Up in Ireland*, Harmondsworth: Penguin, 2001.

Foucault, Michel, 'Questions of Geography', in *Power/Knowledge: Selected Interviews and Other Writings 1972–1977*, trans. Colin Gordon et al., Brighton: Harvester Press, 1980, pp. 63–77.

Freud, Sigmund, *Beyond the Pleasure Principle*, trans. James Strachey, London: Hogarth Press, 1950.

Front Line 1940–1: The Official Story of the Civil Defence of Britain, London: HMSO, 1942.

Glendinning, Victoria, *Elizabeth Bowen: A Biography*, New York: Avon Books, 1979; New York: Alfred A. Knopf, 1978.

– *Elizabeth Bowen: Portrait of a Writer*, London: Weidenfeld & Nicolson, 1977.

Glover, Edward, 'Notes on the Psychological Effects of War Conditions on the Civilian Population, Part III: The "Blitz" - 1940-1', *International Journal of Psychoanalysis*, 23(1), 1942: 17–37.

Gontarski, S.E., *The Intent of Undoing in Samuel Beckett's Dramatic Texts*, Bloomington: Indiana University Press, 1985.

Haggard, H. Rider, *Ayesha: The Return of She* [1904], Whitefish, MT: Kessinger, 2005.

– *She* [1887], Ware, Hertfordshire: Wordsworth, 1995.

Halliwell, Stephen, *The Aesthetics of Mimesis: Ancient Texts and Modern Problems*, Princeton: Princeton University Press, 2002.

Hanson, Claire, *Hysterical Fictions: The 'Woman's Novel' in the Twentieth Century*, New York: St Martin's Press, 2000.

Hardwick, Elizabeth, 'Elizabeth Bowen's Fiction', *Partisan Review*, 16, November 1949: 1114–21.

Harrington, John P., *The Irish Beckett*, Syracuse: Syracuse University Press, 1993.

Harrisson, Tom, *Living Through the Blitz*, London: Collins, 1976.

Hartley, Sarah, *Mrs. P's Journey: The Remarkable Story of the Woman who Created the A–Z Map*, London: Simon & Schuster, 2001.

Heath, William, *Elizabeth Bowen: An Introduction to Her Novels*, Madison: University of Wisconsin Press, 1961.

Hill, Leslie, *Beckett's Fiction: In Different Words*, Cambridge: Cambridge University Press, 1990.

— 'Flaubert and the Rhetoric of Stupidity', *Critical Inquiry*, 3(26), Winter 1976.

hoogland, renée c., *Elizabeth Bowen: A Reputation in Writing*, New York: New York University Press, 1994.

Hopkins, Chris, 'Elizabeth Bowen', *Review of Contemporary Fiction*, 21(2), 2001: 114–51.

Humble, Nicola, *The Feminine Middlebrow Novel 1920s to 1950s: Class, Domesticity and Bohemianism*, Oxford: Oxford University Press, 2001.

Innes, Michael, *Hare Sitting Up*, New York: Berkeley Medallion Books, 1959.

Jordan, Heather Bryant, *How Will the Heart Endure: Elizabeth Bowen and the Landscape of War*, Ann Arbor: University of Michigan Press, 1992.

— 'The Territory of Elizabeth Bowen's Wartime Short Stories', *The Library Chronicle of the University of Texas at Austin*, 48, 1989: 69–85.

Jöttkandt, Sigi, *Acting Beautifully: Henry James and the Ethical Aesthetic*, New York: SUNY Press, 2005.

Kelly, Marian, 'The Power of the Past: Structural Nostalgia in Elizabeth Bowen's *The House in Paris* and *The Little Girls*', *Style*, 36, 2002: 1–18.

Kemp, Sandra, 'But One Isn't Murdered: Elizabeth Bowen's *The Little Girls*', in Clive Bloom (ed.), *Twentieth Century Suspense: The Thriller Comes of Age*, Basingstoke: Macmillan, 1990, pp. 130–42.

Kenney, Edwin J., *Elizabeth Bowen*, London: Associated University Presses, 1975.

Kermode, Frank, *The Classic: Literary Images of Permanence and Change*, New York: Viking Press, 1975.

— *Essays on Fiction 1971–82*, London: Routledge & Kegan Paul, 1983.

Kern, Stephen, *The Culture of Time and Space 1880–1918*, London: Weidenfeld & Nicolson, 1983.

Kershner, R.B., *The Twentieth-Century Novel: An Introduction*, Boston: Bedford, 1997.

Lacan, Jacques, *The Four Fundamental Concepts of Psycho-Analysis* [1973], trans. Alan Sheridan, London: Vintage, 1998.

Lane, Jack, and Brendan Clifford (eds), *A North Cork Anthology*, Millstreet: Aubane Historical Society, 1993.

— *Notes on Eire: Espionage Reports to Winston Churchill 1940–2*, Millstreet: Aubane Historical Society, 1999.

Lassner, Phyllis, *Women Writers: Elizabeth Bowen*, Basingstoke: Macmillan, 1990; Savage, MD: Barnes & Noble, 1989.

Layton, Geoff, *Germany: The Third Reich, 1933–45*, London: Hodder & Stoughton, 1992.

Lee, Hermione, *Elizabeth Bowen*, London: Vintage, 1999.

— *Elizabeth Bowen: An Estimation*, London: Vision Press, 1981.

—'Re-reading Elizabeth Bowen', in Maureen Bell, Shirley Chew et al. (eds), *Reconstructing the Book: Literary Texts in Transmission*, Aldershot: Ashgate, 2001, pp. 148–57.

LeFanu, Joseph Sheridan, *Uncle Silas: A Tale of Bartram-Haugh* [1864], New York: Dover, 1966.

Lefebvre, Henri, *The Production of Space*, trans. Donald Nicholson-Smith, Oxford: Basil Blackwell, 1991.

Lessing, Doris, *The Four-Gated City*, St Alban's: Panther, 1972.

Levine, George, *The Realistic Imagination: English Fiction from Frankenstein to Lady Chatterley*, Chicago: University of Chicago Press, 1981.

Magot, Céine, 'Elizabeth Bowen's London in *The Heat of the Day*', *Literary London*, 3(1), 2005 (http://www.literarylondon.org/London-journal/march2005/Magot.html.

McCluskey, Kathleen, *Reverberations: Sound and Structure in the Novels of Virginia Woolf*, Ann Arbor, MI: UMI Research, 1986.

McCormack, W.J., *Dissolute Characters: Irish Literary History through Balzac, Sheridan LeFanu, Yeats, and Bowen*, Manchester and New York: Manchester University Press, 1993.

McCormick, John, *Catastrophe and Imagination*, London: Longman, 1952.

Melberg, Arne, *Theories of Mimesis*, Cambridge: Cambridge University Press, 1995.

Mengham, Rod, 'Broken Glass', in Rod Mengham and N. H. Reeve (eds), *The Fiction of the 1940s: Stories of Survival*, Basingstoke: Palgrave Macmillan, 2001, pp. 124–33.

Meredith, George, *Collected Poems*, London: Constable, 1912.

Merrifield, Andy, *Henri Lefebvre: A Critical Introduction*, London: Routledge, 2006.

Meyer, Leonard B., *Music, the Arts, and Ideas: Patterns and Predictions in Twentieth-Century Culture*, Chicago: University of Chicago Press, 1967.

Miller, Kristine A. '"Even a shelter's not safe": The Blitz on Homes in Elizabeth Bowen's Wartime Writing', *Twentieth Century Literature*, 45(2), 1999: 138–58.

Morris, J.A., 'Elizabeth Bowen's Stories of Suspense', in Clive Bloom (ed.), *Twentieth Century Suspense: The Thriller Comes of Age*, Basingstoke: Macmillan, 1990, pp. 114–29.

Moynahan, Julian, *Anglo-Irish: The Literary Imagination in a Hyphenated Culture*, Princeton: Princeton University Press, 1995.

Muldoon, Paul, *To Ireland, I*, Oxford: Oxford University Press, 2000.

Nobus, Dany, *Jacques Lacan and the Freudian Practice of Psychoanalysis*, London: Routledge, 2000.

O'Faolain, Sean, *The Vanishing Hero: Studies in Novels of the Twenties*, Freeport, NY: Books for Libraries, 1957; London: Eyre and Spottiswoode, 1956.

Osborn, Susan, 'Reconsidering Elizabeth Bowen', *Modern Fiction Studies*, 52(1), Spring 2006: 187–97.

Parsons, Deborah, 'Souls Astray: Elizabeth Bowen's Landscape of War', in *Women: A Cultural Review*, 8(1) (1997): 24–32.

Pearsall, Phyllis, *A–Z Maps: The Personal Story, from Bedsitter to Household Name*, Sevenoaks: Geographers' A–Z Map Company, 1990.

— *An Artist's Pilgrimage in Business*, privately printed, 1993.

— *Women at War: Drawn and Overheard by Phyllis Pearsall*, Aldershot: Ashgate, 1990.

Pedlar, Valerie, '*The Woman in White*: Sensationalism, Secrets and Spying', in Dennis Walder (ed.), *The Nineteenth-Century Novel: Identities*, London: Routledge, 2001, pp. 46–68.

Pippett, Aileen, *The Moth and the Star: A Biography of Virginia Woolf*, Boston: Little Brown, 1955.

Plain, Gill, *Women's Fiction of the Second World War: Gender, Power and Resistance*, Edinburgh: Edinburgh University Press, 1996.

Potolsky, Matthew, *Mimesis*, New York and London: Routledge, 2006.

Prendergast, Christopher, *The Order of Mimesis: Balzac, Stendhal, Nerval, Flaubert*, Cambridge: Cambridge University Press, 1986.

Radford, Jean, 'Late Modernism and the Politics of History', in Maroula Joannou (ed.), *Women Writers of the 1930s: Gender, Politics and History*, Edinburgh: Edinburgh University Press, 1999.

Rau, Petra, 'The Common Frontier: Fictions of Alterity in Elizabeth Bowen's *The Heat of the Day* and Graham Greene's *The Ministry of Fear*', *Literature and History*, 14(1), 2005: 31–55.

Rose, Jacqueline, 'Negativity in the Work of Melanie Klein', in *Why War: Psychoanalysis, Politics, and the Return to Melanie Klein*, Oxford: Blackwell, 1993.

— *On Not Being Able to Sleep: Psychoanalysis and the Modern World*, Princeton and Oxford: Princeton University Press, 2003.

Rosen, Charles, and Henri Zerner, *Romanticism and Realism: The Mythology of Nineteenth Century Art*, New York: Viking Press, 1984.

Rule, Jane, *Lesbian Images*, New York: Doubleday, 1975.

Sage, Victor, 'Introduction', in Victor Sage and Allan Lloyd Smith (eds), *Modern Gothic: A Reader*, Manchester: Manchester University Press, 1996.

Schmideberg, Melitta, 'Some Observations on Individual Reactions to Air Raids', *International Journal of Psychoanalysis*, 23(1), 1942: 146–76.

Sheridan, Dorothy (ed.), *Wartime Women: A Mass-Observation Anthology*, London: Heinemann, 1990.

Showalter, Elaine, 'King Romance', in *Sexual Anarchy: Gender and Culture at the Fin de Siècle*, New York: Viking Penguin, 1990, pp. 76–104.

Smith, Patricia Juliana, *Lesbian Panic: Homoeroticism in Modern British Women's Fiction*, New York: Columbia University Press, 1997.

Stengel, E., 'Air-raid Phobia', *British Journal of Medical Psychology*, 20(2), 1944: 135–43.

Sturrock, June, 'Murder, Gender and Popular Fiction by Women in the 1860s: Braddon, Oliphant, Yonge', in Andrew Maunder and Grace

Moore (eds), *Victorian Crime, Madness, and Sensation*, Aldershot: Ashgate, 2004, pp. 73–88.

Thacker, Andrew, *Moving Through Modernity: Space and Geography in Modernism*, Manchester: Manchester University Press, 2003.

Todorov, Tzvetan, 'Les fantômes de Henry James', in *Poétique de la prose*, Paris: Seuil, 1971, pp. 186–96.

Trevor, William, 'Between Holyhead and Dún Laoghaire', *Times Literary Supplement*, 6 February 1981: 131.

Wajcman, Gérard, 'The Birth of the Intimate', trans. Barbara P. Fulks, *lacanian ink*, 23, 2004: 57–81.

Watson, Barbara Bellow, 'Variations on an Enigma: Elizabeth Bowen's War Novel', *Southern Humanities Review*, 15(2), 1981: 131–51.

Watt, Ian, *The Rise of the Novel: Studies in Defoe, Richardson and Fielding*, Berkeley: University of California Press, 1964.

Wegner, Phillip E., *Imaginary Communities: Utopia, the Nation and the Spatial Histories of Modernity*, Berkeley: California University Press, 2002.

West, Paul, *The Modern Novel*, London: Hutchinson University Library, 1963.

Wilson, Angus, 'Introduction', in *The Collected Stories of Elizabeth Bowen*, New York: Vintage, 1982.

Worringer, Wilhelm, *Abstraction and Empathy: A Contribution to the Psychology of Style*, trans. Michael Bullock, London: Routledge & Kegan Paul, 1953.

Wyatt-Brown, Anne M., 'The Liberation of Mourning in Elizabeth Bowen's *The Little Girls* and *Eva Trout*', in *Aging and Gender in Literature: Studies in Creativity*, Charlottesville: University of Virginia Press, 1993, pp. 164–86.

Index

This index covers the main body of the text, but not the notes and bibliography. Titles of works are in italics.